THE NEW
AMERICAN LANDSCAPE

THE NEW
AMERICAN LANDSCAPE

LEADING VOICES ON THE FUTURE
OF SUSTAINABLE GARDENING

Edited by
THOMAS CHRISTOPHER

TIMBER PRESS
Portland · London

All photographs are by the chapter's lead author unless otherwise noted.

Grateful acknowledgment to the people who sustained us and made this book happen: Lorraine Anderson, Todd Forrest, Saxon Holt, Sally Widdowson, Matt Moynihan, Mollie and Moxie Firestone, David Kuester, Jess Kaufmann.

Frontispiece: Moynihan-Smith garden, Clayton, Missouri. Photo by John Greenlee.

Published in 2011 by Timber Press, Inc.

The Haseltine Building
133 S.W. Second Avenue, Suite 450
Portland, Oregon 97204-3527
www.timberpress.com

2 The Quadrant
135 Salusbury Road
London NW6 6RJ
www.timberpress.co.uk

Printed in China
Text designed by Susan Applegate

Library of Congress Cataloging-in-Publication Data

The new American landscape: leading voices on the future of sustainable gardening/edited by Thomas Christopher.
       p. cm.
   Includes bibliographical references and index.
   ISBN 978-1-60469-186-3
   1. Sustainable horticulture—United States. 2. Natural landscaping—United States. 3. Organic gardening—United States. 4. Gardening—Environmental aspects. I. Christopher, Thomas.
   SB319.95.N49 2011
   635'.048–dc22   2010034075

Catalog records for this book are available from the Library of Congress and the British Library.

To Lorrie Otto
(1919–2010)

CONTENTS

I've never met a gardener whose aspirations weren't constructive. We may differ passionately in what we find beautiful and appealing, yet one thing we all share. The desire to enrich the earth, at least our own small patch of it, to some degree motivates us all.

That's our intention, but what we actually achieve is frequently far different. Too often, the way in which we nurture our plants depends on extravagant investments of limited or non-renewable resources, and massive inputs of fossil fuels. Instead of enhancing what we find in the landscape, we insist on making it conform to some artificial pattern. Indeed it's a bizarre but prominent aspect of our horticultural heritage that we pride ourselves on imposing the exact opposite of what would naturally occur. We plant lawns in the desert and brag about the subtropical species we manage to nurse through northern winters, or the alpine flowers we have imprisoned in a lowland setting. We neglect the indigenous flora, insisting instead on importing exotic rarities that in our habitat

Queens of the prairie: Lorrie Otto and *Filipendula rubra*. Photo by Krischan Photography.

rampage as weeds. So, beginning with a dream of lush fertility, we end up fostering environmental depletion and degradation.

It doesn't have to be this way. We can change our ways of gardening. By adopting more sustainable practices, we can make our plantings an environmental asset rather than a drain. They can become a haven for wildlife as well as people, and a reinforcement to the local ecosystem. In short, we can make our craft earth-friendly, as we have always imagined it should be.

This is a challenge, but it's also an opportunity. Adopting these sustainable practices isn't about belt-tightening. It's about making our gardens more rewarding, more interesting and diverse than they have ever been before. It's a process of taking on the role of leaders, not just in our own backyards but in our communities as well.

The accepted definition of sustainability (to paraphrase Gro Harlem Brundtland—see "Defining Terms" in Chapter 2) is to meet present needs without compromising the ability of future generations to meet theirs. Applied to gardening, this means using methods, technologies, and materials that don't deplete natural resources or cause lasting harm to natural systems.

This may seem like an obvious goal, especially since gardeners have all had first-hand experience of working with natural systems. Anyone who has ever raised their own vegetables, for example, knows what happens to the plot when you work it over a period of years without nourishing the soil. Or the unintended consequences that are likely to result from heavy-handed use of pesticides: chemically purging the garden of insects kills predators as well as pests, setting the stage for plagues and epidemics. Most of us have also seen how our gardens can benefit from respecting and working with nature rather than against it. We have experienced how feeding the soil's microorganisms with organic matter in turn produces healthier, more vigorous plant growth, how selecting plants adapted to the local climate and soil makes success easy.

There are selfish benefits to be had from gardening sustainably. Gardening sustainably involves reducing not only inputs of resources (which saves money as well as the environment) but also inputs of energy. Much of the energy we'll conserve is the kind that comes out of an electrical wire or a gas pump, but we'll also be saving our personal energy, the push and pull of our own muscles. Gardening sustainably is, by definition, easier.

The environmental problems we now face are seemingly overwhelming in scope. This fosters a feeling of hopelessness and apathy: how can any one of us individually have an impact on the looming global water shortage, climate change, and the loss of biodiversity? If you look at sta-tistics, though, it soon becomes clear that gardeners have an essential role in the answer to any of these crises, and that we *can* have a personal impact.

Reduced consumption of fossil fuels

The gardening style that has dominated the American landscape in recent decades involves an inordinate consumption of fossil fuels and is responsible for a disproportionate share of the pollutants released into the atmosphere every year. Curbing this appetite yard by yard can make a significant impact on resource depletion and air pollution, especially with respect to the release of greenhouse gases. The amount of gasoline we burn every weekend, mowing our lawns, could fuel 1.16 million cars and trucks for a full year of driving, according to recent Environmental Protection Agency estimates.

The EPA has at last released new standards for non-road engines, forcing garden equipment manufacturers to install the kind of pollution-control technology that automobile manufacturers have had to include in their products since 1975. Nevertheless, yard and garden equipment still contributes an estimated 5 percent of our nation's air pollution, from carbon monoxide to volatile organic compounds (VOC) and nitrogen oxides (NO_X). The latter pollutants are particularly troublesome—the VOCs consist largely of vaporized petroleum products and solvents, which are both smog- and cancer-causing, while the NO_Xs lead to the formation of ground-level ozone, which impairs lung function, inhibits plant growth, and is another key ingredient of smog. In fact, according to another EPA study, operating a walk-behind gas-powered lawn mower produces as much smog-forming emissions as driving eleven average automobiles for a similar interval of time; each riding mower produces emissions equivalent to those of thirty-four cars. The actual effect of this particular pollution source is greater than the figures suggest, because it is, by its nature, centered in population centers. These are the very areas where poor air quality already poses the greatest threats to human health and quality of life.

Power equipment takes other tolls on the environment. A report by California's Environmental Protection Agency found that as much as 5 percent of the state's windborne "fugitive dust," a type of pollution implicated in a wide range of respiratory diseases, may be traced to leaf blowers. The material that blowers introduce into the air, according to that report, includes the to-be-expected sediment and pollen as well as fertilizers, fungal spores, pesticides, herbicides, and fecal material.

Imagine if all this pollution and consumption of resources was reduced by 50 percent, or even 75 percent? We could do this tomorrow, simply by adopting more sustainable styles of gardening.

Fresh water—the new oil?

Gardeners' contribution to air pollution, however, pales in comparison to the demand our craft places on America's supply of potable water. This, unlike petroleum or natural gas, is a resource for which there is no substitute. An adequate supply of water is irreplaceable, both for satisfying our personal needs and for the production of foods and all the manufactured products on which we rely. Indeed, as the global population grows and the need for essential goods swells, the world economy is increasingly dividing into haves and have-nots based on the local availability of fresh, clean water. Economists are touting water as "the new oil," the defining resource of the twenty-first century.

The United States is a clear winner by this criterion with an estimated supply of renewable freshwater resources totaling 6,815.8 cubic meters per capita per year. This is wealth indeed, but it doesn't eliminate the need to be frugal in our use of water resources. Much of our fresh water must remain in streams, rivers, and aquifers if we are not to cause an ecological meltdown, and anyway, much of our resources are inaccessible to our existing water supply systems and cannot be tapped without great expense and disturbance to the ecosystem. This is why, from a personal and horticultural perspective, the most meaningful figure is how much water your local utility can supply to your house on a sustainable basis. And the answer to that, increasingly, is not as much as we want. A survey of local water supply systems led the Government Accountability Office to predict that thirty-six of our fifty states will face chronic water supply shortfalls by the year 2013.

This is what makes water—and the conservation of this resource—a gardener's business:

■ Nationwide, 30 percent of the water used by residential customers goes to landscape irrigation, mostly to irrigate lawns.
■ That's 7 billion gallons of this precious resource pumped from streams, rivers, and underground aquifers every day.
■ A standard recommendation in lawn care manuals calls for 1 inch of irrigation per week during hot, dry, windy summer conditions.
■ If your lawn meets the national average of one-third of an acre, 1 inch of irrigation translates into more than 9,000 gallons of water.

Most of this summertime irrigation—if it doesn't run away into a storm drain—serves mainly to cool the lawn's surface, to keep the grass in a state of active growth when it would naturally have fallen into a state of summer dormancy. The growth of Kentucky bluegrass, for example, shuts down almost completely when the ambient temperature rises above 75°F. This causes a dulling of the color of the leaf blades, and eventually their browning, but allows the grass to survive in a state of suspended animation through weeks of summer weather until the cooler temperatures and renewed rains of fall return the grass to an active state. The primary purpose of lawn irrigation during hot, dry weather is to defeat this natural cycle. Most of the water deposited by the sprinklers evaporates off the surface of the turf, cooling it so that it continues in active growth. Relatively little of the moisture actually reaches the grass roots.

Because so few gardeners have adapted their gardening style to match the local climate, landscape irrigation tends to place the greatest demands on the water supply in arid regions, precisely where this resource is most scarce. The EPA asserts that landscape irrigation is the reason that average per capita residential water use is 50 percent higher in the West than the East. But this does not mean that water shortages are a feature only of regions of scant rainfall. South Florida, where precipitation averages 55 inches annually, is locked in a chronic state of water shortage, largely because of excessive withdrawals from the water supply system for landscape irrigation.

Invasive species

The issue of water use is a particularly dramatic one, and lawns have become a popular target for environmentalists as a result. With justice: by changing the style of your garden to fit the local climate, by reducing the area of your lawn or by converting it to more self-sufficient, locally adapted species of grasses, you can reduce your water draw by thousands, or tens of thousands of gallons. This is a solution to celebrate, but we shouldn't give a free pass to other areas of the garden. The perennials and annuals we have imported to color our flower borders, the vines we cover ground with, the shrubs that make up our foundation plantings, and the trees we set around our houses for shade have, in many cases, had a disastrous effect on the surrounding habitat. Just because their environmental impact is less visible doesn't mean it hasn't been profoundly damaging.

The problem is that many of these imports have proven too successful in their new homes. They've escaped from gardens to nearby wild areas. There, by proliferating unchecked, these so-called invasive species have displaced native plant species, thereby robbing native wildlife of the species on which it had previously depended for food and cover. As Rick Darke and Eric Toensmeier point out (in Chapters 4 and 5, respectively), many species with exotic origins have integrated harmlessly into our landscape, and the threat from plant "invaders" is often overblown. Still, as Doug Tallamy in particular (in Chapter 9) emphasizes, plants that evolved in tandem with local wildlife support larger, more diverse, and more complex food webs than do plants that evolved elsewhere. Changing the character of the local flora, clearly, is not something to be undertaken lightly.

Not all invasive species trace back to deliberate importations by gardeners. Many arrived accidentally, inadvertently included with importations of harmless plants or in shipments of agricultural seed. Some early invaders arrived on our shores in sand or soil used as ballast by sailing ships; when the ballast was dumped to make room for goods intended for export, the seeds contained in the soil or sand were released onto our coasts. Still, an impressive array of the worst invasive plant species are the legacy of unwise gardeners. The water hyacinths that now choke southern waterways were brought to the United States from Asia for use in aquatic gardens.

The very successful English ivy (*Hedera helix*) on an American tree. Photo by Allan Armitage.

The ailanthus trees (also natives of Asia) that sprout so vigorously along highways, spreading into adjacent woodlands, were deliberately planted up and down the East Coast because they made such vigorous, indestructible trees for the harsh urban landscape. It's not clear how purple loosestrife, a European native now overrunning countless North American wetlands, first arrived in the United States, but its spread was undoubtedly helped by nurserymen promoting it as a garden perennial. Brazilian peppertree; Japanese honeysuckle, Japanese barberry, and Japanese knotweed; Norway maple; Russian olive; English ivy—the host of invasive species introduced by gardeners affects every corner of our continent. The role that we have played in this environmental problem varies from region to region, but locally, it can be decisive. According to the state of Wisconsin, fully 30 percent of the invasive plant species found within its borders originated as ornamentals.

Unfortunately such ill-considered introductions are not a thing of the past—as gardening has increased in popularity in the United States, more and more exotic material is shipped in to tempt the horticultural consumer. The impact is felt by both wildlife and taxpayers. The annual cost of programs undertaken to beat back purple loosestrife comes to $1 million. The state of Florida spends some $3 million every year to clear dense sheets of water hyacinths from canals and rivers; the total bill for the state's efforts to control exotic plant species since 1980 is reported to have topped $250 million.

In most cases, total eradication of an invasive species, when it has become established in its new home, is impossible. But gardeners can do their part to limit their spread by making sure that they do not plant any known invasives—the National Biological Information Infrastructure (NBII), a division of the U.S. Geological Survey, offers a comprehensive index of local and regional checklists of such plants and guides to their identification on its website, at http://www.nbii.gov/portal/server.pt/community/-_checklists_and_identification_guides/1303. Consider this small measure of restraint as insurance—insurance that our generation's mistaken enthusiasm doesn't wreak havoc with the next generation's habitat and budget.

It's *too* easy being green

Enthusiasm and good intentions are no substitute for practical experience and hard, verifiable scientific data. Unfortunately, this is a substitution that is too often made by promoters of "green" products and practices. When an environmental marketing firm investigated 1,018 self-styled "green" products, it found only one that didn't make false or misleading claims on the product label.

So serious has this problem of "greenwashing" become that the Federal Trade Commission, the government agency charged with protecting consumers against false advertising, has begun deliberating on revisions to its Green Guides, which will establish stricter guidelines for what is a legitimate use of the term "green" versus uses that are untrue or misleading (a note to the wise: manufactured rayon fiber is not "bamboo"). In the meantime, gardeners are well advised to consult independent evaluators, such as Consumer Reports' Greener Choices division, or National Geographic's online Green Guide, which direct readers to products whose manufacture and use have a less negative impact on the environment.

Ultimately, though, an insoluble difficulty underlies any attempt to identify "green" products, which is that the term itself is so amorphous. All that it really communicates is the user's desire to do something good for the environment, and different people define good in widely differing ways. Various green organizations and advocacy groups, for example, have promoted mass tree planting as a means of reducing humanity's carbon footprint. Such programs could reduce, at least somewhat, the atmospheric concentration of CO_2, the premier greenhouse gas, though it wouldn't be the panacea for global climate change that proponents sometimes claim. Still, trees do function as carbon sinks—that is, they absorb carbon dioxide from the atmosphere and they extract the carbon from it, using it as a constituent of the wood they form as they grow. So planting trees must be green.

Not necessarily, according to environmental scientists, and probably not if pursued indiscriminately and in too great a quantity. Some have argued that this practice isn't green at all. Blanketing the landscape with monotonous expanses of nursery-grown trees, these critics point out, reduces the biodiversity of the forest flora, and tree planting, if pursued too enthusiastically, obliterates the patchwork of different habitats—such as woodland interspersed with meadow or brush—that many species of wildlife prefer or require.

Fortunately, "sustainability" has a much more concrete definition than does

It doesn't have to be this way. We can change our ways of gardening.

"green." The extent to which our actions consume resources, the effects of such consumption, and the rate at which resources are naturally replenished can all be more or less precisely measured. Sustainability is, when properly practiced, a matter of data, not intentions.

This being so, it is our responsibility to work from facts. If, for instance, you support the concept of vertical farming, raising food in high-rises, you need to demonstrate that the calories of energy yielded by your harvests will exceed the energy input required for building or retrofitting your farmscraper, and for raising the necessary water, soil, fertilizer, animal foods, and machinery to the height of your high-rise fields. Does producing food in this manner actually consume less energy and resources than would be required to raise the same harvest on conventional farms and ship it to population centers? If such calculations are not your forte, then seek out an unbiased authority who can help you to an informed conclusion. That's what we've done. For each chapter of this book, we've selected different authors, individuals with extensive, firsthand experience in the aspect of gardening they describe, experts who have made an in-depth study of their craft. Such detailed, factual knowledge must be the foundation of true sustainability. Without it, this new campaign will be nothing more than greenwashing by another name.

How this book can help

Creating a truly sustainable garden isn't difficult, but it does require a gentler, more holistic approach. To enable nature to take over such tasks as irrigation and fertilization requires an understanding of the systems involved, and the recognition that they all are interconnected. Ensuring that the plants get the minerals they need for healthy growth, for example, is no longer just a matter of broadcasting fertilizers. Instead, fertility becomes a reflection of a healthy soil with a robust flora and fauna of beneficial microorganisms, which in turns

reflects a more sensitive approach to moisture management and pest control. Which means that the plants must be selected to suit the site and climate. All these things must be managed in a coordinated manner, if they are to work together successfully. That's why this book's relevance begins well before the opening of a nursery catalog or the turning of the first spadefull of soil.

- In Chapter 1, David Deardorff and Kathryn Wadsworth train their knowledge of plant pathology and love of gardening on pests and diseases and how best to cope with them. Like any good physicians, they focus on prevention—their nine-point program provides a sustainable foundation for horticultural health no matter what sort of garden you are contemplating.
- Chapter 2 introduces the new Sustainable Sites Initiative (SITES). Developed at the instigation of the U.S. Green Building Council, these guidelines are intended to do for landscape design what the LEED system has done for green building design and construction. Designers and gardeners will find that SITES provides both a blueprint for planning and a sort of tangible vocabulary in which they can express themselves sustainably.
- The biggest consumer of resources and energy in the average garden is the lawn. That's why in Chapter 3

nurseryman and designer John Green-lee presents alternatives, seducing former mower-addicts, as he has for more than twenty years, with his visions of sustainable meadow gardens. And if you'd still like a bit of clipped turf, as a play space for children perhaps, or a firebreak, prairie-plants guru Neil Diboll contributes a succinct epilogue on "no mow" lawns for ecological—and economical—landscapes.

- In Chapter 4, your guide is Rick Darke, a leading authority on the restoration of native species to their rightful place in the garden and a horticultural polymath who served for more than a decade as Curator of Plants at Longwood Gardens. His expertise is integrating and successfully balancing natives with non-invasive exotic species, and on the design of regionally adapted plantings.

- In Chapter 5, Eric Toensmeier examines how edible and useful plants can be assembled into functioning ecosystems, and how growing food sustainably can transform your garden, your cuisine—and maybe even your community. Broadening the scope of your garden to include the diversity of unconventional fruits and greens Toensmeier touts will reduce the environmental costs of your harvests while also enriching mealtimes with countless flavors you won't find in the corner market.

- Sustainability doesn't just involve the healing of the global environment; it is a way to address the continuing, challenging fallout of our history of abusive exploitation and development. In Chapter 6, David Wolfe of Cornell University shares his insights and offers ways for us to negotiate the inevitable stresses of gardening in an era of climatic upheaval.

- Water is both an essential resource and, potentially, a gardener's most potent tool. I've been studying the issues associated with water use by gardeners for twenty years, and in Chapter 7, I present a guide to reducing water consumption in the garden—and at the same time outline how you can turn your garden into a means for cleansing storm runoff, making it a boost for rather than a drain on the local water supply.

- One of the many benefits of sustainable gardening is that it can take your planting to a new level—literally. In Chapter 8, Ed Snodgrass and Linda McIntyre, leaders in the design and planting of green roofs, outline the potential this new sort of gardening has for reducing water pollution while also furnishing visual pleasure and serving as habitat for wildlife.

- Collaborating with nature in the sustainable garden means inviting the wild back in. Doug Tallamy, professor of entomology and wildlife ecology at the University of Delaware, tells how to manage this re-opening of the borders in Chapter 9, and why doing so will benefit you, your neighbors, and other living creatures equally.

- Gardening sustainably means cultivating the soil as well as plantings. Elaine Ingham, a former professor at Oregon State University, has continued to pursue her research into the ecology of soil life. Chapter 10 tells how different ways of managing the garden affect the many players in the soil food web, and how growers of every kind can use this knowledge to promote plant growth and reduce reliance on inorganic chemical fertilizers and pesticides.

- And finally, Toby Hemenway, a gardener and thinker who has played a central role in translating permaculture principles to fit North American ecosystems, ties it all together in Chapter 11, through the concept of whole system design. For a sustainable gardener, this is the essential process of connecting the dots, of making every element of the landscape work in unison so that each reinforces and extends each other.

There isn't a single solution to any aspect of sustainability, and every one of the authors included in this book encourages experimentation. We view our advice as a beginning rather than an end point, for a diversity of responses is going to be crucial to achieving success in this area.

The payoff

Defenders of the status quo frequently complain that the economic and cultural reforms recommended by environmentalists are immediate in their costs, while the benefits are remote. This shouldn't dissuade us from making such investments in the future, of course. Still, it does make especially welcome the fact that the changes this book proposes are not only inexpensive but also almost instantaneous in their rewards.

Experience has shown many times that it's in response to a challenge that the best, most exciting gardens emerge. Certainly, the landscape we've created through our current lavish consumption of resources is disappointingly bland. Garden equipment powered with fossil fuels, cheap synthetic fertilizers and pesticides, and federal and state water projects that supply irrigation almost for free might seem to have made anything possible, horticulturally speaking. What they've achieved, though, is to make us lazy. They made it easy to impose the same, cookie-cutter model of landscape in every community across the United States, so that our gardens have, over the last couple of generations, lost much of their regional flavor.

The exceptions to this dreary rule have arisen most commonly in response to adversity. It was the droughts of the 1980s that caused gardeners in the western states to experiment with more imaginative, locally adapted garden styles. In Arizona and New Mexico, gardens inspired by the local desert began to emerge. Californians began experimenting with drought-tolerant plants from their own state and from other climatically similar regions. It was in large part the concern over invasive weeds from abroad that drove the rediscovery of native plants over the last couple of decades; now we see prairie restorations and gardens in the Midwest, woodland gardens in the East and Northwest.

This isn't a new phenomenon. It was hunger, a need for a new and more reliable food source, that prompted Neolithic people to create the first gardens, and it is hunger that has enriched our plots since: we have gone back to the wild repeatedly for new crops and new sources of food. The need to protect the garden against animal and human intruders led to the architectural framing of gardens; the desire to create flat growing spaces in hilly terrain led to the terraced landscape masterpieces of the Italian Renaissance; and the scarcity of arable land in Japan encouraged the development of bonsai and other techniques that distilled broad experiences into small spaces. This relationship between need and ingenuity continues today: our newfound concern for sustainability has already created an explosion of rain gardens and green roofs. This is only a beginning. The challenges we confront are sure to pro-duce endless innovation, and it will be our privilege to enjoy the results.

Sustainable leadership

It's a testimony to our democracy, as imperfect as it may be, that in matters of environmental policy Americans have been accustomed to relying on leadership from the top down. We look to elected officials and to state and federal agencies for answers to environmental challenges. Certainly, the laws and regulations they issue will play an essential role. But by itself, these official measures cannot achieve the sort of door-to-door conversion that must occur; politicians and civil servants cannot impose a transformation of personal attitudes. For that, we need bottom-up leadership: we need personal, one-on-one persuasion. We need people willing to set an example in every community across the United States. In short, we need grass-roots activism on a massive scale. We need gardeners.

Grass roots are something gardeners know all about, and not just in the botanical sense. There's a long history in the United States of gardeners organizing for community action. The local garden clubs that began to appear in the late nineteenth century were social meeting places, but virtually all included in their mission statements the preservation of native trees and wildflowers. Despite their white-glove image, these organizations, with current membership in the hundreds of thousands, fund research at the cutting edge of environmental restoration and preservation and are a powerful force in the ongoing self-education of their members. Working together through state and national organizations, they lobby for improved environmental policy.

These links between gardeners continue to evolve. Online gardening forums, many dedicated to the preservation of native plants and wildlife or other environmental causes, spread ideas, debate, and advice literally at the speed of light. These can and should be powerful advocates of sustain-

Gardening sustainably is, by definition, easier.

ability. Surely, though, it is the insistence on personal action—of dirt-under-the-fingernails direct action, of encountering natural systems firsthand—that makes gardening such a persuasive, transformative experience. For more often than not, those who have brought about the most dramatic changes in our field haven't been those who sought to lead but instead were simply responding to what they recognized as a need. The effect of such individuals has made itself felt far outside the boundaries of their gardens.

Consider the story of a sustainable gardening hero, Lorrie Otto, who was working

toward this goal long before the term was coined. Sixty years ago, when she began replanting her suburban Milwaukee lawn with asters, goldenrods, and prairie grasses, she wasn't hoping to spark a revolution. She simply wanted to provide her children with the experiences she recalled from playing as a child in the surviving prairie around her father's Wisconsin farm. It was only when the town sent a crew to mow in her absence that she began proselytizing for natural landscapes. She invited town officials in for a tour, introducing them to the beauties and practical virtues of the plants they had felled. They apologized to Lorrie and paid damages that she immediately invested in more planting.

It was the poisoned birds Lorrie was finding around her yard that subsequently led her to begin agitating for a local ban of DDT. She invited environmental scientists and organizers who shared her concern to join her, hosting them in her own house. These efforts played a fundamental role in the state of Wisconsin's decision in 1969 to declare this pesticide a "hazardous pollutant" and to promote a statewide campaign against its use. This was the first legal victory of the opponents of DDT, a consummation of the message Rachel Carson had preached in *Silent Spring* (1962) and the first step of a legislative process that led to a nationwide ban of DDT in 1972.

Lorrie continued to explore environmental issues. She became a personal advocate for prairiescaping, encouraging gardeners throughout her community and indeed all the area of North American once occupied by grasslands to rediscover the native flora. A lecture about landscaping with native plants in 1979 inspired a member of the audience, Ginny Lindow, to found Wild Ones, a nonprofit organization devoted to promoting that cause. Wild Ones now boasts fifty chapters from Connecticut to Colorado and offers a wide variety of educational programs about growing and using native plants in a domesticated setting, as well as serving as an informational exchange and meeting place for natural landscapers from all over North America.

Meanwhile, the scope of Lorrie's interests continued to expand. During the droughts of the late 1980s and early '90s, when other gardeners were focusing on conserving water, Lorrie recognized that this was only one face of the water crisis.

She became concerned with the role that stormwater runoff played in polluting nearby waterways and reconfigured her yard to serve as a biofiltration system, absorbing and cleansing all the precipitation that fell on it. Twenty years before the EPA began promoting such "green infrastructure," Lorrie Otto was already working out the details of stormwater management on her own.

Very few of us (if any) have the dynamism of a Lorrie Otto. But we all can serve as leaders and examples within our communities. Proving to our neighbors that sustainable gardening is practical—that it offers immediate benefits as well as serving future generations—is how we are going to transform the American landscape. One yard at a time.

THOMAS CHRISTOPHER
Earth Day 2010

CHAPTER 1

Sustainable Solutions

by David Deardorff and Kathryn Wadsworth

THE MORE A GARDEN IMITATES the processes and functions of natural ecosystems, the more sustainable and resilient it becomes. Healthy natural systems are self-regulating. Mutually beneficial transactions between suites of organisms characterize natural systems. Checks and balances between prey and predator keep pests at bay. Soil microorganisms outcompete pathogens (disease-causing agents, most often bacteria or fungi), thus reducing the incidence and severity of disease. Plants that take advantage of the pollinators, native soils, microclimates, and hydrology of their location thrive. Gardeners who choose to replicate these natural processes create sustainable gardens.

As organisms in natural systems adapt to their physical environment, they also co-evolve with one another. Every plant species is native to a particular geographic region of the world. Each region is also home to specific insects, birds, and other animals as well as fungi, bacteria, and

The natural meadow is a system beautifully in balance. Photo by Saxon Holt.

other plants. Some plants have nectar-rich flowers adapted to attract bees, butterflies, hawkmoths, hummingbirds, or bats. These flowers entice animals to move from plant to plant and provide pollination services, for which the animals receive food (nectar). Other plants have fruits adapted to attract birds, monkeys, or other animals that eat the fruit and scatter seeds. Plants often have specific symbiotic or mutualistic relationships with fungi and bacteria in the soil as well. Every plant has developed a repertoire of adaptations to the physical and biological environment of its homeland.

The garden, on the other hand, is, by definition, an artificial construct, a landscape of strangers. Aesthetic or utilitarian criteria—in addition to environmental constraints such as light, water, temperature, and soil—often dictate plant choices, so that plants that originally evolved in western China may be juxtaposed with plants from South Africa, Turkey, and Mexico. In their original homelands, these plants co-evolved over time with suites of animals, fungi, bacteria, and other plants in relationship to one another. Thrust into the garden in an alien environment, each plant is exposed to new suites of pests, diseases, competitive interactions, and ecological transactions.

This artificially constructed community of strangers we call a garden soon begins to form a community of organisms we call an ecosystem. Hummingbirds, found only in the New World, will readily visit flowers from China or Africa, which they have never encountered in their evolutionary past. The hummingbirds get food and provide pollination. Warblers, chickadees, and titmice frequent gardens to forage for food, shelter, and nesting sites. They benefit the garden by eating pests. Bees, butterflies, and ladybird beetles provide pollination

A male Costa's hummingbird, found only in the New World, visits an aloe flower native to Africa. The plant gives food (nectar) to the bird, and the bird brings pollen to fertilize the flowers, a mutually beneficial transaction between strangers.

and insect predation while foraging. Mammals, such as squirrels, raccoons, rabbits, and deer, seek food and sometimes cause damage. But they leave behind fertilizer pellets. Thus, a series of mutually beneficial transactions begins to take place. Gardeners who encourage these transactions create a sustainable garden.

Natural systems are balanced. They need no input of supplemental water from irrigation; all the plants are adapted to the typical water regime of their habitat. They do not require inputs of fertilizer; all the output of plant and animal waste is composted on site and nutrients are recycled. They do not need inputs of pesticides and do not produce outputs of pollution. Beneficial organisms regulate pests and diseases.

To create regenerative, sustainable gardens, we must balance inputs with outputs, as natural systems do. Inputs—water, fertilizer, fossil fuels—are resources that we invest in the garden. Outputs are products that flow from the garden—vegetables, fruit, and flowers, for example. Outputs also include byproducts from the garden: garden waste, runoff water, sediment, excess mineral nutrients, pathogens, and agricultural chemicals. Composting is a classic example of the balancing act that is required. Compost is recycled garden waste (an output) that provides an organic amendment (an input) that improves soil structure, feeds the organisms in healthy living soil, and fertilizes plants. Another example is capturing rainfall runoff (an output) in rain barrels and using it as irrigation water (an input).

Five philosophical approaches

The past three decades have seen the emergence or revitalization of five important philosophical approaches to gardening, each of which incorporates elements of natural ecosystems into the new American sustainable garden.

Xeriscaping. This approach advocates water conservation through the use of native plants and adapted exotics that perform well on the amount of precipitation typically provided by nature wherever the garden is located. The goal of xeriscaping (dry-scaping) is to eliminate the input of supplemental irrigation water. This approach developed to correct excess water usage in the water-thirsty gardens and landscapes of the Desert Southwest, where, in some municipalities, maintaining inappropriate landscapes consumed as much as 50 percent of all available water. Xeriscaping is a technique that can be applied to landscapes well beyond desert ecosystems, however. Every region of the country has a semi-predictable amount of precipitation that is distributed at a specific time of year. In each of these areas, plants that are naturally adapted to the typical conditions thrive. These plants remain healthy without supplemental water, because they avoid water stress.

Native plant landscaping. This gardening movement advocates restricting plant choices to species that are native to the region. It does not permit the use of exotic plant material, even if it is well adapted to local environmental conditions. Every region of the country has a native

flora perfectly adapted to the characteristic rainfall amount and distribution, the winter cold and summer heat, and the pests and diseases of that region. Because native plants are adapted to these conditions, they are more resistant to pests and diseases. Wherever the garden is located, numerous attractive, native plant species can be selected to provide a close approximation to a natural ecosystem.

Wildlife gardening. Gardening for wildlife has also emerged as an important tool for the gardener, partly fueled, we think, by biophilia—the profound human need for contact with nature. This approach to the garden advocates incorporating plant material that provides habitat

Gardens generate waste (an output), which can easily be composted and turned into fertilizer (an input), closing the loop between outputs and inputs. This makes the garden more sustainable. Adding compost to the soil helps to create a biologically active, rich soil ecosystem, which maintains healthy plants.

for wildlife. Although it is not incompatible with the previous approaches, wildlife gardening is not as restrictive as either xeriscaping or native plant landscaping when it comes to choice of plant material.

Birdwatchers, in particular, plant gardens to attract numerous species of birds, both seed- and insect-eaters. Butterfly lovers include plants for butterfly larvae to eat, along with flowers that provide nectar for the adults. These gardeners embrace the concept of sharing their produce with the wild creatures around them. In addition, many of the wildlings attracted to the garden are also efficient partners that help control insect pests. Indeed, attracting beneficial wildlife is a major tech-

This xeriscape garden atop a bluff overlooking Puget Sound features species native to the Pacific Northwest. No supplemental irrigation is applied— these organically grown plants remain healthy on the natural precipitation provided by this environment.

nique to use for the creation of sustainable gardens.

Organic gardening. Organic gardening has, of course, been around for a long time and, although not new, has enjoyed a resurgence of popularity in recent years. Concern for the health and safety of our children, of ourselves, and of our environment has prompted us gardeners to avoid poisons in the garden, in the home, and on our food. This approach restricts the use of agricultural chemicals to natural substances mined from the earth or obtained from plants and animals. The use of modern synthetic pesticides is not permitted on plants grown for food or on ornamental plants. Nor is the use of modern processed fertilizers permitted; fertilizer is instead obtained from natural plant and animal byproducts. Organic gardening, as a philosophy, is applicable to xeriscaping, native plant landscaping, wildlife gardening, and all other gardening systems.

Permaculture. Permaculture (the word combines "permanent" and "agriculture") is a gardening design system developed by Bill Mollison of Australia, in which productive plant materials (fruit trees, berry bushes) combine with herbs and perennials in permanent guilds of compatible plants. Permaculture gardens are designed around these guilds—combinations of plants, animals, fungi, and insects found in healthy natural ecosystems. They mimic the architectural and beneficial relationships found in a natural forest or other ecosystem, in which diverse plants coexist with animals foraging, cultivating, and providing manure. In such "food forests," each "member" contributes something of value to the whole.

Each of these five philosophical approaches attempts to address specific aspects of sustainability. By synthesizing the best of each into a unified whole, we give ourselves powerful tools to achieve the balance we seek. We need gardens that conserve water, that promote native plants, that invite wildlife, that are organic, and that produce food. The new American sustainable garden should do all these things.

Even with this new integrated approach, plants can get into trouble, and the system gets out of balance. When disorders, diseases, and pests show up, it is tempting to throw all our philosophies out the window, because we suspect we cannot maintain the balance we seek. But we can. Sustainable solutions are not as difficult as we imagine.

Nine-point program for preventing and solving plant problems

Prevention is at the heart of any program to reestablish balance in the garden ecosystem. It is always the easiest, cheapest, and most effective solution to any plant problem. The following nine-point program is especially appropriate to the new American sustainable garden.

Put the right plant in the right place. This lets the plant you choose thrive in its own niche, with proper soil conditions and suitable light, water, and temperature to enjoy robust good health. If you do all you

can to provide a stress-free environment, you will have planted for success. Consult plant labels and packaging, reliable books, magazines, and Internet sites to determine a plant's requirements for water, sunlight, temperature, and soils. Use this information to better meet plants' needs or to relocate unhappy plants.

Choose plant varieties that are genetically resistant. Many new varieties of popular vegetables and ornamental plants are genetically resistant to pests or diseases. Certain cultivars of roses (*Rosa*), for example, are resistant to leaf fungus diseases like black spot, powdery mildew, or rust. Some cultivars of sweet corn (*Zea mays*) are more resistant to corn earworms than others because their husks are tighter and keep insects out. Some cultivars of tomato (*Lycopersicon*) are more resistant to aphids than others. To find pest-

The corn earworm (*Helicoverpa zea*). Certain sweet corn cultivars are bred to resist the attacks of this pest; the husks wrap tightly around the ear, blocking the insect's access to the corn.

or disease-resistant varieties, read labels on plants, bulbs, tubers, or seed packets, look in catalogs from suppliers, or do an Internet search. Check with your local Master Gardeners organization or Extension service. Local knowledge is invaluable.

Manage the planting site to permit free air flow and adequate light. Whether they're on your windowsill, on your deck, or out in the garden, plants crowded together and plants with dense foliage are more susceptible to pests and diseases. Make sure each plant has enough room for the air to move freely about it. Prune individual plants to open them up to light and air. Both these tactics allow the foliage to dry quickly after rain and reduce the number and kinds of fungus infections on your plants. Both techniques also expose insect pests to predators, allowing the predators to help you control these pests.

Use the right amount of water. Effective water management often means the difference between gardening success or failure. Too much water, and the roots of your plant suffocate and die, or are subject to invasion by root rot fungi. Too little water, and your plant will die of drought. Even the way you water your plants can affect the incidence of disorders, pests, or diseases in your garden. Apply water to the root zone of the plant, not the foliage. Fungi often, and bacteria and foliar nematodes always, need a film of moisture on the surface of the plant in order to infect the host.

Protect your plants from extremes of temperature—freezing cold or baking heat. Extremes of temperature affect plants in several ways. Obviously, plants can freeze in winter and sustain severe damage or be killed outright. For many plants, excessive heat (above 85°F) causes photosynthesis to slow down or even cease. Warm temperatures at night can cause plants to burn up more fuel (through respiration) than they make during the day (through photosynthesis), causing them to die from starvation. This is why temperate zone plants, like miniature roses, do not survive as houseplants.

Build healthy, biologically active soil. Well-managed soil, amended with rich compost and supplemented with a good organic fertilizer, if necessary, should be adequate to meet your plant's needs. If you find you have a nutritional emergency, use fish emulsion or another liquid organic fertilizer in the form of a foliar spray; the plant can absorb nutrients through its leaves very quickly. Organic fertilizers release their nutrients slowly over time and feed the decomposer community in your soil. This is especially important for nitrogen because nitrogen is highly mobile in the water column and leaches quickly away into the groundwater. Synthetic fertilizers tend to release nitrogen much too quickly.

Plant polycultures, not monocultures. A polyculture has many different plants growing in one location and helps to inhibit the spread of pests and diseases. Distributing flowers, herbs, and vegetables throughout garden beds, so each plant's closest neighbor is different from itself, greatly reduces the incidence of diseases (fungal, bacterial, and viral) and pests (insects, mites, and nematodes). Insect pests, for example, track their food plants from long distances by scent. Upon arrival in the vicinity of their food plant they switch to visual cues. When large numbers of other kinds of plants disrupt their sight line, insect pests become confused and fail to find their food plant.

Incorporating flowers and herbs into the vegetable garden provides multiple benefits in the form of effective pest and disease management. Herbs such as fennel (*Foeniculum*) and dill (*Anethum*) attract beneficial insects to help control insect pests. Flowers like yarrow (*Achillea*), cosmos, and coneflower (*Rudbeckia*) also attract beneficial insects, and marigolds (*Tagetes*) repel root-knot nematodes. Lavender (*Lavandula*), rosemary (*Rosmarinus*), thyme (*Thymus*), and sage (*Salvia*) repel deer.

Rotate plants (or crops) from year to year. Do not put the same plants or the same kinds of plants in the same location year after year. For annuals, vegetables, and bulbs, this is an effective way to avoid soil-borne diseases caused by fungi and bacteria, and pests such as insects and nematodes. When you plant each bed or container, keep in mind that you want polycultures; for example, include marigolds between your tomatoes, and when you move your tomato planting bed each year, move your marigolds to that bed, too.

Attract or purchase beneficial organisms. To attract beneficial organisms to your garden, provide water in very shallow containers, such as a bird bath or plant saucer. Also, grow species of plants these animals prefer as sources of food or shelter. Some examples of plants to grow:

- The carrot family (Apiaceae): coriander, dill, fennel, parsley
- The mint family (Lamiaceae): catnip, thyme, rosemary, hyssop, lemon balm
- The daisy family (Asteraceae): cosmos, yarrow, coneflower

Spiders and birds are also efficient predators of insects and other pests. A spider's web may be a nuisance if its location is in-

Tomatoes, arugula, and sunflowers grow side by side with purple basil and many other kinds of useful and ornamental plants in this urban backyard. Such a polyculture limits the plant-to-plant spread of insect pests and bacterial and fungal diseases.

convenient for you, but it's better not to kill the spider. She's just doing her job—to catch and eat as many insects as she can. Many birds eat insects exclusively, while some are part-time insect eaters. Other birds relish snails and slugs. Attract birds of all kinds to your garden with water and shelter. They are valuable allies.

Resort to chemicals only when necessary

Various chemicals are certified for use in organic gardening. Many of these organic treatments are relatively safe for you and the environment. Some have been in use for hundreds of years; others are quite new.

People have been growing plants for food, beauty, or medicinal value for five

Crop rotation helps avoid the buildup of soil-borne pests and diseases. This patch of the garden will not see green beans and corn again for four years.

millenia. For most of that time, we have successfully grown plants without the significant use of chemicals in the garden. The extensive use of chemicals in the home garden is an artifact of World War II weapons production. Chemical manufacturers needed a market for their enormous surplus after the war ended. Many areas of the world needed food, and they needed it quickly, and research at major universities demonstrated that the use of chemical fertilizers and pesticides yielded just that: more food, more quickly. The chemical revolution was born.

Agricultural use was the basis of all research; once government funding of university research began to dry up, the manufacturers of chemicals began to pay for the research. And whatever was good for large-scale monoculture farming drove the conclusions for the use of all chemicals on plants. No one questioned whether home uses and commercial uses were compatible. No one noted how the source of the money affected the conclusions of the scientists. Until Rachel Carson's *Silent Spring* (1962), few questioned the consequences of this "chemical revolution" in agriculture. As time passed, however, the industry's bright promise became tarnished by harsh realities, a legacy of damaged ecosystems, genetic resistance, increasingly endangered non-target species, and unacceptable risks to our own health and safety.

Sustainable gardeners have alternatives to these destructive practices in certified organic remedies. Remedies acceptable in organic gardening are those derived from naturally occurring substances that come directly from the earth or from plants and animals. They are generally less toxic to humans and to the biosphere than modern, synthetic, designer remedies. They also break down quickly to harmless products. Nevertheless, all chemicals should be stored in a safe place where inquisitive children and pets cannot get at them. Look for OMRI (Organic Materials Review Institute) certification on the label.

Your personal safety and the safety of your family, pets, and neighborhood are important issues when using remedies of any kind, especially on houseplants and edible plants intended for food. Avoid using chemicals, even organic ones, near bodies of water because many fish and shellfish can be harmed by them. Also, remember that many families of organisms have a "bright side" and a "dark side." Some, such as mycorrhizal fungi or beneficial insects, are the ones that help us grow better plants; others, such as fungal pathogens or insect pests, are the ones that harm our plants. Use organic remedies wisely and protect the good fungi and insects while saving your plants from the bad guys.

The new American sustainable garden seeks to achieve aesthetically pleasing landscapes and food production systems that conserve resources, eliminate pollution, and enhance the natural environment. By emulating natural ecosystem functions and processes, the garden becomes more self-regulating and less management-intensive. We highly recommend that you stroll through your garden at least once a week and "visit" with your plants. It is not only a pleasure to witness their health and beauty, it is a means to a more enjoyable life. The best gardens please the senses, lift the human spirit, and reconnect us to nature. How successful we are in these endeavors depends entirely on how we, as stewards of the green world, manage our gardens.

A beneficial insect, a tiny wasp, has laid her eggs inside this tomato hornworm caterpillar. When the eggs hatched, the baby wasps ate the caterpillar alive from the inside out. Now the baby wasps have matured and spun white cocoons attached to the body of their host. Soon a new crop of adults will emerge to lay more eggs inside more caterpillars. Lots of beneficial insects such as these little wasps are ready, willing, and able to help manage the garden.

CHAPTER 2

Managing the Home Landscape as a Sustainable Site

by the Sustainable Sites Initiative™ with Thomas Christopher

You wouldn't be reading this book if you weren't a strong supporter of sustainable landscape practices—and you probably know many others who feel the same way. But do you all agree on how to use water? Native plants? Recycled materials? Does the sustainable garden that you're creating precisely reflect the priorities of your environmentally conscious neighbor? Founded in 2005, the Sustainable Sites Initiative™ (SITES™) provides a way for those that design, construct, and maintain landscapes to measure their success in sustainability by using performance-based benchmarks and guidelines. Although intended mainly for landscape architects, engineers, and other public planning professionals, the lessons of SITES apply equally to the changes every gardener makes to his

or her own residential landscape. Thousands of hours of work and discussion have gone into this effort, and you, the reader, are invited to take advantage of the useful (and free) results and resources by visiting www.sustainablesites.org.

Defining terms

What is a sustainable site? Although the concept of environmental stewardship is not new, the near-universal acceptance of the term "sustainability" can be traced to 1987 and a report by the UN World Commission on Environment and Development led by Norwegian Prime Minister Gro Harlem Brundtland. This report, "Our Common Future," defines "sustainable development" as meeting the needs of the present without compromising the ability of future generations to meet their own needs. SITES' guiding principles align with this definition.

In the years since the UN's report, guidelines for evaluating environmentally sustainable buildings have evolved rapidly, in countries around the world. In the

Interpretive signage for passersby drives home garden/garden's striking side-by-side message (see page 39).
Photo by Deidra Walpole Photography, courtesy of City of Santa Monica.

United States, the LEED® (Leadership in Energy and Environmental Design) Green Building Rating System™, introduced in 1998 by the U.S. Green Building Council (USGBC), has become the standard. A carefully structured procedure for analyzing and rating the sustainability of new construction, the LEED standards have focused architects' and builders' attention on such areas as energy and water conservation, indoor air quality, and the use of recycled and renewable materials. Securing LEED certification, at a silver, gold, or platinum level, has become an important milestone for a builder's public image; environmentally conscious communities offer financial incentives to meet LEED standards, and even the newest constructions on the Las Vegas Strip have spent millions of dollars to obtain LEED ratings. However, although the LEED system doesn't entirely neglect landscape, its standards for the outside environment are more general and much broader than they are for the buildings they surround. An equivalent system for landscape design and construction was needed.

To fill this void, three leaders in the field of landscape and environmental design jointly formed the Sustainable Sites Initiative. The American Society of Landscape Architects' mission, since its founding in 1899, is to lead, to educate and to participate in the careful stewardship, wise planning, and artful design of our cultural and natural environments; the United States Botanic Garden in Washington,

D.C., is a leader in American horticulture and conservation, providing a connection to officials, visitors, and gardeners; while the Lady Bird Johnson Wildflower Center in Austin, Texas, has been a leading advocate for the conservation and sustainable use of North American native plants and their habitats since the day of its founding in 1982. Modeling its program after LEED, SITES resolved to develop comprehensive standards for sustainable landscape design, construction, and maintenance. From its beginning, SITES has been working with USGBC, not to replace or compete with LEED, but to complement it.

The central message of the Sustainable Sites Initiative is that all landscapes—including home landscapes—hold the potential both to improve and to regenerate the natural benefits and services provided by ecosystems before development. These benefits—air and water cleansing, global climate regulation, pollination, erosion and sediment control, to name only a few—are essential to the health and well-being of humans and all other life on the planet.

Perhaps most importantly, SITES provides a common language and set of shared values for the term "sustainability" and all that it might mean for the landscape. Not everyone will agree with every benchmark or philosophy represented in the SITES work, but used holistically the years of discussion, research, and outreach behind the Initiative bring us all closer to a consensus on what is sustainable—and what is not.

GUIDING PRINCIPLES OF A SUSTAINABLE SITE*

Do no harm
Make no changes to the site that will degrade the surrounding environment. Promote projects on sites where previous disturbance or development presents an opportunity to regenerate ecosystem services through sustainable design.

Precautionary principle
Be cautious in making decisions that could create risk to human and environmental health. Some actions can cause irreversible damage. Examine a full range of alternatives—including no action—and be open to contributions from all affected parties.

Design with nature and culture
Create and implement designs that are responsive to economic, environmental, and cultural conditions with respect to the local, regional, and global context.

Use a decision-making hierarchy of preservation, conservation, and regeneration
Maximize and mimic the benefits of ecosystem services by preserving existing environmental features, conserving resources in a sustainable manner, and regenerating lost or damaged ecosystem services.

Provide regenerative systems as intergenerational equity
Provide future generations with a sustainable environment supported by regenerative systems and endowed with regenerative resources.

Support a living process
Continuously re-evaluate assumptions and values and adapt to demographic and environmental change.

Use a systems thinking approach
Understand and value the relationships in an ecosystem and use an approach that reflects and sustains ecosystem services; re-establish the integral and essential relationship between natural processes and human activity.

Use a collaborative and ethical approach
Encourage direct and open communication among colleagues, clients, manufacturers, and users to link long-term sustainability with ethical responsibility.

Maintain integrity in leadership and research
Implement transparent and participatory leadership, develop research with technical rigor, and communicate new findings in a clear, consistent, and timely manner.

Foster environmental stewardship
In all aspects of land development and management, foster an ethic of environmental stewardship—an understanding that responsible management of healthy ecosystems improves the quality of life for present and future generations.

---

* From the *Sustainable Sites Initiative: Guidelines and Performance Benchmarks 2009*

The lessons of the road

In creating its guidelines, the SITES team sought feedback from the general public and contacted thousands of civil engineers, landscape architects, arborists, cooperative extension agents, nursery owners, biologists, horticulturists, ecologists, hydrologists, soil scientists, and representatives of every aspect of the landscape construction industry. The widest possible range of views and expertise was considered. Everyone is a stakeholder in our human-influenced landscape.

Visitors to the SITES website will find two important reports (for information on how to obtain them, see under Chapter 2 in "References, Resources, and Recommended Reading" at the back of this book). The core document is the 231-page rating system, *Guidelines and Performance Benchmarks 2009*, which will be covered in more detail later in this chapter. But just as important for our purposes is *The Case for Sustainable Landscapes*, a concise summary of the important lessons of and philosophies behind the Sustainable Sites Initiative. *The Case for Sustainable Landscapes* highlights the need for all development to address considerations in three key areas: social, environmental, and economic. Environmental sustainability is impossible on its own unless people perceive benefits to themselves and their community. SITES addresses economic issues directly:

> [E]fforts to build landscapes that preserve and restore healthy ecosystems face a significant challenge—namely, persuading decision-makers that the cost of changing conventional methods of landscape design, development, and maintenance is money well spent. Persuasion must begin, then, with an accurate accounting of what the benefits of ecosystems are worth to the economies of our cities and towns, to developers, and to individuals.

Thus, a significant portion of *The Case for Sustainable Landscapes* attempts to make very specific and real the economic value of a healthy environment—going so far as to use the label "ecosystem services" for those benefits an ecosystem provides us and our economies. Several attempts to list these benefits have been made, each with slightly different wording, some lists slightly longer than others. The SITES team has consolidated the research into a list of ecosystem services that sustainable land development and management practices strive to protect or regenerate.

Establishing the value of these benefits isn't easy. How, for example, do you place an exact monetary value on the degree to which forests and woodlands help to regulate the global climate, even though the cost of climate disruption is, clearly, astronomical? A fascinating article published in the British scientific journal *Nature* suggests that a reasonable figure for the economic contribution of the environment worldwide would be $33 trillion (in 1997

U.S. dollars) annually, almost twice as much as the global gross national product.

On a more local scale, sustainable landscaping practices can bring impressive savings to a community. Yard and landscape trimmings, for example, contribute 13 percent of all municipal waste in the United States; more sustainable landscaping would, through more intelligent design, prevent the creation of much of this waste and recycle the remainder on site through composting and mulching. By promot-

ECOSYSTEM SERVICES*

Global climate regulation
Maintaining balance of atmospheric gases at historic levels, creating breathable air, and sequestering greenhouse gases.

Local climate regulation
Regulating local temperature, precipitation, and humidity through shading, evapotranspiration, and windbreaks.

Air and water cleansing
Removing and reducing pollutants in air and water.

Water supply and regulation
Storing and providing water within watersheds and aquifers.

Erosion and sediment control
Retaining soil within an ecosystem, preventing damage from erosion and siltation.

Hazard mitigation
Reducing vulnerability to damage from flooding, storm surge, wildfire, and drought.

Pollination
Providing pollinator species for reproduction of crops or other plants.

Habitat functions
Providing refuge and reproduction habitat to plants and animals, thereby contributing to conservation of biological and genetic diversity and evolutionary processes.

Waste decomposition and treatment
Breaking down waste and cycling nutrients.

Human health and well-being benefits
Enhancing physical, mental, and social well-being as a result of interaction with nature.

Food and renewable non-food products
Producing food, fuel, energy, medicine, or other products for human use.

Cultural benefits
Enhancing cultural, educational, aesthetic, and spiritual experiences as a result of interaction with nature.

* From the *Sustainable Sites Initiative: The Case for Sustainable Landscapes 2009*

ing the retention of stormwater runoff on site and infiltrating it into the soil through rain gardens and other bioretention systems, sustainable landscaping practices could dramatically reduce the cost to local governments of water treatment. The soil erosion caused by stripping the landscape of its cover doesn't just degrade the local landscape, by feeding silt into waterways; it serves as another major source of water pollution (second in its impact only to actual pathogens), also increasing costs of water treatment. Reducing and recycling construction wastes (which total 170 million tons annually in the United States) would dramatically reduce landfill waste, the need for harvesting wood from our forests, and the costs inherent in both.

Some eye-opening examples of specific economic benefits from environmental stewardship:

- Sufficient tree canopy assists home cooling. According to American Forests, an adequate tree canopy in the Atlanta, Georgia, region could amount to a savings of $28 million per year in cooling costs.
- Urban trees in New York City intercept almost 890 million gallons of rainwater runoff each year, resulting in an estimated annual savings of $35 million in stormwater management costs alone.
- Trees in Chicago filter an estimated 6,000 tons of air pollutants every year,

providing air cleansing value equivalent to $9.2 million.

Of course, economics aren't the only reason for acting sustainably, even if they are sometimes necessary to sway financial gatekeepers. SITES also underlines the health and wellness benefits nature provides us; these are impossible to quantify, yet no less important. One can attempt, for example, to calculate the effect of a view of green forest on property values, but that doesn't mean anyone should ignore the purely psychological and social value of having a forest nearby where one can take a walk or have a picnic.

In 2006, SITES announced a call for case studies—examples of sustainable land development and management practices that would inspire and educate the public. More than 130 projects were submitted, including a rehabilitation of 40 acres surrounding Washington's Headquarters at Valley Forge and a 314-acre mixed use development in Calgary, Alberta, but for the purposes of this book, two examples of sustainable home landscapes will be of particular interest. Before we plunge into the nitty-gritty of benchmarks, we can see in them what sustainability looks like on the ground—and how much it costs.

Case study: Santa Monica, California

In 2003, the City of Santa Monica, California, initiated garden\garden, a project designed to encourage city residents and landscape professionals to adopt sustainable garden practices. The city wished to promote practices that would, among other things, conserve water and energy, reduce waste, and decrease urban runoff, the single largest source of pollution in Santa Monica Bay. Although the city already kept a large demonstration garden at City Hall and had conducted seminars and tours of local sustainable landscapes, most residents were not moved to alter their gardening practices, and landscapers continued to recommend and install the traditional kinds of non-native plants with which they were most familiar.

The City of Santa Monica's challenge was to persuade both homeowners and landscapers that sustainable gardening was not only better for the environment than traditional gardening but also was attractive and made good economic sense. To prove their case, the city created garden\garden—adjacent residential front yards, one landscaped in the traditional manner and the other a native garden featuring climate-appropriate plants. Garden\garden is an invitation to the city's residents to make a direct comparison; it serves as a learning laboratory and working example for workshop attendees, garden tour visitors, and for the general public who walk past the garden daily.

Size/type of project. Approximately 1,900 square feet in each garden / urban residence.

Site context. Coastal southern California's Mediterranean climate is dominated by the Pacific Ocean. The air tends to be salt-laden; soils are commonly alkaline and sandy in texture. Average daily temperatures are mild, and morning fog is common, with daily afternoon winds. Average annual rainfall is 11 to 20 inches. The side-by-side bungalows are in an urban residential neighborhood.

Issues/constraints of the site. Both gardens are exposed to unusually high vehicular traffic and resulting air pollution. In both gardens the soil was a sandy loam (moderate permeability), poor in organic matter, and highly compacted. Tests also indicated high alkalinity and high levels of heavy metals, including zinc and copper. The existing landscape on both sites was completely removed to create an identical base condition for study, with all waste exported for recycling. Soil amendments were applied as appropriate for the respective plant material. The intent was to bring the soil to a basic level of balance, facilitate a long-term development of healthy soil life, and to increase plant health.

Practices in the traditional garden (TG). No chemical herbicides or insecticides (per Santa Monica City policy); occasional use of blood meal; exotic plants from northern Europe and the eastern United States; standard, user-controlled sprinkler irrigation system; no provision for runoff mitigation.

Sustainable practices in the native garden (NG). No chemical herbicides or insecticides; climate-appropriate California native cultivars, designed to replicate the chaparral of the Santa Monica Mountains; low-volume drip irrigation with a weather-sensitive controller; system for capturing stormwater runoff for groundwater recharge; wildlife habitat for local and migratory fauna.

Construction costs. TG = $12,400; NG = $16,700. The higher cost of the native garden included demolition and replacement of an existing access ramp, installation of permeable paving, and installation of a rainwater recovery system—rain gutters that tie into an underground infiltration pit.

Monitoring. Construction was completed in March 2004. From 2004 to 2008, the city tracked plant growth and other environmental factors, as well as costs associated with labor hours, water consumption, and green waste production, for both gardens. Long-term, the ever-increasing costs of maintenance, water, and green waste transport/disposal required by the traditional garden will offset construction costs for the native garden.

Maintenance. TG = $223.22/year; NG =

The traditional garden features conventional turf and exotic cultivars from the eastern United States and Europe. Photo by Deidra Walpole Photography, courtesy of City of Santa Monica.

$70.44/year. Difference = $152.78/year—or 68 percent fewer dollars spent on maintenance labor for native garden.

Water use. TG = 283,981 gallons/year; NG = 64,396 gallons/year. Difference = 219,585 gallons/year—or 77 percent less water use in the native garden.

Green waste. TG = 647 pounds/year; NG = 219 pounds/year. Difference = 428 pounds/year—or 66 percent less waste produced by the native garden.

Lessons learned. Collected site data have validated theories that a southern California native landscape would yield signif-icant reductions in resource consumption and waste production as compared to a traditional southern California landscape.

Case study: Portland, Oregon

The Malolepsy/Battershell project is a renovated urban residential landscape in Portland, Oregon. The project objectives included reducing water use for irrigation, managing stormwater runoff, decreasing heat buildup from a concrete driveway, reusing salvaged materials, and increasing water infiltration and productivity of marginal and compacted soil. Client and de-

In the native garden, California native taxa replicate the drought-tolerant chaparral of the Santa Monica Mountains. The native garden uses 77 percent less water than the traditional garden. Photo by Deidra Walpole Photography, courtesy of City of Santa Monica.

signer goals—such as maintaining bioregional characteristics and involving the family in garden implementation—guided the project in all phases of development.

Size/type of project. Approximately 4,700 square feet / urban residence.

Site context. The Willamette Valley ecoregion was historically covered by rolling prairies, oak savannas, coniferous forests, extensive wetlands, and deciduous riparian forests. The climate is Mediterranean, characterized by mild winters and hot summers. Approximately 45 inches of precipitation falls during seven months of the year, while the remaining five months, from June to October, are generally dry. The Malolepsy/Battershell site is located in an urban residential neighborhood of primarily owner-occupied homes.

Issues/constraints of the site. The site was characterized by a lack of shade and compacted soil with a 40 percent slope (elevated 10 feet above street level). The compacted soil as well as the steep terrain (both on site and in neighbors' yards) meant that the site was prone to excessive stormwater runoff; the concrete driveway directed runoff either toward the basement of the house or immediately into the street. The lack of shade trees exacerbated stormwater runoff and contributed to the heat produced from the street, sidewalks, and the driveway. In the backyard, 6-foot-high weeds occupied 80 percent of the open space. The disturbed soil—whether bare, compacted, or contaminated with chlordane (a toxic lawn and garden pesticide commonly used to exterminate ants and termites that is damaging to both the environment and human health)—needed to be restored.

At the inception of the project, a neighbor's large ash tree fell during a windstorm and completely covered the backyard. As much of the tree as possible was salvaged and worked into the landscape design. The remainder was used for building a wattle fence, as firewood in the household fireplace, and as brown material to provide the carbon for the three compost bins that reside in the yard.

Sustainable practices: protect existing soils during construction; restore disturbed soils. Construction work was confined to designated pathways, and no heavy equipment was used on the site. Soil improvement techniques included amending the soil with 25 cubic yards of compost (applied over existing turf to a depth of 6 to 8 inches) and replanting for quick establishment. The design included an aspen forest (nine multi-trunked specimens) in the backyard to ameliorate the soil for chlordane contamination in areas where children would be playing. Exposed soil was mulched heavily with neighborhood leaf litter to supplement onsite resources.

Reduce potable water use. Downspouts were disconnected from the residence and two 55-gallon drums were installed to collect rainwater. This both reduced supplemental watering for the landscape and eliminated stormwater runoff from the driveway. To reduce water needs in the landscape, plants were selected according to site microclimates. A strict and disciplined watering schedule for all plants was implemented, which almost eliminated the need for supplemental water in the landscape, including the steepest terrain. Less than 10 percent of total domestic water is used for outside purposes, including the vegetable garden and lawn.

Preserve and restore vegetation. Existing vegetation was retained and incorporated into the new design. Native ferns and spleenworts, birches, willows, and a couple of species of ceanothus and cistus joined the existing maple tree and several non-native plants (hydrangeas, rosemary, assorted perennials). In the backyard, contiguous nonlinear beds of vegetation with diverse and tiered canopies were strategically placed in order to salvage existing plant material, foster habitat diversity, and create social spaces.

Reuse excess vegetation; use salvaged materials. No materials were purchased other than concrete for setting three 4×4 posts, upon which was mounted a fence of salvaged wood to set off the upper quarter of the driveway. During all phases of construction, landscape waste was recovered and materials salvaged: plant trimmings were composted; bricks from a decommissioned house chimney were used in a large patio and several pathways; broken concrete made stepping stones; drawers from an old chest were used as containers for vegetable starts (which are particularly at risk from slugs and water and soil runoff);

a drywell was constructed in the backyard underneath the lawn and filled with the broken-up pieces of what had been a small concrete slab.

Enhance group and individual experiences. The landscape design included spaces or small outdoor "rooms" to accommodate activities on all sides of the house and to promote free flow of child play from front yard to back. A small playhouse connects to the back patio and side path, doubling as a trellis and shade structure. A winding path connects all outdoor rooms, making them easily accessible. Focal points were created in the landscape for views from inside the house. Although grass was requested in the backyard (for children), multiple microclimates were created for diversity of habitat and plant material. The grass area is large enough to accommodate three children and two parents but small enough to mow with a push mower.

Reduce urban heat islands. Shade was established over the driveway and southwest-facing side of the house. A portion of the driveway was converted to a container garden with furniture and rain barrels to help mitigate other heat effects.

Reduce emissions. Hand tools were used during all phases of construction, including the breaking up of the concrete, with one small exception—a power saw was used for the fence posts.

Construction costs. Of the $16,500 total cost (design, materials, and labor), the majority was spent on design, plants, soil, and sand. All other materials came from the site, were found, or were donated by the neighborhood. Labor costs were $4,500; additional labor was contributed by the homeowner (drywell construction, digging, grading, planting, and mulching), following instruction by project designer Debbie Tolman, who provided hands-on tutoring and thereby facilitated more homeowner involvement in the finished product. The costs of the sustainable strategies in this project may be lower than conventional practices primarily due to onsite reuse of materials and owner labor contributions.

Monitoring. Construction was completed in June 2008. The front yard was completed first and has gone through three full growing seasons; the backyard took an additional year. In 2007, only one watering was required in the front yard during the dry season. Environmental testing for soil quality was recommended for two years. Field tests of the soil structure

Malolepsy/Battershell residence, front yard. Design and photo by Debbie Tolman of Avant Gardens, nw, Portland.

have shown that compost has improved the existing soil.

Maintenance. Because most of the design was intended to be no- to low-maintenance (with the exception of the vegetable garden), maintenance continues to avoid the use of machinery. During establishment (the first year), maintenance and management strategies included weeding in the backyard (two to three hours per season) and deep watering during the dry season (June to October). In the second year there was less weeding and watering as plants were established and covered more ground. In addition to mulching in the spring and fall, the maintenance plan includes adding compost in the garden and to the landscape areas. All fertilization is natural: leaf litter and compost.

With annual visits by the project designer, the Malolepsy/Battershell family continues to be involved actively in their developing landscape—composting and mulching, harvesting and replanting vegetables, espaliering fruit trees, and watering containers in driveway with captured rainwater.

Lessons learned. The rainwater collection system has resolved two issues: reducing potable water needs for landscape irrigation and eliminating stormwater runoff from the driveway. The new landscape design created new spaces for family activities such as gardening, dining, and playing, and continues to provide approximately 60 percent of the garden vegetables for the family's diet.

A guide to the guide— explaining the system

You've read through the case studies. Now ask yourself this question—exactly how sustainable are the gardens in them? Could you objectively measure the degree of sustainability if some features—say, rainwater collection, or avoidance of machinery—were added or taken away? The Sustainable Sites Initiative's LEED-inspired rating system can provide at least partial answers to such questions. Because the rating system,

Malolepsy/Battershell residence, backyard path. Design and photo by Debbie Tolman of Avant Gardens, nw, Portland.

Guidelines and Performance Benchmarks 2009, addresses the whole range of public, commercial, and private landscapes, it may not always be directly relevant to the average gardener; however, the guidelines as a whole can provide even the novice with a summary of new priorities and design practices that work in landscapes of all sizes. To work all this out on one's own would be a daunting task; SITES provides not only a framework for arranging the various steps but also lists of resources to which you can turn for more detailed information.

Like the LEED standards it reinforces, the Sustainable Sites Initiative rating system includes with each landscaping recommendation the number of points that may be earned by successfully implementing it in your project. These are weighted to reflect the relative value each "ingredient" of a sustainable landscape offers. Restoring and stabilizing the channel of a previously degraded stream, for example, can earn you up to 5 points, whereas restoring and revegetating half an acre of soil moderately disturbed by previous activity on the site earns 3. Of course, restoring damaged sites caused by the development process (such as soil compaction to areas that will later be vegetated) is one of the fifteen prerequisites, which can be considered to be the most important elements of the SITES credits.

Accepting that few home gardeners will read every word in *Guidelines and Performance Benchmarks 2009*, we offer in the next few pages a guide to the guide, an extract of the sustainability guidelines most directly applicable to home gardening—with directions on how (if you are so inclined) to refer back to the corresponding sections of the original to pursue the various topics in greater depth (not covered here is Section 2, pre-design assessment and planning, which covers two important prerequisites, one being a full ecological site assessment, which is crucial for ensuring adverse effects from development are minimized and the greatest range of benefits can be garnered from the site). A "perfect" score for sustainability would be 250, but so long as all fifteen prerequisites are met, stars are awarded with as few as 100 points, as follows:

One Star: 100 points
Two Stars: 125 points
Three Stars: 150 points
Four Stars: 200 points

One gauge of the importance of a given section is by the number of prerequisites and its percentage of the total possible 250 points.

Site selection (Section 1; 21 possible points). The first thing to consider on your path to a more sustainable landscape is where to locate it. If your new home is newly built on what was prime farmland (which goes against Prerequisite 1.1), you have already undermined the sustainability of your garden and local community needs. And though few gardeners would choose to locate their homes on a brownfield (Credit 1.5; 5 to 10 points), this is a realistic option for city gardeners and community garden groups seeking unbuilt land. If handled properly, turning such a degraded site into a green and attractive landscape is an excellent example of how human development can enhance the environment.

Another consideration to keep in mind when siting a garden involves respecting the natural hydrological (rain and water circulation) cycle. That is, your garden should be sited in such a way as to protect and preserve existing floodplains and wetlands (Prerequisites 1.2 and 1.3), areas that play an important role in absorbing and biologically purifying precipitation and flood water.

Finally, you can minimize the disturbance your garden causes to the environment by the simple step of locating it within an established community (Credit 1.6; 6 points), especially one that is served by public transit (Credit 1.7; 5 points). Popular mythology in the United States has glamorized the pioneer, but the time has come to redefine "breaking new ground." We must instead seek out new and more intelligent methods for developing and maintaining the land we already occupy.

Site design: water (Section 3; 44 possible points). This section suggests techniques and technologies (many of them covered in Chapter 7 of this book) for protecting fresh water, an essential and increasingly scarce resource—everything from rehabilitating lost streams, wetlands,

and shorelines (Credit 3.4; 2 to 5 points) to managing rainwater so it is used in your garden. For instance, homeowners who confront problems with runoff during wet seasons could skip the traditional solution of installing a subsurface system of drainage pipe and instead take advantage of the flow to add a seasonal stream to their garden.

One recommendation in this part of the report is to protect and restore riparian, wetland, and shoreline buffers (Credit 3.3; 3 to 8 points). Replanting these margins with adapted native species markedly decreases the flow of lawn fertilizers and other pollutants into such sensitive habitats; reduces the erosion of stream and river banks and thus the flow of silt into waterways; and provides shade for greenways and habitat for wildlife. Another is to reduce potable water use for landscape irrigation by 75 percent or more, compared to conventional gardens in your region. This can be accomplished by adjusting your plant selection—the most drought-tolerant groundcovers, shrubs, and trees require only about one-third as much irrigation per square foot of area as do the most drought-tolerant turfgrasses.

You'll also find here an analysis of the uniformity of water distribution (a key to irrigation efficiency) offered by different technologies. A drip irrigation system equipped with pressure-compensating emitters emerges as the clear winner, providing 90 percent efficiency in this respect, 20 percentage points more than the next most efficient technologies. Additionally, taking advantage of other sources of water through rainwater collection systems or greywater recycling can further reduce or even eliminate potable water use in the home landscape.

Site design: soil and vegetation (Section 4; 51 possible points). Preserving and enhancing the soil quality on your site and selecting plants adapted to the site and local climate are obvious ways to enhance the sustainability of your garden, but as this section of the report indicates, that's just a beginning. Identifying any invasive plants already on site and making a plan for their ongoing control is also fundamental (Prerequisite 4.1), as is identifying any plants protected by local, state, or federal regulations and planning for their protection (Credit 4.5; 5 points). Planning the landscaping in such a way as to minimize disturbance of the soil on your site (Credit 4.4; 6 points) is the most efficient way to enhance the quality of your garden soil. Confining construction equipment to clearly designated zones during the installation of driveways and garden paths is an easy and effective way to protect soil in other areas. Using locally adapted native plants and entire native plant communities (Credit 4.7; 1 to 4 points / Credit 4.8; 2 to 6 points / Credit 4.9; 1 to 5 points) is suggested as a means of reinforcing the natural ecology of your area.

Among the less obvious measures the report recommends are planting a wind-break of evergreen trees and shrubs to keep the prevailing winter wind from striking your house and so reducing heating costs (Credit 4.10; 2 to 4 points); and planting deciduous trees and shrubs to shade the south, west, and east walls and roof of your house to reduce summer cooling bills (Credit 4.11; 2 to 5 points). Especially in areas where wildfires are common and perhaps even an essential feature of the regional ecology, sustainable design should also include limiting the planting within 30 feet of the house to species of low stature and low flammability (Credit 4.13; 3 points).

Site design: materials selection (Section 5; 36 possible points). What you buy and how you use it has a major impact on the sustainability of your gardening. It's important to keep this in mind while you are in the planning stages of creating your garden; otherwise, you may include features that will impose an unnecessarily heavy burden on the environment. For example, don't even contemplate using wood harvested from threatened tree species (Prerequisite 5.1). Rather, you should consider using lumber certified by the Forest Stewardship Council (Credit 5.6; 1 to 4 points) and recycled materials (Credit 5.5; 2 to 4 points), or salvaged materials and plants (Credit 5.4; 2 to 4 points), perhaps including as elements of your design plants and rocks removed during the clearing of your site. Reuse and adapt existing structures, **paving**, and other amenities

(Credit 5.2; 1 to 4 points). Use locally produced materials and plants to minimize the energy used and emissions produced in transporting them from the producer to your garden. Including locally produced materials in your design will also give your garden a more genuinely regional character, helping to root it into the surrounding landscape (Credit 5.7; 2 to 6 points). Finally, purchase plants and materials produced in a sustainable manner. In the case of plants this might mean purchasing from a nursery that uses compost (a recycled material) rather than peat (which is strip-mined from wetlands) as a growing medium, or that irrigates with water collected on site rather than drawing on the municipal water system (Credit 5.9; 3 points). In the case of materials, you might look for a manufacturer that uses energy from renewable sources or uses non-potable water in its manufacturing processes (Credit 5.10; 3 to 6 points).

Site design: human health and well-being (Section 6; 32 possible points). This section begins with the advice: "During construction of the site, ensure that the project provides economic or social benefits to the local community." Gardeners who landscape their own lots won't have to worry about many "human" aspects of construction, such as paying a living wage to workers or providing disability access (both measures covered in this portion of the guidelines). However, can a private garden really be sustainable if it ignores the community that surrounds it? This portion of the guidelines has many excellent ideas for people who want to build "community benefits" into their home landscape:

■ If your garden is open to public areas and public viewing, do you provide opportunities for neighbors to enjoy the view—or even provide a bench for passersby to take a rest? (Credit 6.2; 1 to 4 points)
■ Have you taken care that your plantings (particularly trees) will not obstruct the views of neighbors? (Credit 6.7; 3 to 4 points)
■ If you're making an effort, say, to use native plants and avoid irrigation, can you use your garden as a teaching tool, adding some signage for passersby to explain your efforts? (Credit 6.3; 2 to 4 points)
■ If you own a historic house or live in an historic area, have you carefully studied the impacts of your garden plans on cultural sites? (Credit 6.4; 2 to 4 points)
■ If you include outdoor lighting, do you minimize light pollution and only use lighting consistent with safety needs? (Credit 6.9; 2 points)

One suggestion not explicitly stated as a credit in the rating system but worth considering—if your garden includes fruits, vegetables, and other edibles, do you set aside part of your harvest to share with food banks, shelters, or other charities?

Construction (Section 7; 21 possible points). Good design may be the foundation of a sustainable garden, but the means by which the design is implemented is a critical piece of this process. This is not a place to "bend the rules." Construction pollutants must be controlled and retained (Prerequisite 7.1); such pollutants include toxic chemicals, such as spilled fuels and pavement sealers, but also sediments washed or blown off areas of soil disturbed during construction or grading. The guidelines also require that 100 percent of soil disturbed during construction be restored (Prerequisite 7.2) and provide criteria for successful restoration based on the following:

1. Organic matter (required for all sites)
2. Compaction
3. Infiltration rates
4. Soil biological function
5. Soil chemical characteristics

Digging compost or other organic matter into compacted or otherwise disturbed soils during construction boosts sustainability in two ways: it restores healthy functioning to the soil, a source of important ecosystem services such as water filtration, and it reduces the need for irrigation, fertilization, and other supplementary measures later on. Restoring soils that were disturbed by previous development (Credit 7.3; 2 to 8 points) is also recommended, as is minimizing construction waste and recycling such waste products and composting on site whenever possible (Credits 7.4 and 7.5; 3 to 5 points each). Scrap lumber can be recycled for use in other projects. Woody material collected during land clearing can be chipped on site and used as mulch; soil excavated from one area can be used as fill in another. Rock exposed during excavation and grading can be reused in retaining walls or as garden features.

Maintenance (Section 8; 23 possible points). This section begins with two prerequisites: plan for sustainable site maintenance (8.1) and provide for storage and collection of recyclables (8.2).

Minimize the production of greenhouse gases as a result of garden maintenance (Credit 8.7; 1 to 4 points). The best way to accomplish this is to plan ahead: avoid features such as hedges and lawns that require constant trimming. Gardeners are likely to find that in a well-designed home landscape, hand clippers and push mowers are sufficient. If they are not, use electrical or solar-powered tools; these are better options than gas-powered equipment, as the gasoline engines used in garden equipment are typically inefficient and highly polluting. If you must, use power equipment that has been shown to meet the EPA's new standards for non-road engines.

Recycle organic wastes such as autumn leaves and tree and shrub trimmings on site through composting and chipping into mulch (Credit 8.3; 2 to 6 points). This simultaneously reduces the garden's contribution to the waste stream and eliminates the need to import organic materials such as peat to maintain soil health.

Use electricity generated from renewable sources (Credit 8.5; 2 to 3 points) and use only energy-efficient fixtures, such as water-feature pumps and lights (Credit 8.4; 1 to 4 points). This can result in a substantial savings: according to the report, exterior lighting alone represents an estimated 1.34 percent of California's total energy use.

Monitoring (Section 9; 18 possible points). The final step in gardening sustainably is to keep track of resources. For the average gardener, keeping track of monthly water usage and the various inputs (fertilizers, maintenance hours) required by different garden areas or amenities (mixed bed, water feature, vegetable garden) is sufficient. Use these records to periodically assess how the existing design can be further refined. Look to the record-keeping evident in both case studies to get an idea of what is meant by monitoring. Many gardeners keep a journal or notebook for these and all records, including climatic data, records of purchases, and wildlife sightings.

SITES' two-year pilot program, set to conclude in 2012, will help ensure that the *Guidelines and Performance Benchmarks 2009* are both practical and effective as a tool for recognizing projects that incorporate sustainability at every stage of development. Specifically, the pilot program will evaluate the appropriateness of the point system and of performance benchmarks in a variety of climate zones, geographic areas, and project types and sizes—public and private, urban to rural, greenfield to greyfield. The Sustainable Sites Initiative will make refinements as needed, releasing a new version of the credits in 2013. SITES shows that even small landscape projects can be conducted in a way that *adds* to the health of the ecosystem. Gardeners on the typical quarter-acre lot should feel there are no barriers to being completely sustainable at home!

CHAPTER 3

The New American Meadow Garden

by John Greenlee with Neil Diboll

IF YOU HAVE A TYPICAL American lawn, chances are good that no matter where you live, you already have the perfect place for a meadow or a natural lawn. Chances are also really good that the conventional lawn you have fits into one of two categories. Either it is in poor or unsatisfactory condition, suffering from weeds, lack of sun, or lack of attention, and honestly does not look very good. Or you are putting down lots of chemicals, water, and resources in order to have a thick lush carpet, and thereby trashing the environment. Why have a bad lawn when you could have a great meadow? or a lawn that is a "natural" lawn, a native or regionally adapted lawn that does not consume the same kind of resources as a conventional lawn? Meadow gardening is an idea whose time has come.

The traditional American lawn is iconic to the point that having a good-looking lawn is equated to being a good citizen. But current research says the conventional lawn is downright bad for the planet and makes you a not-so-good eco-citizen. Sure, we are always going to need sports turf for athletic endeavors. But most American gardeners strive for the perfect lawns they see on TV during baseball games and golf tournaments and in doing so cause serious ecological harm. The pollution caused by conventional turfgrass culture is real and significant. The promotion of this kind of gardening by large corporate interests is insidious and threatens our own health and the planet's as well. Cookie-cutter lawns in traditional suburban neighborhood settings are the perfect place to plant meadows and natural lawns that are better for us and the environment.

The crazy thing is, my own design and consulting work has convinced me that the vast majority of Americans really do not even know what their lawn is really made of. Is it rye, Bermuda, fescue, or all three? They might have started with one, but what's there now? I will bet your lawn, like most, probably has lots of different components—for better or worse. Besides, anecdotal evi-

---

A meadow garden is a place where man and nature meet halfway. The simple green "carpet" here, a mixed sedge lawn near St. Louis, Missouri (see page 65), is actually a matrix of four different sedges.

SOME FACTS ABOUT AMERICAN LAWNS

- According to a NASA study using satellite imaging, lawns in America cover 40,411 square miles, an area larger than the state of Kentucky. That makes lawns the country's largest irrigated crop.

- A 2002 Harris Survey suggests as a nation we spend $28.9 billion yearly on lawns. This translates into approximately $1,200 per household.

- Fifty to 70 percent of residential water use is needed for landscape, mostly lawn. This translates into about 10,000 gallons of water per summer per 1,000-square-foot lawn.

- According to the Safer Pest Control Project, 67 million pounds of synthetic pesticides are added to U.S. lawns each year. We use three times as much pesticide on our lawns per acre as we do on our agricultural crops.

- According to the EPA, 54 million Americans mow their lawns each weekend, using 800 million gallons of gas per year and producing tons of air pollutants. Garden equipment engines, which had unregulated emissions until very recently, emit high levels of carbon monoxide, volatile organic compounds, and nitrogen oxides, producing up to 5 percent of the nation's air pollution. One older gas-powered mower emits the same pollutants as forty-three cars being driven 12,000 miles per year. Newer models emit eleven times the pollutants of a new car.

- Seventeen million gallons of fuel, mostly gasoline, are spilled each year while refueling lawn equipment.

dence suggests that the average time it takes to mow a lawn each week far exceeds the amount of time homeowners actually use their lawn for recreation or enjoyment. Most people just look at their lawns.

Michael Pollan calls the American lawn "nature under our boot." So why not partner with nature instead of trying to defeat it? Why not learn about the native and regionally appropriate plants and replace your barren lifeless turf with a glorious meadow? A place where, as Pollan says, we can "meet nature halfway."

Why not plant a meadow instead? Meadows can be a compromise where there is something for us, and for nature. People like Neil Diboll, Rick Darke, and I have been promoting the creation of meadows and natural lawns as alternatives to conventional American lawns.

What is a meadow?

So just what is a meadow? Meadows are generally acknowledged to be grassy openings in landscapes with trees, often associated in nature with streams or creeks. Meadows can comprise indigenous species, or they can be mixes of both native and introduced or exotic species. Although grasses will always dominate in any meadow, a true meadow ecology will be rich in many kinds of plants, with bulbs, sedges, mosses, and perennials in a beautifully woven cloth. A meadow is a symphony of color, light, and texture. Filled with diverse plants, meadows support a diversity of life—from microscopic organisms to birds, bees, and butterflies. There is nothing more beautiful than a natural meadow, but I'd like to think that a designed meadow—using the natural meadow as its inspiration—comes a close second.

The beautifully woven cloth of a wild meadow. Photo by Saxon Holt.

What is a natural lawn?

What is a natural lawn? A natural lawn is lawn composed of native grasses and sedges or regionally adapted grasses and grass-like plants that, by nature and habit, make a lawn-like carpet that can be enjoyed like conventional lawn, without the negative ecological impact imposed by the conventional lawn. Every region of the country, no matter the soil or climate, whether in sun or shade, has native sods that, once established, will make a natural lawn. A natural lawn is earth-friendly and alive, not a dead zone of chemicals and fume-belching machines that scare away the birds and bees. Natural lawns stay lawn-like with a minimum of mowing, so that flowers and bulbs can bloom right in the lawn. Many of these natural lawns are new to the American nursery trade but are increasingly offered by regional plant growers to help Americans get away from conventional lawns.

Growing a conventional lawn is the path of least resistance for most gardeners. Once you put it down, you don't have to think about the lifecycle of the plants. You keep cutting them, so they never flower or set seed. You are always mowing, hence birds and bees cannot hang out. Having something else would require learning about plants, about what your property used to be, and about what is there now. How does this information affect the environment, and what resources are required to make it "look good"?

Fortunately, there are new solutions and new thinking for American gardeners. It is all about putting the right plant in the right place and letting the plants do the work. Scott Ogden and Lauren Springer Ogden call it "plant-driven design." Instead of planting turf that needs constant watering, mowing, and input to thrive, choose a "turf" that thrives naturally in your soil and climate. If you can find your original native sods, once established they will thrive with minimum input. Most homeowners, given the choice, will choose the solution that combines both beauty and ecology. Nature can be right outside your door, not just fenced off in a national park.

Chances are that natives will play an important role in the new sustainable American lawn. I'm often asked why we don't use only natives in our designs. I'm passionate about natives, and I think understanding the native grasses in your area is critical to creating a successful meadow, but meadow gardens are not always habitat restoration projects in which only natives would be proper. A meadow garden is a balance of ornamental design needs and habitat restoration, and we must recognize the following truths.

You can't stop evolution—there is no way-back machine to make a perfect habitat without human influence, human traffic, and introduced plants. You could find only the plants that grow within a hundred miles of your site, but they might not work with the lovely trees, or changes in soils or exposure you have in your particular site. Many of the treasured and beautiful pasture grasses across the northern tier of our country are in fact exotics that have pushed natives out. Many natives have cycles and needs—such as fire ecology—that are incompatible with homes. By all means, I would choose an equivalent native first over an introduced plant, but this just isn't always practical or feasible in residential gardens. Non-native plants, if they are well behaved, might make a fine meadow that can be managed, instead of killing everything and starting all over.

Thomas Church, beloved American and landscape architect, wrote the classic *Gardens Are For People* (1955). If he were alive today, I bet he would revise that and declare, "Gardens are for all living things." I would like to think he would agree that nature belongs in the garden.

Wherever I've traveled and found remnant native grass habitats, they're doing the same things lawns do except they're the "real deal." Such habitats are windows into our ecological past, and they're not an idealized notion. Part of embracing the American meadow is putting some of it back where it belongs.

What would it have been to walk on a native meadow along the Salt River right through Phoenix? Do you know that Las Vegas means "the meadows"? It was an area with native sedges like *Carex praegracilis* (western field sedge) and *Distichlis spicata* (saltgrass). People first came to Las Vegas because there was water and grass, and now there are over a million people in that valley. The native meadows are long

gone. Native to grasslands thousands of miles away, Bermuda grasses and fescues have replaced the native desert grasses—it makes no sense.

The greatest argument for planting a meadow instead of a lawn is a positive rather than a negative—people might get out and actually enjoy their yards if they're full of life and beauty rather than synthetic chemicals and gasoline fumes. I think meadows are really seductive. If you look at meadow gardens, you want to be there. You can sense that it's going to be a place that's romantic—nothing catches light or moves like grasses. Most foliage is translucent—light passes through it. Very few other garden plants can move in the wind and even create sound like grasses do. People don't think of grasses as flowers, but many have amazing flowers. Meadows can be simple and elegant and quiet. Or they can be energizing, with exploding colors and textures—bulbs that come and go throughout the season. I do understand what lawns do aesthetically—a place where the eye can rest that is cool and calming—but you can achieve the same thing with a grass that doesn't need to be mowed, fed, and watered as heavily as a conventional lawn.

A celebration of regions

One subtle point I make in my new book, *The American Meadow Garden* (Greenlee and Holt 2009): lawns are what make Tucson, Baltimore, Portland, Des Moines, and Los Angeles all look the same—like a chain store, the same in every city. Conventional lawns will look the same anywhere they are planted. This is a terrible waste, because Maine really is different from Arizona, which is different from California. We can celebrate the beauty and variety of American regions with American meadows—not one standard turf that's applied everywhere, even when it's an unsound choice. Instead, why not celebrate your local grass ecology? I guarantee you that there are some natural lawn grasses that "look right" just for your region and nowhere else.

Meadows can honor regionality instead of trying to homogenize the country. If it doesn't need to be a lawn, meadows can really capture the essence of a region. By doing so, they will not just add beauty but actually enhance the local ecology. Plant native grasses and wildflowers, and you will attract native insects and butterflies, which will attract native birds, creating a valuable habitat. Even lawns maintained "organically" cannot offer the beauty and versatility of a meadow.

Almost every region of the country has a "no mow" turfgrass, a grass or sedge blend that needs little mowing. It is important to know, however, that there is no universal "no mow" lawn for this vast and varied country of ours. For example, Neil Diboll of Prairie Nursery in Wisconsin (www.prairienursery.com) has developed a fine fescue turfgrass blend for customers who, in addition to the prairie-type plantings that are Diboll's specialty, want to maintain some area of lawn. When

planted as recommended (see the Epilogue to this chapter), his "No Mow" fine fescue seed mix typically performs as advertised, providing a less labor- and resource-consuming alternative to the conventional lawn through the northern tier of our country, the region with cool summers and low humidity. But Diboll (who has a degree in ecology) doesn't recommend this mix for the dry Southwest or the hot, humid Southeast. Trying to force a plant to grow where it does not want to will always be a losing proposition. The southern tier of this country needs its own native sods.

The solutions are out there in nature, what little is left, and—finally—nurseries are making these plants available for our gardens. Instead of searching for a "holy grail" lawn, plant a meadow.

Getting started

If you've decided you want to replace lawn with a meadow, the first question is "Where are you?" Do you know your soil, your exposure, your climate and microclimate? Are you in a hot, windy zone or a cold inland valley? Are you willing to do a little bit of work and find out what native grasses were probably growing in fields and meadows in your area or on your property before the bulldozers came? Even if these grasses are unavailable commercially, they may be able to tell you what nursery plants are good substitutes. The essence of meadow gardening is to completely study the site first, to be sure you are choosing plants that will need little chemical or water inputs once it's established. Gardening is about the process, and enjoying the change from one season to another and one vision to another. Creating a natural lawn is going to be a challenge. You will have to learn the plants, or pay someone else who does know them.

If you have a difficult time with these questions, and especially if you're a newcomer to understanding plants and garden habitats, don't be afraid to ask for help. There are designers around the country who specialize in ecological designs and habitat restoration. It might be hard to find designers who have experience with meadows, but you might track down a landscape architect who knows habitat restoration and has been dying to design a residential meadow garden. Talk to nursery wholesalers who sell grasses—they may have relationships with designers who use their products.

Along with absorbing other revelations about common gardening practices, many experts are rethinking how we prepare the soil. Many, myself included, believe that adding lots of organic matter or trying to "change" or "improve" the soil they have is old school thinking. More and more the notion is to work with what you have. "Do not fight the site" is the new rallying cry. Raping a peat bog to rototill into the top 6 inches of your ground makes no significant "change" to the soil whatsoever. Adding organic matter, which will quickly decompose, will not change the nature of the soil.

The new thinking says if you have sand, plant sand-loving plants. If you have clay, there is a myriad of potential candidates that thrive in clay soils. Plant them. The plants will thrive, and your garden will consume less energy. Improving the soil for food production is an exception, but even food crops have diversity that favors some varieties over others, depending on your soil type. It is really all about learning the plants.

Weeds and chemicals

Perhaps the most important factor, after choosing the right plants for your soil and climate, is to be weed-free. Before you plant, to be successful, you need to understand what weeds are, what weeds you have, and what constitutes a disturbed ecology. The real definition of "weed" is a plant out of place. A plant that is considered a weed in a conventional lawn may not be a weed in meadow. It depends on the nature of the plant. Weeds compete for nutrients and light. The worst ones are aggressive and will overrun the more desirable plants. They may spread by seed, by stems above and below the ground, or from all three. The really bad ones, noxious weeds, are truly plant bullies. These include grasses both annual and perennial, like cheat grass, Bermuda grass, Johnson grass, and plants like Canadian thistle and morning glory. Many of our worst weeds take real effort to eliminate. But the rewards are usually worth the fight. To beat your enemies, you have to know them. A surprising number of American gardeners do not even know their own weeds. They might think Bermuda is crabgrass. Crabgrass is an annoying annual that is somewhat easy to pull, but trying to eliminate a mature stand of Bermuda, by hoeing it out, is next to impossible. So if you are not sure what your weeds are, be smart and find a professional who does.

Getting back to square one: being as weed-free as possible. This can be accomplished by chemicals or organically. Some people want to be all organic, and it is an admirable goal, but it is important to know

Why have a bad lawn when you could have a great meadow?

that many noxious weeds may require at least two years of control before they are eliminated.

The debate over chemical use is a complex one. Many people, myself included, believe the proper use of chemicals can be a valuable tool for creating meadows and natural lawns. In most cases, they need to be used only once in order to establish the "good guys." Organic methods almost always take longer and can be ineffective on some really noxious weeds. There is a lot of information in *The American Meadow Gar-*

den (Greenlee and Holt 2009), and a lot of information on the Internet on organic gardening sites. Remember, you have to know your weeds before you can kill them. Organic methods include tilling, mechanical removal, sheet mulching, soil baking, and "organic" acids, like vinegar. Again, you have to know what you are fighting to be successful with these methods.

Weed control with glyphosate weed killers (like Roundup), applied properly, can eliminate noxious perennial weeds in one season. The most effective method involves multiple grow-kill cycles: encourage weeds to grow, with water and fertilizer, then spray with Roundup; repeat the process every four to six weeks until the soil is free of weeds. A minimum of three grow-kill cycles is a must for most noxious perennial weeds, and the weeds must actually be growing in order to be killed. This usually means killing in the spring, summer, or while it is still warm in the fall. Irrigating and fertilizing the bare soil will stimulate any weed inoculum to grow. Then it is time to spray again.

Once the grow-kill cycles have done their work, if you are planting from plugs or pots, it is best to cover the soil with bark mulch to a depth of 2 to 3 inches. This will prevent new weed seeds from blowing in while also conserving moisture until the desirable meadow plants are established. Almost any locally available mulch will work, as long as it is weed seed free.

If you are seeding, you are now ready to seed and topdress. Keeping weeds out of your new meadow or natural lawn will be easier if you eliminate disturbance. That is, do not till the soil, which allows weed seeds an entry to the clean site. Mulching helps eliminate disturbance; try to avoid disturbing the soil or leaving bare soil exposed. Bare soil is the devil's workshop. Mulch on the surface is the key to successful meadow plantings.

I am convinced that the limited and temporary use of some herbicides may be less harmful to the environment if it means the space becomes established sooner. Whatever method you choose for the site of your meadow, it needs to be weed-free and properly graded before planting.

Your lawn may not be so easy to kill. It might look dead to you, but may actually be drought dormant and will spring to life as soon as you apply water and fertilizer. Or your lawn may be brown from frost or winter cold. Your existing lawn may be the worst weed possible in a meadow or natural lawn. If you have decided to make a meadow or a natural lawn, you have to know all the components of your lawn, and the best way to do this is to get the lawn actively growing. It helps to add fertilizer, even if it looks like nothing is there. Chances are good that weed seeds are lurking and weed inoculum are waiting to grow. Nature abhors a vacuum and usually fills it in short order, and hardly ever with the plants you want. It is a war, and you have got to know the good guys from the bad guys.

Getting the plants

Meadow grasses are sold by seed, divisions, transplants, and rooted pots. Seed is usually available year-round, but late fall is when inventories for seed stock are flush with fresh seed. Always look out for the highest percentage of pure live seed, and the lowest percentage of weeds. Seed can be sown by hand broadcasting, hand-operated spreaders, or larger mechanical farm implements or drills, or hydroseeded. Meadows planted from seed take longer to establish—usually at least two years, more often three. Depending on the components, the first season will usually be a year in which plants get started; grasses will grow, but many, especially the perennial grasses, will need a second season to show their true character. This is why adding flowering plants that will perform in the first season is a good idea—it helps a meadow look good as early as possible. While seeding can appear to be the least expensive way to plant a meadow, the true cost might not be readily apparent. For best results, a weed-free environment has to be maintained for two years (weeds compete with selected meadow plants for water, nutrients, light, and space), and the costs related to this can be more than you might imagine.

Meadows planted from divisions, transplants, and rooted pots generally are established in the first season. They essentially mature in 60 to 120 days, depending on the region and time of year. In addition to this faster rate of maturity, pre-emergent herbicides (chemicals that inhibit the growth of plants from seed) can be used to help new plantings establish with less weeding. There are both organic and inorganic forms of pre-emergents; most work only on inhibiting the germination of seeds, and do not affect newly planted grasses and meadow plants.

Meadows planted from rooted pots and plugs like these will mature more quickly, in as little as two to three months. Photo by Saxon Holt.

Groundcover grasses

Some of the most desirable meadow grasses, like the sedges that make such excellent natural lawns, are not usually offered as seed and can only be planted as plugs. Some plants (like *Pennisetum* 'Fairy Tails') are seed sterile hybrids or clones and can only be planted from plugs or divisions. Depending on which grasses I use in a meadow, I can plant plugs or pots of the grasses that are difficult or impossible from seed and overseed the ones that are easy to grow from seed. Remember that some grasses are best planted from seed when it is cool; others need spring, early summer, or fall warmth to establish. Do not be afraid to experiment and do not be afraid to edit either.

Filler grasses are grasses that grow between clumps of the primary meadows grasses. Many good filler grasses are sold as seed, but some meadow grasses can only be grown from seed in a greenhouse setting because their seed is either very expensive or not readily available to sow directly into a landscape.

Many meadow grasses are sold as transplants. Transplanted grasses should always have their foliage and roots cut back to an appropriate proportion. On average, the amount cut back is usually one-half to one-third, depending on the size of the division. Divisions can vary greatly in size, and specialty grass nurseries can propagate grasses from single or two-shoot propagules. Most divisions sold for landscape purposes are three- to five-shoot clumps at a minimum. Usually, both the roots and the foliage are cut at the time of division to encourage new growth in both.

Bareroots, transplants, and divisions are usually available only in late winter, spring, and fall, depending on the grass. Once the heat of summer is on, it becomes a riskier proposition to dig and divide many grasses, and many nurseries will not ship grasses to customers in hot weather. This all works out just fine, as most grasses are best transplanted in spring and fall (midwinter divisions in southern tier states are a possible exception to this rule). Unless the plant is a tropical grass, actively growing during hot summer months, divisions and transplants in landscape settings should not be attempted during summer heat. Another factor to be considered, as you make your best laid plans, is that any change in "normal" weather patterns—unseasonably hot, dry fall weather, for example—means that your supplier might postpone the digging and dividing or transplanting of your grasses, or you may have to supply extra irrigation as needed.

If you're going to need large quantities of grasses or sedges, it's best to have them contract-grown by a specialty nursery. This will assure you can get the best price on the sizes and varieties you need. Contract growing usually involves a minimum of 150 days' lead time and 30 to 50 percent of the crop price in advance. Groundcover grasses, like *Carex pansa* (California meadow sedge) are often needed in large quantities; because these base grasses are

relatively new on the scene, availability can be a problem, so it's best to contract early, especially for large amounts, to ensure they'll be there when you need them. Remember, not all grasses are available at all times of the year, especially in the small, economical sizes. Failure to order your plants in advance can result not only in not having the plants that you want for your meadow when you need them but also in having to pay more for them, or having to buy larger, more expensive, plants.

Most groundcover grasses are grown in plugs, liners, 4-inch pots, and 1-gallon

"Do not fight the site" is the new rallying cry.

cans. I plant from smaller sized pots whenever possible: smaller plants get their roots out into the native soil on site more quickly, and they are also faster to plant—shallower planting holes save time and money. Plants with larger root balls, in addition to being more costly to buy, are more expensive to plant. They have a greater volume of nursery soil around their root systems, requiring deeper planting holes, and nursery soil is, of course, not the soil the plants will eventually have to grow in. This difference can lead to slower plant establishment and potential rotting or drying out. It is also important to note that a liner, depending on the time of year in which planting takes place, is often only a few weeks behind the 4-inch pot in growth. In turn, a 4-inch pot is not that far behind a 1-gallon can, which in turn is not that far behind a 5-gallon can. The cost of a liner could be three to five times less than a 1-gallon can, and not only that, it will establish quicker and be a healthier plant in the long run.

Specimen grasses are often available in larger sized pots or tubs, and provided they are properly planted, they should grow just fine. Just remember that most grasses planted from pots grow quickly. Rooted plants from pots can often be planted in the heat of summer, where seeding, divisions, and transplants might be ill advised, as long as the newly planted plants can be kept moist. But this may require round-the-clock monitoring of irrigation demands.

Meadow sweeteners

While grasses and sedges are the foundation of the meadow, it is the flowering plants that really say "I am a meadow." They are the candy that makes your mouth water and catches your eye. Flower color can come from annuals, perennials, bulbs, and even vines. Meadows can be layered with color so that almost any time of year there are flowers or seedheads to delight the eye and provide habitat for beneficial insects, birds, bees, and butterflies. Meadows can be "spring loaded" to have a burst of color in the spring, or plant varieties can be chosen to spread the color out over the seasons, with some plants blooming in the spring, some in summer, and some in fall. As flowers turn to seed, many have showy seedheads that provide dramatic winter skeletons and food for wildlife.

Bulbs are particularly effective in mead-

Plants with grasslike foliage, like daylilies (*Hemerocallis*), are especially suited to meadows as their foliage blends effortlessly with the grasses. Flowers on long stems make great meadow sweeteners, dancing in the breeze and, along with hummingbirds and other pollinators, adding animation to the scene.

ows and add a certain romance that is loved and appreciated by all. Many southern and southwestern climates can have bulbs blooming throughout the year. Since natural lawns are mowed so infrequently, they too can serve as canvases for bulbs and mowable flowers like English daisies or violas.

Color coordination in the meadow can be every bit as complex as the most sophisticated border planting. When I choose flowering plants for my meadows, I try to find flowers with low or basal foliage but with flower stems that throw their flowers up to the tops of the grasses. Flowers on long stems dance in the breeze and animate the color. Do not forget, though: for the flowers to work, there must be a solid foundation of groundcover grasses. The grasses create the frame for color to hang on.

Maintenance

Proper establishment is the key to good meadow maintenance. Most meadows or natural lawns are cut to the ground at least once a year and sometimes two or three times in order to keep the foliage tidy and good-looking. Depending on the grasses, cutting back can be done with a groundcover mower or a weed eater with a blade. Small meadows or natural lawns are easily cut by hand. Meadows are usually cut back in late winter or early spring. We call this the Big Chop, and it's a good time to tweak the plantings, editing here and there and adding color. Sophisticated meadow plantings need trained professionals who

know the plants. Remember, as Roy Diblik of Northwind Perennial Farm in Wisconsin says, "It's not 'No Maintenance,' it's 'Know Maintenance.'" Properly designed, a meadow can easily be classified as low maintenance. Still, every garden setting is unique, and you should design your meadow to require no more than your available resources.

Case study: Clayton, Missouri

A small meadow garden that I was particularly pleased to be involved with was a collaboration with my good friends Matt Moynihan and Brian Smith on their average-sized suburban property near St. Louis. Moynihan owns a landscape architecture firm and Smith is a brilliant architect, so working with them was a lot of fun. Matt and I have known each other since I began gardening over twenty years ago. He has watched my designs and I his.

The traditional 1920s brick Tudor house is situated on a corner in the Wydown neighborhood of Clayton, Missouri. Typical of most of the homes, it was landscaped in the time-honored American fashion with a lawn to the sidewalk and foundation shrubs against the house. Matt removed the lawn and added a dry stacked retaining wall of local limestone to create a flatter front yard and flagstone paths and steps to give the garden some great bones.

Matt has long been a connoisseur of boxwood and uses them in very traditional fashion in many of his residential designs. But at his own house, he planted a collec-

Softly sheared boxwoods (*Buxus*) are just high enough to block the views of the street, and the cars, but low enough to let in the light, a meadow "essential." In this jewel box of a garden, you'll hear songbirds instead of mowers, blowers, and edgers.

Yellow tulips, cream-colored narcissus, and miniature starflowers (*Ipheion*) edge the path in early spring. Later, across the path, daylilies will add summer color, and the spring-flowering bulbs will take a step back.

The informal flagstone terrace
with table and chairs beckons
you to sit and enjoy the designed
meadow throughout the seasons.

tion of rare boxwoods to create a bit of privacy from the street. He planted the boxwoods along the edge of the wall above the sidewalk and then wove them around the house in drifts and groups. Flowering trees and shrubs got sprinkled in. At this point, Matt gave me a call to ask if I could help him create a meadow to accompany his boxwood collection.

The area for a meadow was relatively small, maybe 40 by 60 feet, and wrapped around the front of the house going from shade to sun and back to shade. With remnants of the traditional perennial border here and there, many of the pieces of the puzzle were already on hand. When the retaining wall was built, most of the conventional lawn was removed. Once we de-

Seslerias, or moor grasses, are the workhorses of many of the small meadows I make. Here, a sweep of *Sesleria* 'Greenlee's Hybrid' borders a St. Louis lawn. Meadows don't have to be big to be effective.

cided on a meadow, we removed the rest. Most of the old lawn was dug out by hand, and occasional remnant pieces of the old lawn peeked through the sedge matrix that we used to create the foundation of the meadow.

The sedge matrix was augmented by drifts of species ophiopogons (*Ophiopogon chingii* and *O. planiscapus*) or lilyturf (*Liriope minor*) in the deep shade of trees and shrubs and in the shadows of the house. These grass-like plants are the foundation of the shadier parts of the garden. Matt was looking for a mostly evergreen look, and the sedges and lilyturfs get the job done. But you can't put a shovel or trowel in the ground without exposing a handful of bulbs or some seasonal perennial. Matt is an avid cook, and the meadow is interplanted with herbs and flowers for the table. Matt and Brian both love the passing seasons, and the garden has a constant succession of color that gives the meadow a lively air. Late winter snowdrops give way

MOST IMPORTANT SEDGES AND GRASSES IN THE MOYNIHAN-SMITH MEADOW

- *Calamagrostis brachytricha* (Korean reed grass). A beautifully flowered grass that reaches 3 to 4 feet high with inflorescences. Spring foliage is an energized green, transitioning to an orange-yellow in fall. Light shade to full sun. Zones 4 to 9.

- *Carex divulsa* (Berkeley sedge). Native to Europe, this green clumper is one of the important workhorses for designed meadows. It's cold hardy and tolerant of sun, shade, clay, and sand. Evergreen in all but the coldest parts of its hardiness range. Zones 5 to 9.

- *Carex perdentata* (golden Texas sedge). Native to the southeastern United States and a good choice under trees like oaks—or boxwoods in this case. Can tolerate a variety of light conditions and is even hardier than Berkeley sedge. Zones 4 to 9.

- *Carex remota* (European meadow sedge). A good clumping groundcover sedge, also evergreen. Neat and tidy, it is especially good for massing in a garden situation. Zones 5 to 9.

- *Carex texensis* (Texas sedge). Another southeastern U.S. native that can tolerate hot, humid climates with at least some shade. Zones 5 to 9.

- *Miscanthus sinensis* 'Morning Light'. One of the best grasses for winter color in a winter climate—absolutely outstanding fine-textured variegated foliage and striking inflorescences. Zones 5 to 9.

The backdrop and flowering accents here will be
familiar to most gardeners. What's new on the scene
are the low, mostly evergreen sedges that are the base
of the Moynihan-Smith meadow—a matrix of *Carex
divulsa*, *C. perdentata*, *C. remota*, and *C. texensis*.

As the irises finish, here come the drumstick alliums. A succession of flowers, expertly put together by Matt and Brian, keep the meadow constantly changing throughout the seasons. Personalize your meadow with your favorites.

to daffodils, which then yield to camassias and irises, which mingle with the tulips, which are replaced with alliums and lilies as summer comes on. Cannas, daylilies, and crocosmia blaze through the summer, and the fall crocus push the flower color to the first frost. Matt and Brian's new grass ecology, composed mostly of sedges, carries the green into all but the coldest winters.

Perennials include dozens of "prairie"-type plants such as coreopsis, lobelias, asters, and echinaceas. The edibles Matt sows directly into the garden include arugula, asparagus, dill, fennel, cilantro, thyme, mint, chives, basil, and tomatoes.

The Moynihan-Smith garden is not maintenance-free—it does require mowing twice a season as well as some weeding. Some tidying around paths, vegetable

Here, the foliage of the lilies (*Lilium*) blends seamlessly with the blades of northern sea oats (*Chasmanthium latifolium*), the grass from which the lilies emerge. Combining grasses and bulbs of similar colors and textures simultaneously adds diversity and simplicity.

Low, evergreen, long-lived, and never messy are the attributes of a good groundcover grass, the foundation of the meadow. In Roy Diblik's Wisconsin meadow, it's the autumn moor grass (*Sesleria autumnalis*) that holds the planting together.

beds, and seating areas is inevitable. However, this planting succeeds because it has the whisper of wild beauty even as it welcomes human visitors. To some, this style can seem a bit unkempt at first glance, but familiarity soon breeds devotion. An ever-changing garden always rewards you for coming by.

For Matt and Brian the great joy was watching their garden change the aesthetic of their neighborhood. Not everyone understood it at first. But slowly, as their neighbors became more familiar with the meadow and its changing moods, some also began converting their lawns to meadows. The revolution has begun! People can't help but stop and linger to enjoy the flowers and all the birds, bees, and butterflies that animate the garden. The ultimate joy was having a neighborhood child knock on the door and ask if they could see the garden up close. The meadow revolution happens one garden at a time. How about your garden?

Planting a meadow can be a daunting undertaking, and I'm realistic about the fact that this lawn alternative will not be commonplace until our practices and resources catch up with the idea. Designers will be unwilling to plant meadows until nurseries grow more meadow grasses and sedges, and nurseries won't grow grasses until designers are prepared to purchase them. (They'll keep producing $1.99 pots of bedding plants for stores instead.) However, we have to start somewhere—Mother Na-

ture's brilliant idea for the meadow garden is just too good to pass up, and our planet is too much in need of a good thing. Learn about your region and start small if you can—how about that dying strip of grass next to the driveway, or that hell strip be-

Start small. Grasses, sedges, and dwarf bamboos can handle the tough conditions, including tree root competition, of a "hell strip" between the street and sidewalk.

tween the street and the sidewalk? Support the nurseries that are willing to provide grasses for habitat restoration. Meadows are about doing the right prep work on the front end and letting nature do the hard work from there. Meadow gardening is about partnering with nature. It's a place where gardening and nature come together. It's not a bad place to be.

Epilogue: "No mow" lawns for ecological landscapes

by Neil Diboll

Lawns are increasingly reviled as chemically dependent, energy-hogging, two-dimensional deserts. And rightly so. But not all lawn grasses require a steady diet of fertilizers, pesticides, irrigation, and grooming. A select few turf types survive quite nicely with a minimum of fuss and maintenance.

In hot, dry climates, buffalograss (*Buchloe dactyloides*) has proven a good choice. This native of the Great Plains thrives in well-drained soils, including clay in southern states, in areas that receive 15 to 35 inches of rain per year. Low growing and drought resistant, this warm season prairie grass has been touted as the all-around solution for ecological lawns. There's only one problem: it performs poorly in northern climates, where cool season grasses tend to dominate.

In the late 1980s I tested buffalograss

in Wisconsin as an ecological, low-maintenance turf alternative. It failed miserably. It was slow to germinate, grew at a glacial pace, and was easily outcompeted by non-native cool season grasses and weeds. In retrospect, it should have been obvious that a grass native to the Great Plains would struggle in the cooler northern climes of America's Dairyland.

Undeterred, I then tested various blends of cool season, fine fescue grasses. These germinated quickly, established readily, and were highly competitive against other cool season species. After five years of testing various blends, we introduced our "No Mow" fescue lawn mix in 1994. It has since proven itself to be an excellent alternative to high-cost, high-maintenance traditional bluegrass lawns.

How does it work? Fine fescues exhibit low nitrogen requirements, high drought tolerance, and slow growth rates. It is rare that a "No Mow" lawn would ever require fertilizing. They simply don't need it. The root systems of the fine fescue grasses reach deeper into the soil than most other turfgrasses, making them more drought tolerant. When most other lawns are turning brown during summer dry periods, fescue lawns will remain green longer. With deeper root systems, "No Mow" lawns require little or no watering, so expensive irrigation systems are not required for a reliably green lawn. Couple that with the savings realized by eliminating fertilizers and drastically reducing the number of mowings per year, and a "No Mow" lawn is both an ecological and economical landscape.

Where will "No Mow" grow? The fine fescues do best on well-drained soils, such as loam, sandy loam, and even dry sandy and rocky soils. They prefer slightly acid soil but will thrive in a pH between 5.0 and 7.5 (with a pH of 7.0 being neutral).

"No Mow" is an excellent choice for light sandy soils that will not support other turfgrasses. "No Mow" is not recommended for heavy clay soils with less than 4 inches of loose, friable topsoil, or for wet soils subject to regular flooding and high soil moisture conditions.

"No Mow" will grow in surprisingly shady situations and is one of the most

Buffalograss (*Buchloe dactyloides*).
Photo by Saxon Holt.

shade-tolerant turf blends available. It will grow successfully under oaks, hickories, ashes, pines, and similar trees with relatively open canopies. "No Mow" is not recommended for planting in dense shade, or under black walnuts. When planting under trees and on woodland edges, fallen leaves should either be removed in autumn or shredded using a mulching mower to prevent smothering of the turf.

When allowed to grow, the grasses form a flowing carpet, 5 to 6 inches tall, that requires only one or two annual mowings. In early June the plants will send up seedstalks about 2 feet tall. This is when most people will mow their "No Mow" lawn, to

This "No Mow" fine fescue lawn was established on well-drained, loamy soil in Madison, Wisconsin. It maintains a 5- to 6-inch "flowing" appearance throughout the year and is mowed only in early June, when the fescue seedstalks appear. Photo by Neil Diboll.

maintain a lower profile. The grass should be cut at a height of 4 to 5 inches, typically the highest setting on most lawnmowers. Never remove more than one-third of the leaf material, as this will weaken the root systems and open the lawn up to potential invasion by weeds.

For a more manicured look, a "No Mow" lawn can be mowed every four to six weeks at a height of 3.5 to 4 inches. Fine fescues should never be mowed more closely than 3 inches, as this will damage the plant and reduce its vigor and competitiveness. Mowed material should be left on site to break down and return nutrients to the soil.

Recent research has indicated that fine fescue grasses have the ability to reduce weed competition naturally using "chemical warfare." Apparently these grasses produce substances in their roots that discourage the growth of other plants. This does not ensure other plants or weeds will not become established in your "No Mow" lawn, but it does help reduce the amount of weed control required.

Like most cool season turfgrasses, "No Mow" is best seeded in early fall (September and early October). The cool weather and gentle fall rains encourage germina-tion so that the grasses become established before the onset of winter. Most weeds germinate in spring, so your "No Mow" lawn will grow unimpeded in autumn. In spring, it will be in full control of the site, and weeds will struggle to germinate and compete against it.

All existing vegetation should be killed prior to seeding your new "No Mow" lawn. The area to be seeded can be smothered with newspapers, cardboard, old carpets, or black plastic from spring to early fall to kill most weeds. Alternatively, the area can be tilled repeatedly every few weeks during the late spring and summer to kill existing grass and weeds. Another option is to spray the existing vegetation with a glyphosate herbicide, such as Roundup. If perennial weeds are present on the site, it will require at least three such applications at eight-week intervals, beginning in late May or early June in order to kill all weeds or the existing lawn.

Once your "No Mow" lawn is established, you will reap the benefits of a lawn that requires only occasional mowing, no fertilizers or regular watering, and limited (if any) pesticides to keep it healthy and you happy!

CHAPTER 4

Balancing Natives and Exotics in the Garden

by Rick Darke

I BELIEVE THE MOST sustainable gardens are artful balancing acts. They respond, they evolve. They tell stories, then update the stories and retell them. They balance dreams and resources, desire and possibility. They balance our needs and wants with those of others. In my tenure as a gardener, no act of balance has been more conflicted than that of balancing natives and exotics. Instead of succumbing to frustration or choosing a narrow path for the sake of simplicity, I've come to appreciate the nuance and complexity of this issue as wonderful catalysts to an exploration of why we garden, what our gardens do for us, and how they contribute to sustaining diverse cycles of life.

Think back. What inspires any one of us to begin gardening? Though I spent hours in my grandmother's and mother's gardens, no matter where we lived the local creeks, woodlots, old fields, and parks were always most alluring for me. I know now that the changing nature of these places— their unprogrammed qualities—was what I found exciting. I was sustained by their uncertainties. And yet I found great satisfaction in knowing I could count on climbing a favorite hemlock, oak, or beech, or hiding out inside of a virtual house formed by a mass of blooming forsythia. I counted on the blue beauty of pickerel weeds along the creek I learned to swim in. I counted on the pleasure of fingering four-winged silverbell seeds in late summer, on the fragrance of fermenting katsura leaves

---

The White Clay Creek wends its way through my local landscape in early November. I've lived in this watershed and drawn sustenance from it for more than forty years, and though it can appear as pristine wilderness when viewed from high above, I know it is not. Its woods and wetlands are in constant flux and the balance of indigenous and introduced species is ever-changing. This is a vibrant, cultural landscape and a home to many living things. I've come to view it as an extension of my garden, and to view my garden as an extension of it. I find inspiration in the resiliency of both, and am sustained by their uncertainties.

in early autumn, on finding salamanders under moist rocks in the glen. Were these pleasures native or exotic? The thought never occurred to me, although I was certainly aware that they were all local, and that's all that mattered then.

I didn't even make the distinction between "the garden" and "the landscape" until I'd finished college and begun a career in horticulture. The transition from rented rooms with potted coleus on sunny windowsills to owning a tiny downtown patch of earth also put a finer point on the pleasures and pitfalls of individual stewardship. My inclination in that first garden was to populate it with plant species I knew and loved in native habitats. I was working at Longwood Gardens by this time, immersed in the exotic diversity of the world's flora, yet I personally identified most strongly with the sense of local places. My botanical knowledge far exceeded my gardening skills, but these quickly grew as I introduced natives from varied niches into the homogeneity of my urban eighth-acre of compacted clay. Despite my efforts to "amend" the soil, a wealth of locally indigenous wildflowers taught me the absolute necessity of standing over them, watering hose in hand, during summer droughts. Eastern hemlocks, my favorite native evergreen trees from my childhood landscapes, taught me how an introduced pest (the hemlock woolly adelgid) could eliminate a species' viability in less than a lifetime. Flowering dogwoods were already under stress from an introduced anthrac-

nose disease in their traditional moist woodland habitats, but I still loved them and wanted to live with them. I knew of an abandoned hilltop pasture where they'd seeded in and were thriving in full sun, so I brought two tiny seedlings home to my city yard. Nearly thirty years later, that little house and garden have changed hands and human tenants multiple times. The hemlocks and most of the wildflowers survive only in memory, but the two dogwoods endure, and each autumn birds take their berries. The Japanese magnolia I planted for a neighbor is now one of the largest trees on the street and has witnessed all of this.

What do we mean by "native"?

One of the first challenges in balancing natives and exotics is defining your terms. When I began gardening I had little doubt about what was native. For years I'd been observing and studying the plants that made up my regional flora: those growing wild in northeastern North America. My botanical training taught me to rely upon well-documented professional manuals for the correct names and known ranges of plants. My choice at that time was the eighth edition of *Gray's Manual of Botany* (Fernald 1951). The book's 1,632 pages indicated the status of every species within the flora of central and northeastern United States and adjacent Canada. All plants accepted as indigenous, which was Fernald's (and my) preferred alternative to the term "native," were indicated by bold typeface.

Plants of foreign origin were in uppercase. In the introduction Fernald suggested that plants of foreign origin belonged to two main groups: introduced species that were intentionally brought in by human activity, and adventive species, which arrived uninvited. Fernald further explained that some introduced and adventive species had become naturalized, a term meaning that they were firmly established as members of the wild flora, and needed no human assistance in self-perpetuating. He also pointed out that plants that were truly indigenous in one area might be only adventive or naturalized in another. The *Manual* provided more detailed information in

The term "native" is often used so loosely as to be almost meaningless. This unirrigated, unfertilized, pesticide-free planting in our Pennsylvania garden comprises species native to North America; however, only the cinnamon ferns (*Osmunda cinnamomea*), Jack-in-the-pulpits (*Arisaema triphyllum*), Christmas ferns (*Polystichum acrostichoides*), and American witch hazel (*Hamamelis virginiana*) are truly local natives. The sweetshrub (*Calycanthus floridus*) at right and the bluestar (*Amsonia hubrichtii*) are native to the southeastern United States, and do not occur naturally within hundreds of miles of this garden. All, however, are well adapted to existing conditions on this site and are sensible choices for a sustainable palette in this garden.

the individual species descriptions. All entries for indigenous species described the preferred habitat, indigenous range (by state), and any applicable comments about migration into new areas, naturalization, or known hybridization with other species. Entries for non-indigenous plants described preferred habitats, range of occurrence, and notes about origin.

Gray's Manual provided much of what I wanted to know about the native status of plants I encountered growing wild. After

---

Native status
is a function
of time and place.

---

identifying a plant using botanical keys I'd check the range to see if the species was indigenous. If I wanted more detailed information than the state-by-state ranges, I'd consult a local flora such as Robert Tatnall's *Flora of Delaware and the Eastern Shore* (1946), which included precise information about where a species was native within my state. Habitats in Delaware, tiny as it is, vary from moist Piedmont forests in the north to sandy, salty coastal dunes in the south. Many species native in southern Delaware never occur in the northern part of the state, and such information is highly relevant to gardeners.

Native status is a function of time and

place. To be considered native, or indigenous, in *Gray's Manual*, and most floras, there must be scientific evidence that a species has inhabited an area for a great length of time, often thousands of years or more. The reasoning is that such long periods are necessary for the species to have developed and adapted along with other organisms, both plant and animal, in the regional environment. The terms "native" or "indigenous" then mean that the species in question is an integral part of local evolutionary relationships. Barring catastrophic events, usually precipitated by distant forces, environments populated by co-evolved species enjoy relative stability. Their ecologies are constantly changing, but the change is slow. Many popular definitions of native plants are based on species being present prior to a major event in human history, and in North America that event is often the arrival of European colonists, just a few hundred years ago. The logic here is that the historic evolutionary processes responsible for speciation were disrupted when human activity suddenly became the major force reshaping regional ecologies, and vast numbers of species were displaced or introduced. This is true, however it begs the question: now that we're here and our presence is so pervasive, will there ever be any new native plant species?

Historic examples of profound ecological change not caused by human activity are common, and they offer evidence of the long-term resiliency of living organisms.

The New Jersey Pine Barrens is an example of intense ecological flux. Although pollen and fossil records show that plants recognizable as belonging to modern genera including *Pinus* (pine), *Quercus* (oak), and *Magnolia* (magnolia) were present in the region during the Cretaceous period, more than 65 million years ago, few if any of these would have withstood conditions during the Wisconsin glacial period, which ended approximately 10,000 years ago. The vegetation then probably was much like tundra. The makeup of today's Pine Barrens flora is almost entirely due to migration and hybridization since the glaciers receded.

Considering all this, I'm reminded that my botanical and ecological training provided me with an early appreciation not just of native ranges, but of the often dramatic difference in habitats within relatively small areas, and of the constant flux in all living populations. Perhaps our thinking will evolve away from worrying about whether plants are native or not, and toward a valuation of how they function in today's ecology. After all, it's the only one we've got.

Why natives?

For anyone, like myself, who takes pleasure both in gardening and in understanding undesigned regional habitats, growing native plants is a highly rewarding, meaningful way to combine these interests. My top three motives for cultivating indigenous plants are to make a garden that reflects local materials, patterns, and processes, to live closely with species that represent my region, and to ensure that my garden plays an authentic role in sustaining local life and natural resources.

We learn best what we live with. No matter how often we visit wild places, few of us spend as much time in them as we do in the landscape we live in. Because of this, our home gardens are usually the landscapes we learn the most from and are most influenced by. A garden populated with natives makes them part of our daily routines and provides easy opportunities for close observation at all hours and in all seasons. I've always been inclined to believe that real intimacy breeds respect. The intimate knowledge that results from growing indigenous species most often results in a greater appreciation of them as elements in regional habitats. So many wondrous details in the life cycles of plants are revealed by gardening. When do seeds ripen? When do they germinate? What colors are displayed as new foliage unfurls from spring buds? What time of day are flowers most deeply scented? What pollinators visit at dusk? Such insights make us more informed observers, augmenting and enhancing our ability to see into the myriad patterns and processes of local ecologies, and this is reason enough to invite natives into our home habitats.

Although the case for native plants being best adapted is often overstated, there is still considerable truth in it. Natives may or may not be adapted to the specific growing conditions in a garden, but they are generally adapted to long-established regional climate patterns and seasonal cycles. For example, native deciduous trees and shrubs growing in temperate regions of eastern North America are usually unfazed by the typical late frosts that so often damage deciduous species introduced from eastern Asia. Adaptation to such frosts is the result of long evolution by na-

Well-designed gardens composed largely or entirely of native plants can be extremely evocative of regional ecologies. Though few residential gardeners are likely to grow natives exclusively, many botanic gardens include native gardens. The meadow at the Santa Barbara Botanic Garden in California is a superb example of an entirely indigenous planting that speaks eloquently of place. In this mid March view, California poppies (*Eschscholzia californica*) bloom with deergrass (*Muhlenbergia rigens*).

tive species. Beyond similar issues of hardiness and adaptation to conditions, indigenous species possess long-evolved traits that make them well adapted to support complex relationships with other flora and fauna. For example, native species often serve as critical food sources for specialist insects, which are not adapted to eat exotics. Native plants growing where they are adapted to existing conditions are among the most sustainable means of supporting local diversity.

Another argument for embracing natives in our gardens is the empirical evidence that they are in relative balance in established ecologies. All plants and animals are naturally evolved to reproduce and perpetuate themselves, and they compete for resources as they do this. The dynamic between species that have co-evolved in regional habitats is such that no one species suddenly displaces another. All gains and losses happen incrementally, in response to slowly changing environmental con-

Hamamelis virginiana blooms in autumn and the seed capsules ripen the following autumn. The capsules of this witch hazel are explosively dehiscent, which means they literally burst open upon ripening and propel the seeds outward with considerable force. This makes a lasting impression on anyone who happens to be close by at the time. Living closely with plants provides unique opportunities to learn intimate details of their life cycles, and this can better equip us to appreciate the roles plants play in local habitats.

ditions and through adaptive evolution. Growing locally or regionally indigenous plants in a garden eliminates the potential of inadvertently introducing a species that has the capacity to disrupt the balance of nearby natural habitats.

Why not natives?

The most sustainable gardens are those that consume the fewest resources. Native or not, plants poorly adapted to existing conditions are among the least sustainable choices. The frequent claim that we should grow native plants because they are best adapted is misleading or outright false when it fails to include a realistic assessment of current local conditions. The majority of residential gardens are made on land that doesn't even remotely resemble the natural habitats native plants evolved in and are adapted to. In most cases the topography, drainage characteristics, soil structure and chemistry, and the patterns of sunlight and shadow have been pro-

The berries of *Crataegus viridis*, a hawthorn native to eastern North America, attract a cedar waxwing in early February. In addition to perpetuating plant communities in the garden, seeds and fruits remaining on plants into dormant seasons are important to wildlife.

foundly altered. This is especially true in urban conditions but is also typical for most of suburbia. Although the traditional horticultural model has been to modify site conditions to suit the needs of desired plants, this is completely contrary to sustainable practices. Even if herbicides and pesticides are eliminated from the equation, the initial modifications to soil and grade, combined with subsequent needs for watering, pH adjustment, and fertilizing all consume resources. The most sustainable, low-maintenance approach is to select plants based upon their true ability to thrive without our constant support.

Gardens, by their nature, serve multiple human purposes. Even if preservation of local diversity is a primary goal, as it is for me, there are still many practical design considerations which depend upon a diverse palette of materials. In greener gardens, those materials are mostly plants. In my local landscape, the indigenous vegetation is primarily deciduous, and in order

Formed by a dynamic and eclectic mix of indigenous and exotic species, this tapestry is constantly in flux. The two major forces are Japanese painted fern (*Athyrium niponicum*) and perfoliate bellwort (*Uvularia perfoliata*). Situated on the shady north side of a suburban home, the planting is adapted to site conditions and thrives with minimal input of resources. Gentle editing is occasionally used to adjust patterns in the matrix.

to retain a "sense of place" and to utilize as many native species as practical, I favor deciduous plants in my designs. Despite my best efforts to use deciduous trees and shrubs for screening, I live in suburbia and sometimes evergreens are the only good solution. If I consider only locally indigenous evergreen shrubs, my single option is mountain laurel, *Kalmia latifolia*. Beautiful as it is, kalmia is difficult to cultivate, is not suited to conditions on our property, and is especially vulnerable to disfiguring browsing by white-tailed deer, a member of our native fauna that is completely out of balance with local ecology due to human impact on habitat. If I extend my search from my Piedmont region to the Coastal Plain, inkberry holly, *Ilex glabra* becomes an option. This regionally native evergreen shrub is adapted to conditions in my garden, and I grow it for this reason. It is, however, unlike any locally indigenous shrub found in forests, meadows, or wetlands within many miles of my garden, and it actually works against creating an immediately local sense of place.

The situation regarding evergreen trees is similarly problematic. I no longer plant eastern hemlocks, *Tsuga canadensis*, because the only way to prevent them from succumbing to the introduced hemlock woolly adelgid is to spray them regularly with oils or worse. Red-cedars, *Juniperus virginiana*, are durable local natives that are quite elegant until the deer prune them into lollipops. Regionally native American holly, *Ilex opaca*, is one of my practi-

cal options but it, like inkberry holly, is not an authentic part of my locally indigenous flora. The need for evergreen screening is only one example of a sustainable design goal that may not be fulfilled if the garden palette is limited to local or regional natives.

Why exotics?

Over the ages, gardeners have delighted in the new and the different, and the romance associated with plant exploration and acquisition seems undimmed in our age. Even in circles dedicated to growing native plants, "New!" is often the operative word. Beyond the superficial appeal of the unfamiliar, the underlying motive for the introduction of plants from distant places is that exotics often serve real purposes that can't be fulfilled by natives alone. Around the world, the earliest botanic gardens were primarily gardens of "acclimatization," dedicated to acquiring and learning how to cultivate plants useful for food, shelter, medicinal, and artful purposes. In mostly good ways, exotic plants have become so integral to our modern ways of life that it is almost impossible to imagine living without them, and this is true in the garden, too. The majority of exotic species grown by North American gardeners are benign or innocuous: they cause no harm or injury.

At their best, exotic plants contribute to our sustenance, our sensual pleasure, and to the practicality and sustainability of our landscapes. Many of the food plants in any

North American garden are likely to be of exotic origin. The range of colors, scents, forms, and sizes represented by the global flora vastly exceeds that of any local or regional flora, for obvious reasons. As an exercise, make a list of the fragrant plants you know or grow, then discount the exotics and see what remains. The evocative power of exotics is often another reason we grow them. They may not speak to our immediate sense of place; however, they have the ability to remind us, pleasurably, of distant lands we've visited or lived in. Perhaps most important to sustainable practices, the adaptive capacity inherent in a diverse palette of exotic species provides us with a greater range of planting choices to suit challenging conditions such as extreme heat or cold, alkalinity or acidity, excessive moisture or drought. Disease-resistant qualities of introduced species are undesirable when they upset the balance

Growing under a native pin oak (*Quercus palustris*), in our Pennsylvania garden, spike winter hazel (*Corylopsis spicata*) is a good example of a well-adapted, benign exotic that is visually and seasonally in sync with the local native landscape. Introduced to North America from the mountains of Japan over 150 years ago, this species has shown no capacity for seeding into North American habitats. It is long-lived and virtually maintenance-free.

of indigenous ecosystems; however, these qualities sometimes result in exotics being the only viable choices for specific purposes in the modern landscape. Although exotic plants may not provide the broad range of ecosystem services that co-evolved indigenous species do, all plants sequester carbon and give of oxygen, and these traits are unquestionably desirable.

Why not exotics?

When I first began gardening, my main aversion to exotic plants was that their widespread use tends to homogenize the landscape on a large scale. I didn't expect gardens to be perfect mirrors of regional ecologies, but I was distressed by the sameness I saw in garden plantings over vast distances. Theoretically, the wealth of ex-

Fothergilla is one of the most popular native shrubs for gardens in temperate North America. Its spring flowers (above) are delightful, and its autumn color (right) is rarely surpassed by any shrub, native or exotic. One of the primary reasons for its popularity is that very few native shrubs offer fothergilla's combination of beauty, adaptability, and relatively small stature. Most grow too tall too fast for many residential settings. The plants growing off this glassed porch are only 5 feet tall after nearly twenty years, with only minimal pruning. Recent

research has determined that the majority of fothergillas in cultivation in North America are actually *Fothergilla ×intermedia*, a hybrid of *F. major* and *F. gardenii*. Although the hybrid is the most useful garden plant, its fertility is very low. It rarely produces viable seeds and is generally unable to perpetuate itself. So although it may qualify as native, it is dependent upon humans for its survival and will never be a fully functioning part of regional ecosystems.

otic species available to gardeners should contribute to increased uniqueness, but in real practice a relatively limited set of broadly adapted exotics is endlessly repeated. A preference for local or even regional natives in our gardens is an authentic way to counter this.

Although some exotics possess a hardiness and durability that makes them well suited to sustainable garden design, many popular exotics are very poorly adapted to conditions where they are cultivated, requiring that significant resources or toxic substances be employed in their life support. Classic examples are tropicals grown in cold climates that require winter storage in heated greenhouses, plants from moist habitats that need regular irrigation in dry gardens, short-lived species that require regular replacement, and disease-prone plants that can't survive without the use of herbicides or pesticides.

In recent decades, my discomfort with introduced species is also due to a growing awareness of how rapidly a relative few are displacing huge numbers of indigenous species in habitats across North America. My Mid-Atlantic region has been especially impacted, in part because growing conditions here are so similar to those in the eastern Asian and European regions where most of our weeds evolved, and in part because this area is so densely populated by our species.

I'm comfortable with the word "weed." As I learned it, and use it, it means a plant out of place. It is commonly understood that the concept of weeds was developed by humans, to serve a human perspective: we're the ones deciding which plants are out of place. Weeds, as so defined, are generally unwanted.

I'm not comfortable with the term "invasive." Instead of recognizing the scientific facts of population dynamics, it suggests some plants have a warlike consciousness and are deliberately doing harm. So-called invasive plants wouldn't exist unless they were better adapted to current conditions than so-called native species. In fact, most natives are no more than earlier arrivals that established themselves because, at the time, they had a competitive advantage. Whether we call them exotic, alien, introduced, or invasive, it is critical that we recognize that the displacement we are witnessing is primarily the result of plants responding to human impact on the environment. The changes we've wrought are providing new opportunities for a different set of plants. We could logically call them opportunists, but in today's culture that still sounds as if we are impugning the plants and placing ourselves on the high moral ground.

I believe most of us are alarmed not simply by change, but by the startling rate of change. Although evolutionary biology suggests cataclysmic change is typically followed by the blossoming of new species, the initial effect of rapid displacement is species loss. We accelerate the displacement process when we create disturbance in or adjacent to intact ecosystems, and when we deliberately or unintentionally move plants at greater rates than they disperse unaided. For this reason we should use utmost caution in all activities that involve the introduction or transportation of exotic plants. Ultimately, to minimize the displacement we must minimize the disturbance.

Sustaining the balance

In the vital balance, the plants we choose to grow and the ways in which we grow them them should be guided by our personal values—our ethics. Making note of these and referring to them offers a practical way to stay on course, or to determine when the course needs to be adjusted. For me, in my

Naturalized populations of Virginia bluebells (*Mertensia virginica*) and European wood tulip (*Tulipa sylvestris*) have persisted by self-sowing for decades in a wooded section of our suburban Pennsylvania garden. Though one is native and the other exotic, they are both in sync with the color range and flowering period of spring ephemerals in nearby natural habitats. Both species are adapted to completing their growth and reproductive cycles in spring, when rainfall is plentiful. Both go dormant when summer droughts arrive, which is why they can persist without irrigation even while sharing root space with river birches (*Betula nigra*) and various shrubs.

garden, the dominant ethic is to do good, and the corollary is to do no harm.

Few gardeners are true purists, and this is good. I'm not sure I've ever known anyone who grows only natives, or anyone whose garden is entirely devoted to exotics. Although I've always had a strong preference for local plants, all the gardens I've made, my own current one included, have been a mix of plants from near and far. I believe residential gardens can contribute meaningfully to the conservation and enhancement of local biological diversity, and so my planting choices include a healthy complement of indigenous species. Many of the local plants I grow, including beeches, oaks, and asters, produce fruits and seeds that provide critical sustenance for local fauna. Many also provide shelter for those same animals. At the same time, I believe the wise use of resources is essential to sustaining a healthful global ecology, and so I limit myself to plants that are truly adapted to place, whether they are native or exotic. For example, my garden is situated on high ground and has well-drained soil but no truly wet places. I delight in growing a multitude of plants that thrive in the conditions my garden has to offer, but I don't grow aquatic plants or others that need more moisture than falls from the sky. None of the plants I grow require watering beyond initial establishment, fertilizing, or pesticides.

Years ago, following my ethic of doing no harm, I removed a large burning bush, *Euonymus alatus*, from the garden. Origi-

nally a gift from a close friend, the plant was beautiful and completely adapted to conditions in my garden. It required no watering, fertilizing, or pesticides, and its berries were taken each autumn by local birds. Over time, however, my walks in the adjacent woodland preserve made me aware that this species was self-sowing and displacing significant parts of the indigenous shrub layer. Was my lone plant responsible? Certainly not. Would removing my plant reverse the incursion of this species into the preserve woods? Again, no. My decision was based on not wanting to contribute to the problem, even in a small way. Ten years later the same spot in my garden is occupied by an ironwood, *Carpinus caroliniana*. Grown from a seed of local provenance, this indigenous tree is as beautiful in its own ways and is equally well adapted to my conditions. It does good and does no harm.

Combining natives and exotics is more than a matter of style. Natives or exotics can be arranged and managed formally or informally—this isn't the issue. Most important is how plants function in the garden. I grow a number of plants because they are truly local species and they provide genuine connections with nearby wild lands. These are properly called natives by any reckoning. I grow others, such as oakleaf hydrangea (*Hydrangea quercifolia*), that are often called native but to me are not. This handsome shrub ranges from northern Florida to Mississippi, Alabama, Georgia, and into Tennessee, but no further

An outdoor shower is enclosed by a durable mix of native and exotic plantings. In autumn American witch hazel, *Hamamelis virginiana*, blooms bright yellow as the leaves of Korean spice viburnum, *Viburnum carlesii* 'Compactum', turn rich wine-red. In May the viburnum envelopes the spaces with its sweet clove scent. An inkberry holly in the foreground provides strategic evergreen screening. Although the witch hazel is locally native, the holly is regionally native, and the spice viburnum is exotic, all three shrubs are part of a sensible plant palette for this part of Pennsylvania. All are superbly suited to the site conditions: drought tolerant and tolerant of periodically saturated soils. All are in sync with the textures, colors, and sequences common to the local indigenous flora. Though the spice viburnum is exotic, more than a century of cultivated use has proved this species to be innocuous. Unlike some other exotic viburnum species it does not spread beyond the garden or pose any threat to regional ecosystems.

north. It doesn't occur naturally within hundreds of miles of my Pennsylvania garden, yet almost all nurseries in my region and many native plant societies here refer to it as native. It is truly native to North America, but this continent is much too large and varied to be thought of as having any universal nativity or unified sense of place. I know oakleaf hydrangea firsthand from its habitats in the Southeast, but my guess is that the majority of gardeners in the Mid-Atlantic who grow it as a native only know it as a commodity—they've never seen it in its natural habitat and are unaware of the plant and animal species it normally cohabits with. I grow it not because it's native but because it is a beautiful shrub that is perfectly adapted to conditions in my suburban Pennsylvania garden. Its form, fall color, flowering period, durability, and relative ability to withstand deer browsing combine to make it a highly functional design element in my home landscape. My only ambivalence is that its large leaves and bold texture are unlike any indigenous tree or shrub in the entire Mid-Atlantic region. Even to the untrained eye it looks like an exotic, which, from a truly local perspective, it is.

The notion of plants evoking a sense of place is actually much more complicated than we often admit. For me, the place I most want to evoke is intensely local, and for this reason I seek out and cultivate as many authentically local species as practical in my garden. My suburban acre-and-a-half is also part of a cultural landscape—one shaped by human culture—that is rich in local history that is meaningful to me. I made a point of meeting the couple who built this house on a former pasture sixty years ago. I invited them over, and they told my wife, Melinda, and me about trees they'd planted when they first arrived. Among these were two apple trees, both of which are still thriving. Though we do no spraying at all, and devote no time to either tree except occasional pruning, both fruit heavily enough in alternate years that the ground beneath them turns red for a while. A bench below, shaded by the apple's arching branches, offers an especially delightful place to sit amidst the sweet fragrance of the fallen apples. Melinda usually gathers them up, avoiding hungry yellow jackets and other insects that feed on the fruit, and makes applesauce. The tree is a reminder of the people who planted it and a connection to the orcharding tradition that still survives in our local area. It is among the most resource-efficient plants in the garden, and I can't imagine devaluing it because it is not native.

I'd estimate at least three-quarters of the plant species in my garden are indigenous to the Piedmont region of eastern North America, and of these a significant number are indigenous to my local watershed. The remainder are carefully selected exotics from other parts of North America and from as far away as Japan and China. Chosen in keeping with the ethic of doing no harm, none of the exotics I grow are known to spread into local ecosystems, and

Ecological concepts of stable "climax" vegetation types are moving toward more complex models of a global flora that is itself continually evolving in character. With this perspective, the cosmopolitan wildness of urban places acquires new meaning and value, providing insights into successional process in habitats profoundly altered by human activity. Plantings on New York's unique aerial park, the High Line, were directly inspired by the wild vegetation that established itself along the former freight line during three decades of dereliction. Many of the patterns in the spontaneous communities were virtual portraits of available resources. In a typical pre-construction scene, lines of little bluestem (*Schizachyrium scoparium*) and tall thoroughwort (*Eupatorium altissimum*) vie for sun and root room between abandoned rails and ties. Traditional horticulture rarely addresses questions such as "What will grow in gravel, in full sun, 35 feet in the air in the middle of a city, without irrigation, fertilization, or pesticides?" As we develop sustainable models for urban and suburban landscapes, we need to ask and answer such questions.

none are dependent upon irrigation, fertilizers, or pesticides. Beyond these criteria, I limit my choices to species that are visually and physiologically in sync with the local flora. Most are deciduous. The flowering trees and shrubs mostly bloom in spring along with the natives, are green in summer like the natives, turn color in autumn and drop their leaves along with the natives, and are bare in winter like the natives. Only a trained eye would know they are not native, and that is my goal. I'm able to enjoy a bit of visual and sensual diversity borrowed from the global flora, yet the sense of my garden—its seasonality, architecture, color, texture, and translucency—are all nearly indistinguishable from that of surrounding natural habitats.

The ability of plants, both native and exotic, to adapt to disturbed habits is often essential to their sustainability in modern gardens. Here, ebony spleenwort (*Asplenium platyneuron*) thrives in the cracks between joints in a stone wall that once supported railroad tracks. The colorful graffiti is irrelevant to the plant's well-being. This site bears little resemblance to the traditional habitat of this eastern North American species, which often occurs on natural ledges and rock outcrops, especially in limestone regions. What matters to the fern is that this curious niche provides well-drained soil and alkaline conditions resulting from remnant pieces of mortar.

I've come to believe that simply placing native plants in the garden and tending to their care is not enough to make a difference in the long run. If our gardens are to become sustainable parts of regional ecologies, the indigenous species we grow must be established and managed in ways that enable them to be self-perpetuating, and ever-evolving. A useful exercise for gauging this important aspect of sustainable landscapes is to ask, "Which of the herbaceous plants in my garden has survived or is likely to survive for twenty years or more?" and "Which of the woody plants in my garden has survived or is likely to survive for a hundred years or more?" In most cases the likely answer to both questions is none or very few. Native or not, individual plants have limited lifetimes, but populations can go on indefinitely. Establishing self-sustaining populations requires matching plants to growing conditions, beginning with plants capable of producing viable seed, and allowing them the freedom to self-sow. As authentic, productive wildness becomes established in our gardens, maintenance naturally shifts, from deliberate planting and replacement to editing. There is real efficiency in this, and it contributes greatly to the ultimate sustainability of the landscape.

The idea of naturalizing plants in the garden isn't new, but it takes on new meaning if we imagine our gardens playing major roles as repositories of existing diversity, and as engines for the diversity of the future. Freedom and autonomy have been essential to the origin of today's species and will remain so for tomorrow's. No garden or living landscape remains static, no matter how much we intervene. Change is the signature of our age, and many of our local and global ecologies are in a period of intense transition. Truly sustainable design anticipates this flux and seeks a continuous balance between shifting resources, consumption, and regeneration.

CHAPTER 5

The Sustainable Edible Garden

by Eric Toensmeier

WHEN I WALK OUT my back door in summer I enter a landscape of abundance. Fruits, nuts, berries, edible leaves, shoots, and roots abound. Every day from May through October I enjoy a double handful of fruits, a different mix every week. Two hundred species of useful trees, shrubs, vines, and perennials create a mosaic of habitat patches, interspersed with annual vegetable beds. All on a 45 by 90 foot lot!

I must admit that what first comes into my mind when I am snacking on strawberries in June is not the environmental benefits of such a garden. I am simply enjoying the incomparable quality of home-grown strawberries. However, the context of gardening in a time of ecological crisis is never far from my mind.

Yield of small fruit in my Massachusetts garden in July, including jostaberry (*Ribes ×nidigrolaria*), 'Hinnomaki Yellow' gooseberry (*R. uva-crispa*), clove currant (*R. odoratum*), raspberry (*Rubus idaeus*), goumi (*Elaeagnus multiflora*), highbush blueberry (*Vaccinium corymbosum*), alpine strawberry (*Fragaria vesca* var. *alpina*), and dwarf mulberry (*Morus macroura*).

The ecological footprint of your food

Our food system is among humanity's greatest impacts on the environment. That impact can be positive or negative, depending on what kinds of practices are used and the amount of land used for agriculture. Our current industrial agriculture system has tremendous negative impact on the environment, particularly in the areas of carbon emissions, land degradation, water use, and chemical pollution. Home food gardening can contribute to solutions to all these issues.

First of all, most of our food is grown far from our homes and shipped great distances to us. According to ATTRA's National Sustainable Agriculture Information Service, the average number of "food miles" traveled by produce in the United States is 1,500, with processed foods traveling 1,300 miles. This constitutes a tremendous amount of fossil fuel use and creates significant global warming pollution. Purchasing food from local farmers and processors can be an improvement, but somewhat less than it would appear because of the larger numbers of trips made by smaller vehicles. Growing food on site at home, school, or workplace means that some portion of what you eat has zero food miles, reducing your carbon emissions.

Industrial agriculture is an incredibly water-intensive system. Much of our food is grown in California and Mexico and irrigated with fossil groundwater at a rate that is lowering groundwater tables and impacting ecosystems adversely. Many of the customers of this fossil groundwater–irrigated food live in regions with plenty of rainfall, such as the eastern third of the country. In humid areas, and even arid regions, home food production combined with water-conserving irrigation practices and especially use of harvested rainwater can help to ease the burden on overused aquifers.

Agrichemical contamination, erosion, and loss of habitat are also ecological costs of our industrial farming system. The corn and soybeans that make up most processed foods grow in what were once our great prairies. Author Toby Hemenway (see Chapter 11) makes the interesting argument that by growing food at home, we can free up farmland for restoration—and that large parcels of farmland in rural areas are far more likely to become healthy, intact ecosystems than bits and pieces of yards in highly developed areas. Our home food production practices, of course, can also be far more environmentally benign than the fossil fuel– and chemical-intensive, soil-de-

grading practices of industrial agriculture.

To slow climate change and address critical ecological issues, we must overhaul our industrial food system and replace it with a more sustainable and localized model. Producing more food in our landscapes is an essential building block of that transformation.

Updating our concept of nature

Until recently our picture of North America before European arrival was of an old growth ecosystem largely undisturbed by human activity. Most of us learned in school that Indian populations were small and had a minimal impact on the landscape. Native plant gardening and ecological restoration efforts have been built to some degree on the notion of restoring these pristine, pre-European "virgin" ecosystems.

However, new research has dramatically transformed our picture of Indian land management across the Americas. Perhaps the best of these new publications is *Tending the Wild*, in which M. Kat Anderson presents the history of 12,000 years of sophisticated Indian land management through practices like burning, irrigation, propagation, weeding, pruning, and harvesting. Many unique species and ecosystems have virtually disappeared in the absence of Indian management.

Scientists and land managers are still debating what this means for conservation and ecological restoration efforts. Meanwhile, as gardeners, we may take this to encourage a more active interaction with our landscapes, a reminder that active management and productive use do not have to be in conflict with ecosystem health.

A balanced approach to species selection

The gardening world has gained a lot from the focus of the last few decades on native plants. Many fine native species have been brought into greater cultivation, which benefits us all. The discussion about "invasive" species helped us lift our heads and look beyond our property lines to think about the ecological impact of our gardening practices. However, a dogmatic insistence on growing only native plants was rather a loud voice in that discussion. It was necessary for the pendulum to swing toward native species for a time, but perhaps it swung too far. Now it appears that a more balanced discussion of plant species selection is possible.

In part this is a result of advances and reevaluations in invasion biology itself. Mark Davis' recent *Invasion Biology*, a review of the state of the science, calls in fact for the abolition of invasion biology and the end of the use of loaded terms like "invasive." He makes the case that most claims of harm from non-native species have been exaggerated or are based on biased interpretations of the data. Davis suggests the creation of "species redistribu-

tion ecology," a broader study of dispersal, establishment, and geographic shifts in populations over time. Citing hundreds of studies, he advocates managing species that cause health risks for humans or economic harm to the agricultural and forestry resources on which we depend, but proposes that we may be mistaking change, a fundamental characteristic of life, for harm when it comes to naturaliza-

American persimmon (*Diospyros virginiana*) is an underutilized, low-maintenance eastern native food plant. Improved varieties, including the self-pollinating 'Szukis' (shown), are available.

tion of new species. For example, he demonstrates that the claim that "invasive" species are the second biggest threat to imperiled species—though widely repeated and taken as gospel—is based on a flawed study, since discredited. It is generally not plants but rather insects and pathogens that cause these kinds of measurable harm. As Davis writes, "Given that [as of 2005] there was not any evidence that a single native North American plant species had been driven to extinction, or even extirpated from a single U.S. state, due to competition from an introduced plant species, concluding, or implying, that non-native plant species threaten a large portion of the U.S. flora with extinction seems quite unjustified, even reckless."

The danger is this: if we focus exclusively on native plants in our landscapes, we are externalizing the ecological cost of our food production (this is, of course, also true of ornamental gardening of any kind). Food production and ecosystem services can easily coexist in any garden. The next section of this chapter will address some of the species and practices that can help us take responsibility for providing some of our human needs at home while still providing ecological benefits, and indeed while maintaining an attractive ornamental landscape.

Certifying organizations

The Sustainable Sites Initiative (SITES) has brought a message of ecological gardening to a broad and influential audience of design and landscape professionals. This certification system provides incentives for reducing negative impacts and improving or maintaining ecosystem services. Their hard work in developing and implementing these standards is to be commended. SITES's list of ecosystem services addresses the need for landscapes to be productive, listing provision of food and renewable non-food products among the key twelve benefits provided by landscapes. Unfortunately, SITES does not provide any credits for practices that address this benefit. The Leadership in Energy and Environmental Design (LEED) standards are similar, offering credits for provision of habitat and sustainable water use but ignoring onsite production of food and other resources.

The absence of recognition of the benefits of food production from both leading national standards has a major impact on the practices of professionals. Many designers have requested changes to this aspect of the standards without success. Sustainability is about more than just conservation, water, and native plants. It is about understanding where our food and fuel and building materials come from—not to mention where our wastes go. With time and pressure from gardeners and landscape and design professionals, perhaps SITES and LEED will update their standards to reflect current understandings of historical native land management and species redistribution ecology. Advocating for lovely native landscapes that provide ecosystem services alone, when our food, energy, and building materials are produced with destructive practices and shipped great distances, is too limited a perspective on what sustainable land care can be.

Land use patterns

Food production can be quite compatible with other sustainable gardening concerns. Many new and traditional practices provide yields while sequestering carbon, improving microclimates, improving rainwater capture and infiltration, and providing habitat for wildlife. And certainly any of the practices profiled here can be combined with other gardening techniques to create a productive mosaic of habitat patches to benefit wildlife, humans, and the larger ecosystem.

While practices will necessarily vary in different regions and sites, some general patterns of land use are applicable broadly to new ecological food gardens across climates and at diverse sites and scales. Many of these practices have emerged from the design system known as permaculture, defined by designer Rafter Sass as "meeting human needs while improving ecosystem health." Permaculture provides an integrated design approach and principles for design, and serves as an umbrella for a range of ecological strategies from food production to housing, transportation, and energy.

Biointensive. The biointensive technique is a great way to produce the maximum amount of food on a small piece of land in an ecologically friendly way. Biointensive production involves growing your own raw materials for compost and mulch, minimizing offsite inputs. This is a high-labor, high-productivity, organic land use pattern. To learn more, visit the website of Ecology Action, www.growbiointensive.org. Biointensive beds can of course be incorporated in a broader ecological garden featuring native perennial borders, tree crops, and other elements.

Edible ornamental landscaping. In *Edible Forest Gardens* my co-author Dave Jacke and I describe a land use pattern called the "suburban landscape mimic." This technique is essentially the imitation of popular ornamental landscapes, but substituting edible and functional plants for strictly ornamental species. Many useful species are outstanding ornamentals, and in fact many commonly used ornamentals are actually edible, such as *Amelanchier* species. Low-maintenance productive species are particularly useful in this kind of landscaping.

Edible living structures and water gardens

Some fantastic work has been done in recent years on living walls, arbors, green roofs, and other living structures. Many edible plants are very well suited to these kinds of production. A wide range of food-producing vines can serve as living air conditioners, frame outdoor rooms, and provide other microclimate moderation services to buildings and outdoor spaces. Candidate fruiting species include grapes and muscadines (*Vitis* spp.), kiwifruit (*Actinidia* spp.), and passionfruits (*Passiflora* spp., including the surprisingly hardy eastern native *P. incarnata*). Perennial vegetable vines include climbing spinach (*Hablitzia tamnoides*), Malabar spinach (*Basella*

alba), yams (*Dioscorea* spp.), and chayote (*Sechium edule*). Annual bean and cucurbit crops can also be used very effectively for seasonal living structures.

Candidate crops for living roofs depend on the depth of soil available. The thinnest living roofs support little more than sedums, but at greater soil depths many herbaceous species (e.g., garden chives, *Allium schoenoprasum*) and subshrubs (e.g., lowbush blueberry, *Vaccinium angustifo-*

Biointensive production can be part of an ornamental landscape. This garden is located at Las Cañadas in Veracruz, Mexico. Large plants in the background are clumping timber bamboo (*Bambusa oldhamii*) and ice cream bean (*Inga jinicuil*), a Mexican native nitrogen-fixing tree with sweet edible pods.

Edible landscape at Educational Concerns for Hunger Organization in Fort Meyers, Florida. Almost all the species pictured are edible, including variegated cassava (*Manihot esculenta*), cranberry hibiscus (*Hibiscus acetosella*), taro (*Colocasia esculenta*), Surinam cherry (*Eugenia uniflora*), and *Monstera deliciosa*.

lium) can be integrated. Rooftop gardens with container plants can of course produce many crops.

In Asia many food crops are grown in aquatic conditions. In fact many of the ornamental water garden species we grow in the United States are actually crops in their native land. Edible water gardens can be highly productive without losing their sublime ornamental value. Species are suited to a range of water garden types and depths. Aquatic crops include sacred lotus (*Nelumbo nucifera*), taro (*Colocasia esculenta*), water chestnut (*Eleocharis dulcis*), native and Chinese arrowheads (*Sagittaria*

The author's edible water garden featuring sacred lotus (*Nelumbo nucifera*), arrowhead (*Sagittaria latifolia*), water mimosa (*Neptunia oleracea*), and watercress (*Nasturtium officinale*).

spp.), watercress (*Nasturtium officinale*), rice (*Oryza sativa*), and native wild rice (*Zizania aquatica*).

Rain gardens, which capture and infiltrate roof runoff, are increasingly common. In arid areas these gardens enable production of species that would otherwise need additional irrigation (such as apples and gooseberries). Rain gardens in more humid areas can produce food crops that are tolerant of periodic inundation like elderberry (*Sambucus canadensis*), water celery (*Oenanthe javanica*), and achira, or edible canna (*Canna edulis*).

Backyard micro-livestock

Increasing numbers of gardeners are incorporating backyard livestock. Poultry and honeybees in particular are riding a wave of popularity. Keeping a few hens or other fowl can provide valuable garden services. In many cases the food benefits of backyard livestock, though significant, are less important than their ability to improve nutrient cycling. Chickens can eat weeds and other garden waste, and convert it into eggs, meat, and manure. They accelerate the composting process, as can rabbits and other herbivorous micro-livestock. Ducks are as noted for their appetite for slugs as for their tasty eggs and meat.

If we seek to emulate ecosystems, making a place in our gardens for animals only makes sense. But in most cases we can't just let livestock (even as small as chickens) roam where they please. Movable pens or portable electric fencing allow us to safely harness the scratching, weed- and insect-eating, and fertilizing abilities of chickens. Honeybees are another popular backyard livestock option, when safely sited to keep flight paths away from neighbors, visitors, and children. They can pollinate the neighborhood while providing large yields of honey.

Ecosystem mimicry

To dig a little deeper, we can pattern our gardens after healthy wild ecosystems. These gardens strive to create cultivated food-producing ecosystems by mimicking the structure and function of native vegetation communities. Gardeners using this technique will pick a model ecosystem to imitate, and analyze architecture (layers, density, diversity), social structures (niches, mutualisms), and successional dynamics using observation and research.

In addition to mimicking these structural and dynamic elements, individual species are analyzed. Useful or functional species may be incorporated directly, or perhaps an improved variety may be utilized. Stretching further, perhaps a different and more productive member of the same genus, or even family, might be utilized. Finally, gardeners can analyze the niche of a model species and replace it in the garden with an analog species—for example, replacing mast-bearing oaks (*Quercus* spp.) with Chinese chestnut (*Castanea mollissima*).

Perennial polycultures of multipurpose plants construct novel ecosystems from the ground up. There is an emphasis on low-maintenance food plants, both native and non-native. Functional plants are in-

A portion of my edible forest garden, an ecosystem mimic featuring multipurpose perennial plants including many underutilized natives.

corporated to attract beneficial insects, fix nitrogen, and suppress weeds. In regions where rainfall allows forest, these polycultures are often called edible forest gardens, or food forests. In other regions they take the form of edible prairies, wetlands, or desert scrub. Perennial polycultures are usually ecosystem mimics to some degree, but they may have a more formal look and be used as a form of edible landscaping, or be primarily production-oriented.

Though it is not often emphasized in native plants literature, our continent has produced a wealth of edible species. Many gardeners are incorporating these species in their designs to yield food as well as the many visible and invisible ecosystem benefits native plants provide. Because they are frequently well adapted to local conditions, native food plants tend to require a minimum of care.

Mycoscaping

Mycoscaping is a revolutionary new approach to gardening pioneered by Paul Stamets, author of *Mycelium Running*. While it includes growing mushrooms in various kinds of log culture, it goes far beyond those techniques to the raising of edible mushrooms in mulch and compost. In this fashion, mushrooms can be grown below annual or perennial crops or ornamentals; mushrooms thrive in the shade below crops and help decompose carbonaceous materials and turn them into plant food. In my own garden we have had excellent success with wine-cap stropharia (*Stropharia rugoso-annulata*), simply transplanting rhizobium (fungus "roots") from the previous year's patch to areas where new, fresh mulch will be spread. Mycoscaping is also concerned with inoculation of mycorrhizal fungi for optimum soil food web health and bioremediation of contaminated soils.

Case study: Tucson, Arizona

The single-home, eighth-acre lot of brothers Brad and Rodd Lancaster of Tucson, Arizona, demonstrates most of the patterns just discussed. When these pioneers of the new sustainable edible garden began in 1994, their lot was just another water-wasting, sterile part of a barren neighborhood. Today their edible xeriscape is a rainwater-capturing oasis—the nucleus from which they have transformed their community and begun a global impact with the publication of Brad's three-part series, *Rainwater Harvesting for Drylands and Beyond*.

Tucson is at the northern edge of the Sonoran Desert and receives about 12 inches of rain per year. The summers are extremely hot with intense sun, but winters are fairly mild. Tucson is AHS heat zone 12 and USDA zone 9.

Brad and Rodd's driving goal is to live within their rainwater budget and the natural limits of their environment. Home food production is an essential part of realizing this goal. By producing 10 to 25 percent of their own food on site, entirely with rainwater, greywater, and runoff, they are reducing their dependence on water-depleting and fossil-fuel intensive foods from outside their region. They are proud that no potable groundwater is used to produce their home harvest. Brad reports that they eat much more fresh produce than they did before, and that they have become the life of the party at community potlucks by bringing fresh greens in winter and fresh fruits all year. They also appreciate the diversity and variety of foods available to them, many of which are commercially unavailable. Poultry and honeybees provide additional yields and help with nutrient cycling and pollination.

Brad and Rodd observed their site carefully and performed an integrated design process. At the heart of their design is careful calculation of the rainwater harvesting potential of their site. They determined that between rainfall on their

Lancaster residence in late winter. Photo by Brad Lancaster, reprinted with permission from *Rainwater Harvesting for Drylands and Beyond*, www.harvestingrainwater.com.

roof, yard, and right-of-way, runoff from adjacent streets, and the neighbor's roof, which drains onto their yard, they had over 100,000 gallons per year of rainwater both to capture in tanks and infiltrate into their landscape with small-scale earthworks. The design also called for use of vegetation as "living air conditioners" to shade their home and yard from the intense summer sun. Trees and shrubs were placed around the house to the north, west, and east, and an arbor built to the south side for queen's wreath (*Antigonon leptopus*), a native edible herbaceous vine that provides summer shade without impacting winter passive solar heating.

What is exciting about their approach is that the Lancaster brothers decided to emphasize multipurpose species for these cooling roles, with an emphasis on useful Sonoran natives. They divided their landscape into zones of water use and grow different kinds of plants in each.

Roofwater harvest for greens and herbs. Brad and Rodd grow a great diversity of greens and culinary herbs. The most intensive water use is for beds of mixed annual greens. Roof-captured rainwater provides abundant and clean irrigation for winter salad crops. Not only is the weather cool in that season (ideal for salad crops), but prices for salad greens go up in winter.

Crops vary from year to year and include arugula (*Eruca sativa*), four varieties of chard (*Beta vulgaris* var. *cicla*), four varieties of mustard (*Brassica juncea*), two varieties of kale (*B. oleracea* var. *acephala*), broccoli (*B. o.* var. *italica*), cabbage (*B. o.* var. *capitata*), a dozen different lettuces (*Lactuca sativa*), sorrel (*Rumex acetosa*), calendula (*Calendula officinalis*) for edible flowers, snow peas (*Pisum sativum*), potatoes (*Solanum tuberosum*), fava beans (*Vicia faba*) for edible leaves, flowers, and beans, cilantro (*Coriandrum sativum*), parsley (*Petroselinum crispum*), oregano (*Origanum vulgare*), rosemary (*Rosmarinus officinalis*), sage (*Salvia officinalis*), thyme (*Thymus vulgaris*), Welsh onions (*Allium fistulosum*), garlic (*A. sativum*), and southwestern heirloom i'itoi onions (*A. cepa*).

Greywater with earthworks for exotic fruits. A number of excellent fruits enjoy Tucson temperatures but require irrigation. In addition to the rainwater-infiltrating earthworks on their site, Brad and Rodd provide these species with additional water through a greywater system that takes dish, sink, and laundry waste water and diverts it to productive fruit trees.

Fruits in this category are also central to cooling their home in summer. These species include conadria fig (*Ficus carica*), the creamy and delectable white sapote (*Casimiroa edulis*), Valencia sweet orange (*Citrus sinensis*), 'Desert Gold' peach (*Prunus persica*), and 'Wonderful' and 'Spanish Ruby' pomegranates (*Punica granatum*). Brad has calculated water use requirements for evergreen species, like citrus, which are substantially higher than deciduous fruits.

Rainwater and diverted runoff for drought-tolerant tree and shrub crops. Rainwater is collected from the residential street, patio, and driveway and diverted to earthworks and sunken, mulched basins featuring a diverse array of productive xeriscape species. Non-natives the Lancasters grow that can tolerate these conditions include nopale (*Opuntia ficus-indica*), a Mexican cactus with spineless forms for edible pads and six varieties for fruit production, as well as olive (*Olea europaea*), pomegranate (*Punica granatum*), and Chinese jujube (*Ziziphus jujuba*).

Brad and Rodd's favorite native Sonoran-region edibles include desert ironwood (*Olneya tesota*) and yellow or foothill palo verde (*Parkinsonia microphylla*), both with edible seeds; fruiting cacti including saguaro (*Carnegiea gigantea*), barrel cactus (*Ferocactus wislizenii*) for edible fruit and flower buds, and Engelmann prickly pear (*Opuntia engelmannii*); spiny staghorn cholla (*O. versicolor*) for edible flower buds; chuparosa (*Justicia californica*) for edible flowers; wolfberry (*Lycium fremontii*); and chiltepine (*Capsicum annuum* var. *aviculare*), the fiery wild ancestor of peppers.

Mesquite, an edible xeriscape staple. The most remarkable food plant that the Lancaster brothers have worked with is mesquite, including velvet (*Prosopis velutina*) and screwbean (*P. pubescens*) mesquite. Drought-tolerant mesquite thrives in mulched basins irrigated only with rainwater runoff from the street. Brad

Chi Lancaster eating velvet mesquite pods beside a tree planted ten years earlier in Desert Harvesters' first annual neighborhood tree planting. On the ground are jars including backyard honey, dried chiltepines, salt-cured olives, Engelmann prickly pear jam, and mesquite flour—all grown in a public right-of-way. Photo by Brad Lancaster, reprinted with permission from *Rainwater Harvesting for Drylands and Beyond*, www.harvestingrainwater.com.

and Rodd have planted mesquites in their home landscape, along the street, and now throughout the city of Tucson through Desert Harvesters (www.desertharvesters. org), a nonprofit they helped found. The sweet pods of these native, nitrogen-fixing trees can be eaten fresh or ground to produce a nutritious flour high in protein and carbohydrates.

Inspiration and impact in Tucson and beyond. After getting their home landscape in shape, Brad and Rodd organized their neighbors and set about transforming their community. They began by working with the city to install a traffic circle featuring runoff-harvesting infiltration

Pods of velvet (*Prosopis velutina*) and screwbean (*P. pubescens*) mesquite, velvet mesquite leaves, mesquite flour, and mesquite honey. Photo by Brad Lancaster, reprinted with permission from *Rainwater Harvesting for Drylands and Beyond*, www.harvestingrainwater.com.

basins and multipurpose plantings. Soon they had created a greenbelt along their street, turning stormwater runoff into irrigation for native shade and food trees.

Desert Harvesters continues the work, helping neighborhoods around Tucson plant edible native street trees and install runoff-capturing earthworks to provide irrigation and prevent flooding. In 2005 the nonprofit received a grant for a portable community-access hammermill to grind mesquite pods into flour; the mill moves to various neighborhoods during the fall, helping residents process the bounty of their edible native xeriscape. Desert Harvesters hosts an annual fundraising mesquite pancake breakfast and will soon publish *Eat Mesquite!*, a native foods cookbook.

Brad observes that as a result of Desert Harvesters' annual tree planting initiative (more than 1,200 trees and counting), some two dozen species of birds and hummingbirds now frequent the neighborhood. Residents feel a sense of place, a connection to the Sonoran ecosystem, when they see species like Gila woodpecker, Gambel's quail, and cactus wren.

Brad's books have been well received, and Brad and Rodd's home garden and community efforts have been an inspiration to gardeners, farmers, and regional planners around the globe. In any given region, the climate challenges and ideal productive low-maintenance species will be different, but what the Lancaster brothers have done is a model that can (and should) be applied anywhere. Their "sustainable landscape of productive regeneration" is a recipe for success, and the transformation they have made in their community is the icing on the cake. Brad's motto, wherever he goes, is "plant the rain before you plant the trees."

Low-maintenance food crops

There are hundreds of low-maintenance food crops from which to choose. These crops can thrive with less care and less inputs for fertility and pest control. The following list is intended to introduce a few promising species that are not yet widely grown as foods. The publications and organizations we suggest at the back of this book (see under Chapter 5 in "References, Resources, and Recommended Reading") can assist you in selecting and acquiring appropriate species, and there are wild edible plant guides for all regions of the United States, which can be used to determine locally adapted food plants. Some

A 1996 planting of trees in streetside water-harvesting basins, ten years on. Photo by Brad Lancaster, reprinted with permission from *Rainwater Harvesting for Drylands and Beyond*, www.harvestingrainwater.com.

desert species that have already been pro-filed in the Lancaster brothers case study are not repeated here.

Fruits

Amelanchier **species.** This native genus has a representative in every mainland U.S. state, some hardy to USDA zone 2. The flowers are cream-colored and early. The berry-like fruits have a blueberry-almond flavor and vary in quality consid-

Asian pears (*Pyrus pyrifolia*), like their European counterparts, are much less susceptible to pests and diseases than apples (as long as fireblight-resistant varieties are selected). They are a fine example of a productive, delicious ornamental crop.

erably between and within species. Forms range from 50-foot trees to running sub-shrubs. Several cultivars with superior fruit characteristics are available, including many selections of the western native saskatoon (*A. alnifolia*).

Annonaceous fruits. This mostly tropical family features a range of species that can fruit in much of the United States. The pawpaw (*Asimina triloba*) is an eastern native with potato-sized fruits with a sweet flavor and luscious texture. It bears through USDA zone 5 but does require some winter chilling. In cooler areas of coastal California, the cherimoya (*Annona cherimola*) provides one of the world's finest fruits. South Florida has many annonas from which to choose, among them the sublime atemoya (*A. ×atemoya*).

Kiwifruits. The several cultivated species of kiwifruit hail from Asia. The species found in stores is fuzzy kiwi (*Actinidia deliciosa*), which is well suited to warmer climates like the Southeast and West Coast. Other species have sweeter, smaller "fuzzless" fruits and are significantly hardier. These include hardy kiwifruit (*A. arguta*), hardy to USDA zone 5, and arctic kiwifruit (*A. kolomikta*), to zone 3.

Persimmons. Two primary species are grown in the United States. The American persimmon (*Diospyros virginiana*) is an eastern native. This tough survivor tolerates a wide range of conditions, from the Florida Keys to Michigan. Fruits are smaller than kaki but rich and flavorful. Grafted trees of superior varieties are available. The kaki persimmon (*D. kaki*) is an Asian species that has been domesticated for thousands of years. The fruits are much larger than *D. virginiana*, but to my taste a bit more insipid. Trees are very productive, though the range of this species is restricted to somewhat warmer climates. Both species are very ornamental when in fruit.

More low-maintenance fruits to try. Our most popular fruits—apples, cherries, plums—tend to have fairly high maintenance requirements due to pest and disease problems. Some low-maintenance fruits with wide adaptability include pears (*Pyrus communis*), Asian pears (*P. pyrifolia*), mulberry (*Morus* spp.), gooseberries and currants (*Ribes* spp.), blueberries (*Vaccinium* spp.), grapes and muscadines (*Vitis* spp.), and hardy passionfruit (*Passiflora incarnata*). Warmer climates offer additional options including fig (*Ficus carica*), loquat (*Eriobotrya japonica*), pomegranate (*Punica granatum*), pineapple guava (*Feijoa sellowiana*), avocado (*Persea americana*), olive (*Olea europaea*), tree tomato (*Cyphomandra betacea*), and even date palms (*Phoenix dactylifera*). And truly tropical climates like south Florida and parts of San Diego have a treasure trove of fruits from which to choose, such as banana (*Musa acuminata*), lemon, lime, orange, and grapefruit (*Citrus* spp.), mango (*Mangifera indica*), starfruit (*Averrhoa carambola*), jackfruit (*Artocarpus heterophyllus*), papaya (*Carica papaya*),

and the delicious Florida native, cocoplum (*Chrysobalanus icaco*).

Nuts

Chestnuts. Though our native American chestnut (*Castanea dentata*) has been largely wiped out by blight, Chinese chestnut (*C. mollissima*) and its hybrids bear well across much of the United States. These trees are dramatic in the landscape and highly productive. Fresh roasted chestnuts should once again become an American harvest-time tradition.

Hazelnuts. Remarkably cold hardy (USDA zone 3), hazels are bushes or trees that can produce very heavily. Hazelnuts are a commercial crop in the Northwest and Upper Midwest, but they could be grown much more widely as a home crop.

Nut-bearing pines. Pinion pines of one species or another cover much of western North America. Although they are slow growing, the Colorado pinion (*Pinus edulis*) and single-leaf pinion (*P. monophylla*) are tolerant of poor soils and arid conditions, and will bear for centuries once mature. The Italian stone pine (*P. pinea*) is suited to coastal California. Nut pines are also adapted to much colder climates, including the Korean nut pine (*P. koraiensis*), hardy to USDA zone 4. The available grafted varieties of many nut pine species are much more precocious, cutting back the wait for those first nuts from decades to just a few years in some cases.

Pecans and walnuts. The United States has an abundance of native species in the walnut family (Juglandaceae). They tend to be very tall trees not suited for smaller gardens. The pecan (*Carya illinoinensis*), though an eastern native, is now grown in much of California and the Southwest with irrigation. Mature pecan trees are magnificent landmarks. The walnuts grown in California are a Eurasian species, *Juglans regia*, which features very thin, easy-to-crack shells. Our eastern native species are much thicker-shelled but more tolerant of cold and humidity; they include black walnut (*J. nigra*) and butternut (*J. cinerea*).

More low-maintenance nuts to try. Many other nuts thrive in some of our regions. Macadamia (*Macadamia* spp.) and monkey puzzle (*Araucaria* spp.) thrive in Florida and coastal California. Other California nuts and nut-like crops include pistachio (*Pistacia vera*), almond (*Prunus dulcis*), carob (*Ceratonia siliqua*), and holly oak (*Quercus ilex*). South Florida gardeners are fortunate to be able to grow coconuts (*Cocos nucifera*) and Malabar chestnut (*Pachira aquatica*).

Perennial vegetables

Allium **species.** Edible *Allium* species are tremendously diverse, suitable for tropical climates through extreme cold mountaintops and plains. Scallion types include Welsh (*A. fistulosum*) and walking onions (*A. ×proliferum*). Garlic chives (*A.*

tuberosum) and garden chives (*A. schoenoprasum*) are lovely edible ornamentals. Our eastern native ramp or wild leek (*A. tricoccum*) is a beautiful spring ephemeral in deciduous woods; its strong rich flavor has made it a favorite of Appalachian residents for generations, prompting ramp festivals when it is in season.

Aroids. Taro (*Colocasia esculenta*) and tannia (*Xanthosoma sagittifolium*) are closely related crops, from the Old and New World tropics, respectively. Both species have some toxic, strictly ornamental forms, as well as varieties that are among the world's most important crops. Even the crop forms are striking ornamentals, with large arrow-shaped or "elephant ear" leaves. Most crop types have edible corms (tuber-like structures), and some have very good-quality edible stems (notably *C. esculenta* 'Celery Stem') or leaves, or taioba (as the leaves of some low-oxalate forms of *X. sagittifolium* are known). Tannia is root hardy in USDA zone 9, but taro is surprisingly hardy, to zone 7b. I have seen established colonies in Summertown, Tennessee.

Brassicas. Several perennials in the brassica family make very good eating. For coastal California and perhaps the warmer Southeast, tree collard (possibly a sterile hybrid between *Brassica oleracea* var. *acephala* and *B. napa*) is a truly fantastic vegetable, growing to 12 feet or higher and producing copious harvests of purple-tinged leaves. Sea kale (*Crambe mari-*

tima) and Turkish rocket (*Bunias orientalis*) produce broccoli-raab-like flower buds. Sylvetta arugula (*Diplotaxis muralis*) is a shrub arugula with a sharp, nutty flavor. Though it comes from the Mediterranean, it overwinters as a perennial in my Massachusetts garden.

Chayote. This perennial vegetable produces zucchini-like squashes, edible young leaves, and large, sweet tubers. Chayote (*Sechium edule*), or mirliton as it is called in the Gulf states, is originally from Mexico and Central America. It is an attractive vine worth a place in any garden warm enough to grow it. Florida, the Gulf Coast, southern Texas, and southern and central California are all viable locations. Chayote fruit comes in many shapes and colors— those available in our supermarkets are generally of poor texture and flavor.

Climbing spinach. This central European crop is little known here but has a bright future. *Hablitzia tamnoides* is in the spinach family, and the leaves are excellent and spinach-like. This is a vine crop that tolerates cold and arid conditions. It has survived three winters in my Massachusetts garden and has become one of our favorite leaf crops. The spring shoots are also of gourmet quality.

Dioscorea **species.** The genus *Dioscorea* includes the true yams, as distinguished from the unrelated sweet potato (*Ipomoea batatas*). Large and starchy, yam tubers are an important staple in much of the world. More than sixty species are edible; at least ten are in cultivation. All are highly ornamental vines. Chinese yam or cinnamon vine (*Dioscorea batatas* or *D. opposita*) is a cold-hardy species that grows from very large edible tubers. It also produces chickpea-sized tubers on the vines. Yields of these "yam berries" can be very high; they are fairly easily harvested, as if they were little fruits, and when boiled for a few minutes are remarkably like new potatoes.

Climbing spinach (*Hablitzia tamnoides*) is a cold-hardy member of the spinach family. This 9-foot herbaceous vine produces edible leaves of excellent quality.

White yam (*D. alata*), probably the most important commercial species in the tropics, is suited to conditions in warm areas with a ten-month growing season. Air potato (*D. bulbifera*) has a bad reputation in the Southeast because toxic wild forms have naturalized aggressively, but cultivated forms are more mild-mannered; this crop is unique in that it produces apple-sized tubers on the vines, providing a

Edible pads of the spineless form of *Opuntia ficus-indica*. This species has a surprisingly large range, thriving in hot and humid and even cool humid climates in addition to arid lands.

huge harvest without disturbing the soil. It is surprisingly hardy, to USDA zone 7.

Edible canna. Known as achira in its Andean homeland, edible canna (*Canna edulis*) resembles its ornamental relatives but has large, sweet edible tubers. It is an important commercial-scale starch crop in Australia, where it is known as Queensland arrowroot. The prospect of an edible canna is quite promising for edible landscaping, and one has to wonder why more work has not been done to develop this crop in the United States, including hybridizing to create multicolored forms.

Moringa. This remarkable crop should be much more widely grown in our hotter regions. A tree in frost-free areas, and a dieback perennial reaching 15 feet annually in warm climates, moringa (*Moringa oleifera* and *M. stenopetala*) is incredibly nutritious. The leaves and pods (cooked) are so high in protein and minerals that six dried tablespoons of leaf per day provides 42 percent of the protein and 272 percent of the vitamin A of the USDA's Recommended Daily Allowance (RDA) for children. Moringa is easily grown and tolerates arid and humid conditions.

Nopale cactus. Nopales (*Opuntia ficus-indica*) are cultivated cacti. They are (mostly) spineless, with forms grown for fruit and others for edible pads. The fruits are very popular in many parts of the world; the pads are an important vegetable, reminiscent of okra or green beans to the palate, and they help to lower cholesterol. Nopale cactus loves warm, arid climates but is hardy through USDA zone 8 and grows in cooler climates as well as humid ones.

More low-maintenance perennial vegetables to try. Sadly our continent, so rich in native fruits and nuts, has not provided us with many strong native perennial vegetables. Some candidates include arrowheads (*Sagittaria* spp.), sunchoke (*Helianthus tuberosa*), groundnut (*Apios americana*), and camas (*Camassia* spp.). More popular exotics are asparagus (*Asparagus officinalis*), rhubarb (*Rheum* ×*hybridum*), and globe artichoke (*Cynara* *scolymus*). Other hardy perennial vegetables include giant fuki (*Petasites japonicus* var. *giganteus*), skirret (*Sium sisarum*), and water celery (*Oenanthe javanica*). Tropical selections include katuk (*Sauropus androgynus*), chaya (*Cnidoscolus stimulosus*), and hoopvine (*Trichostigma octandrum*), a rare Florida native. Coastal Californians and Pacific Northwest gardeners can enjoy many crops of Andean origin, including the tubers of oca (*Oxalis tuberosa*) and mashua (*Tropaeolum tuberosum*), and the melon-like fruits of pepino dulce (*Solanum muricatum*).

CHAPTER 6

Gardening Sustainably with a Changing Climate

by David W. Wolfe

WE GARDEN IN PART for the pleasure of being out in nature, but it is also a battle—with Mother Nature, and with the weather. Gardeners just about everywhere have something to complain about regarding their local climate. In low latitude regions like the southern or southwestern United States, it can be too hot, or too dry, or too humid, with too many insect and disease pests. In higher latitude locations it is too cold, the summers are too short, or the springs are too wet. The grass looks a little greener . . . just a little south or north or east or west.

Now things have become much more complicated because it is not just the familiar day-to-day weather challenges associated with our local climate that we must contend with. The climate itself—the fundamental meteorological characteristics defining where we live and garden—has become unpredictable, a moving target. We are in the unfortunate situation of being the first generation of gardeners, *ever*, who cannot rely on historical weather records to tell us what our climate is, or what to expect in the future. Our weather records can tell us only how far from "normal" our local climate has strayed.

Those currently gardening in cool higher latitudes might celebrate the thought of a warmer, longer growing season, and indeed they should be prepared to take advantage of any opportunities that climate change might bring. But we should be careful what we wish for. It is not clear that climate change will be a benign and smooth transition to a "better" climate for anyone. Instead, we are entering an era of great uncertainty that makes gardening even more challenging than it was before.

Climate change in perspective

Isn't the climate always changing? The short answer to that question is yes: the climate has been changing throughout

Mountain pine beetle damage in Rocky Mountain National Park.
Photo © iStockphoto/Sylvia Schug.

the entire 4.5-billion-year history of our planet. Modern human civilization, particularly our use of carbon-based fossil fuels, has emerged as a factor in climate change only during the past 150 years. However— and this is the most important part of the story—seldom has the pace of change been as rapid as projected for the next several decades. Over the long history of our earth, the ups and downs in global temperatures have typically occurred over tens of thousands or millions of years. Consider, for example, that during the past 15,000 to 30,000 years or so, as much of the northern hemisphere transitioned from being covered by a deep glacial ice sheet to the vast green landscapes we see today, the planet warmed by about 15 degrees Fahrenheit. Now, in many parts of the same region, climate scientists project we could have almost an equivalent amount of additional warming within a single century— our century. That will be *more than a hundred times faster than the warming of the most recent ice age transition.* The human race has never experienced this pace of climate change, so perhaps it is not surprising that, as a species, we are having a hard time coming to terms with the possibility.

For decades, gardeners have used plant hardiness zone maps, based on minimum winter temperatures, to determine what plant species are adapted to where they live. In the United States such maps, periodically produced by the U.S. Department of Agriculture (USDA), are based on the past fifteen years of weather records from

the same network of NOAA weather stations our local meteorologist uses for daily forecasts. The last version published by the USDA appeared in 1990. In 2006, the Arbor Day Foundation published an updated map using the same methodology as the USDA, which shows a dramatic "zone creep" northward throughout the country. Almost no matter where you live, there has been a shift toward a warmer zone based on the minimum winter temperature.

Several years ago the New York Botanical Garden in the Bronx, New York, planted a small test garden of sorts, with numerous woody perennials one hardiness zone warmer for their region than indicated by the 1990 USDA map. Thus far all appear to be doing all right (T. Forrest, NYBG, personal communication). This can be interpreted as success; but despite this, and the additional anecdotal evidence of a warming trend it provides, most experts agree that gardeners should be very cautious and do their own experimenting on a limited basis.

As climate zones continue to shift, with longer growing seasons and milder winters in temperate regions, it will undoubtedly open the door to cautious exploration of new food crops, ornamentals, and flowers in the garden. Gardeners like to experiment, and, unlike farmers, they have the luxury of being able to be adventurous without risking their entire livelihood on it. In this way gardeners can lead the way to what is possible in a changing climate. On the down side, we are likely to lose some of our favorites. Some traditional garden and native plants will suffer from changes in the local climate while new and exotic species, including aggressive invasives, could thrive.

Plant responses to climate change

An earlier spring. It is not just thermometers and the weather record, as depicted in Figure 1, telling us the climate is changing. We now have clear evidence that the living world is already responding, particularly in the form of an advance in spring biological events such as spring bloom date and spring arrival of migratory birds and insects.

The study of seasonal biological events is called "phenology." Phenological calendars, based primarily on spring bloom dates, were used by the ancient Chinese and Romans to guide agricultural operations. Plants, particularly woody perennials, are like sensitive weather instruments, indicators and integrators of complex changes in winter and spring conditions. Scientists are now seeking out historical phenological records and using them to study regional climate change trends. In the United States, one of the best data sets was initiated in the 1930s by conservationist Aldo Leopold, at his family farm in Wisconsin. His children continued the tradition, and in 1999 published an analysis of over fifty years of record (Bradley et al. 1999). They found that among

fifty-five species monitored, there was an advance in spring earliness of about six days during this time period. Wolfe et al. (2005) utilized a particularly robust data set for the period 1965–2001 based on

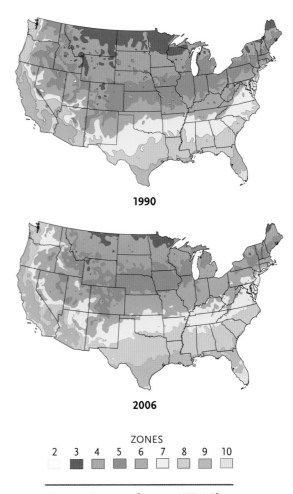

Figure 1. Compare the 1990 USDA Plant Hardiness Zone Map (top) to the 2006 arborday.org Hardiness Zone Map (above): the "zone creep" northward is obvious. Maps courtesy of the Arbor Day Foundation.

seventy-two locations in the northeastern United States where genetically identical lilac plants (*Syringa ×chinensis*, clone 'Red Rothomagensis') were planted and monitored for first flower (bloom) date. These plantings were originally established by a USDA project designed to optimize farming operations (e.g., to establish the most effective time for sowing seed or the control of spring-emerging insects) and predict harvest dates and yield potential. What they found was that on average lilacs are blooming about four days earlier today than they were in the 1960s, corresponding with a warming climate during the same time period. The researchers also used a more geographically limited data set for the same time period for grapes and apples, and found bloom dates for these species had advanced by about six and eight days, respectively. Similar evidence for earlier spring has been found from historical phenological records gathered in the western United States (Cayan et al. 2001), Britain (Fitter and Fitter 2002), and throughout Europe and other parts of the world (Walther et al. 2002; Parmesan and Yohe 2003).

Historical records of botanic gardens such as those maintained at Harvard's Arnold Arboretum have proven particularly useful in documenting climate change effects on local spring phenology (Primack et al. 2004), and this suggests an emerging role for public gardens (Primack and Miller-Rushing 2009). Gardeners now have an opportunity to become personally involved as "citizen scientists" in monitoring efforts, such as "Project Budburst," associated with the U.S. National Phenology Network (www.usanpn.org), Canada's Nature Watch (www.naturecanada.ca/cwn_naturewatch.asp), and the U.K. Phenology Network (www.naturescalendar.org.uk).

One concern among ecologists is that climate change could disrupt important species interactions. For example, if a plant is blooming earlier, will its pollinators respond to climate change in a similar manner and be active earlier? Will insect pests and their natural enemies that currently keep their populations under control remain in sync? As spring arrives earlier and climate zones shift, one thing we know for certain is that entire complex communities of plants and other species are not going to respond en masse in exactly the same way. Disruptions are almost certainly going to occur, but thus far we have very little research to document whether they are occurring, or whether there is enough redundancy in particular ecosystems (or gardens) to overcome such disruptions.

Warmer winters and perennial plants. As discussed already in relation to the hardiness zone maps, warmer winters will affect which plants are adapted to each region, and for gardeners in cold areas this should gradually expand the palette of species one might experiment with in the garden. However, the situation has been confusing in recent years due to several well-documented examples of an increase in winter freeze or spring frost damage, despite the fact that winters overall are getting warmer.

This apparent paradox can be explained by the variability we are seeing in winter temperatures. For example, in the winters of 2004 and 2005 there were millions of dollars of vine damage to non-native European wine grape (*Vitis vinifera*) plantings in upstate New York associated with unusually warm periods in December, followed by "normal" severe cold (i.e., below −5°F) in January (Levin 2005). It is suspected that the warm Decembers either delayed "hardening" of the vines, or actually "dehardened" them, increasing their susceptibility to freeze damage (Anisko et al. 1994). A more widespread phenomenon has been reported in recent years in both the United States and Canada, where extended warm periods in late winter have caused premature leaf-out or bloom of temperate perennial plants and bulbs, leaving them susceptible to subsequent frost damage when temperatures dip below 32°F (Gu et al. 2008).

Another issue for temperate perennial plants is that most undergo a winter period of rest or dormancy and have a "winter chilling requirement"—a required period of temperatures below about 45°F—in order to be capable of normal hormone production and leaf-out and bloom in the spring. In some regions winter warming might create a situation where the chilling requirement is not met, and this will negatively affect flowering and crop production. Figure 2 illustrates the range of chilling hours required for several tree fruit and nut species. Apples, adapted to colder regions, have relatively high winter chill requirements of 800 to 1,800 hours, peaches are intermediate (about 500 to 1,000 hours), and almonds, adapted to warmer regions, have chill requirements from about 50 to 600 hours. The potential for inadequate winter chill hours could be a problem where these crops are being grown near the fringe of their optimum range. Some fruit growing areas of California may be particularly vulnerable. In another study by Wolfe et al. (2008) that focused on the northeastern United States, a simulation model projection for apple suggested that by mid- to late-century, apple growers may need to switch to varieties that require less than 1,000 hours

These avocados suffered freeze damage during an unexpectedly severe winter— on the temperate coast of California. Photo by David Deardorff and Kathryn Wadsworth.

of winter chilling for maximum yield potential.

Summer heat stress. For gardeners in warm lower latitude locations there is little "silver lining" to a warming trend. Warmer temperatures will exacerbate any existing problems with summer heat stress. Gardeners in some historically cooler regions will for the first time have to consider heat stress and a possible increase in the frequency of summer days when temperatures exceed thresholds that negatively affect flowering, fruit production and quality, growth, and survival. Even a species like tomato, adapted to warm climates, can be negatively affected by temperatures over 90°F during critical reproductive stages. In many cases, gardeners can look to regions that have been historically warmer for options—new heat-tolerant varieties or new species. Several guides to selecting plants for heat tolerance have been produced (e.g., Cathey and Bellamy 1998), and in 1997 the American Horticultural Society produced a heat zone map for the United States (visit www.ahs.org and select "publications"). As with the hardiness zone maps, such heat zone maps will need continual updating if they are to reflect the reality of our rapidly changing climate.

Water: too much, too little, or both. Climate change is likely to bring new challenges in the process of water management—challenges such as water shortages, or increased frequency of high rainfall events and flooding, or some combination of both. For those in already dry-prone areas like the western United States, more severe water shortages are projected, due to reduced total annual rainfall and also reduced storage of water in winter high-elevation snow packs. As society grapples with severe water shortfalls in some regions, the use of precious water resources for gardening will almost certainly be constrained, requiring a shift to slower growing drought-tolerant varieties and species in the garden.

Even for regions like the northeastern United States, where climate models do not project any clear trend toward reductions in rainfall, summer plant water re-

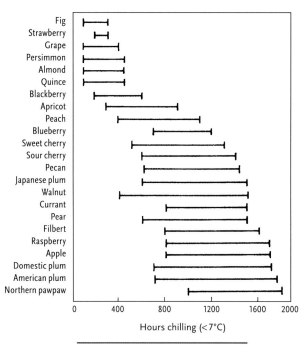

Figure 2. The range of chilling hours required for fruit and nut species.

quirements and the frequency of summer drought is projected to increase by mid- to late-century (Hayhoe et al. 2007). This is because as summer temperatures go up, plant transpiration water losses will go up, increasing water requirements. If this is not compensated for by an increase in rainfall, water deficits will increase.

Throughout much of the northern hemisphere, a recent historical trend is that a greater proportion of rain comes in intense high-rainfall events (i.e., more than 2 inches in forty-eight hours) (Trenberth et al. 2007), and this trend is expected to continue for many regions. This creates numerous problems for the gardener, such as "wet feet," root disease, and direct crop flood damage. Other issues are lack of access to the garden for extended periods of time, delayed spring planting, soil compaction due to entering the garden when soils are wet, wash-off of foliar pesticides, and erosion and runoff. For landscapers and planners in urban areas, heavy rains can be particularly damaging to plants growing with constrained root zones, and can create flooding problems in areas that are covered with asphalt or other impermeable surfaces.

The potential carbon dioxide (CO_2) "fertilization" effect. Carbon dioxide, in addition to being a greenhouse gas, has a more direct effect on plant life because plants take up CO_2 in the process of photosynthesis to produce sugars for growth. Atmospheric CO_2 is projected to increase from current levels near 390 ppm to at least 550 ppm and possibly 970 ppm or higher this century (Nakicenovic and Swart 2000). This could potentially increase the growth of many plants, particularly those with the so-called C_3 photosynthetic pathway, under optimum conditions. About 90 percent of vascular plants are C_3. Experiments examining the effect of a CO_2 doubling from today's levels have found large variation in response depending on species and environmental conditions. Crops grown in greenhouses or growth chambers at optimum temperature, optimum water and nutrient supply, and free of pest or weed pressure, have shown yield gains of 20 to 30 percent or more (Kimball 1983) with a CO_2 doubling. More recent studies where crops were grown at higher CO_2 under field conditions found smaller benefits of 5 to 10 percent (Long et al. 2006). Under high temperature or other forms of stress, or with limiting nutrients, the CO_2 effect on photosynthesis and growth can be negligible (Wolfe 1995). Unfortunately for gardeners, it appears that fast-growing invasive plants and aggressive weed species tend to benefit most from high CO_2 (Ziska 2003), and weeds are more resistant to herbicide control at high CO_2 levels (Ziska et al. 1999). Most studies conducted to date have found that the photosynthetic stimulation diminishes and saturates at CO_2 above about 800 to 1,000 ppm (Wolfe 1995); this benefit will not go on forever, therefore, but could affect plants for much of this century.

Increased weed, insect, and disease pressure

The same minimum winter temperatures that constrain which ornamental plants can be grown where, also constrain the habitable range of many weeds, insects, and disease organisms. The scientific literature of the last two decades has documented many examples of northward range spread of everything from plants to insects, birds, and mammals (for reviews, Walther et al. 2002; Parmesan and Yohe 2003; Montaigne 2004). At Britain's Kew Gardens, oaks have recently been plagued by larvae of the moth *Thaumetopoea processionea*, which had been considered a more southern pest (Marris 2007). As the climate continues to warm in the coming century, these trends are expected to continue. A recent assessment of future climate impacts on the northeastern United States projected a rapid spread northward of the hemlock woolly adelgid (*Adelges tsugae*) (Paradis et al. 2008), an aphidlike insect pest that has already devastated stands of the important native evergreen hemlock trees in more southern regions. As part of the same northeastern U.S. regional assessment, Wolfe et al. (2008) projected a spread northward of the notoriously aggressive weed kudzu (*Pueraria montana*) into the region, and increased spring populations of flea beetles (*Chaetocnema pulicaria*), an insect pest which now only marginally overwinters in the region. The flea beetles typically do only minor damage to plants, but they often transmit Stewart's wilt, a bacterial disease, to corn and other crops.

In addition to shifts in habitable range bringing new pests to a region, we are also seeing examples of increased, sometimes devastating, pressure from native pests that historically have been a tolerable problem. One explanation is that longer, warmer summers means more time for weeds to establish and produce more seed, and more generations per growing season for some insects and pathogens. A particularly frightening example is the mountain

Woolly adelgid damage.
Photo by Eli Dickerson.

pine beetle (*Dendroctonus ponderosae*), a native species of the western United States that has co-existed with conifer trees in the region for thousands of years. In just the past decade, however, the magnitude of recurring outbreaks is causing unprecedented mortality to trees from the Rocky Mountains to British Columbia (Logan et al. 2003). Nearly 5 million lodgepole pines were lost in 2006 alone in Colorado. A number of factors are involved, including milder winters that have favored survival of the insect's larvae, and increased vulnerability of trees due to recent drought and high summer temperatures in the region.

Climate change causing earlier emergence or migratory arrival of familiar pests is another issue. In the United Kingdom, aphids that carry the barley yellow dwarf virus have advanced their spring migration by three to six days (Goho 2004). In the northeastern United States, integrated pest management (IPM) specialists have had to begin monitoring for the corn earworm (*Helicoverpa zea*) several weeks earlier than in the past (Wolfe et al. 2008).

Adapting to unavoidable change

Climate change will bring both opportunities and challenges for gardeners and landscapers. For historically cool regions, a longer growing season and warmer summers and winters will allow experimenting with new things that in the past you couldn't grow. That will be the fun part. However, as the aforementioned reports of recent cold damage to perennials (even as winters warm) show, we are entering an era of uncertainty, so gardeners should be cautious. Here are several adaptation approaches to take advantage of opportunities and minimize negative effects from a changing climate.

Plant selection. This can be an exciting opportunity for gardeners to experiment with new plant species and new varieties as plant hardiness zones and other aspects of climate continue to shift. However, we may have to give up on some of our former stand-bys. Trying to maintain our traditional favorites even as they become less suitable to our climate will require more inputs and work against any interest in a low-input, sustainable garden. Often it will be difficult to know when it is time to give up on one species or variety and try another. In the context of such uncertainty, more diversity in the garden and a watchful eye will be the best approach. Also, find out what gardeners in other regions are doing. Sometimes there may be an alternative variety available "off the shelf." Also, keep an eye on new developments from plant breeders for varieties tolerant of heat or drought stress, and tolerant of new insect and disease pests you are coping with.

Shifting planting date. For annuals, changing planting and/or harvest date can be an effective, low-cost option to take advantage of earlier springs and a longer growing season, or to avoid crop exposure to adverse climate (e.g., high temperature stress, low rainfall). Predicting the optimum planting date will be very challenging in a future with increased uncertainty regarding climate, however, so gradual and cautious experimentation should be the approach rather than radical changes in a single year.

Pest, disease, and weed control challenges. Climate change is an incentive to work closely with local IPM or Extension service specialists to keep track of potential new pest threats whose habitable range is expanding into your area. Gardeners can play an important "citizen scientist" role in monitoring and informing regional specialists of new pests they are observing. Also, as an important stakeholder group, gardeners can express their support of local and regional IPM and Extension programs to universities and policy makers. Increasing insect, disease, and weed pressure may require increased applications of chemical controls to grow certain species in the garden, working against an interest in low-input, sustainable gardening. To avoid this, gardeners may need to shift to new plant species resistant to the pests, or contact IPM and Extension specialists for information about non-chemical control strategies.

Freeze and frost protection for perennial plants. Perennials are long-term investments and choosing the right ones to plant is the first step. With an uncertain climate you cannot rely entirely on some-thing like the 1990 USDA Plant Hardiness Zone Map, particularly if you are on the southern fringe of a minimum temperature range. Consult your local nursery and Extension service for information on the latest climate trends and suitable species and varieties for your area. The second step is site selection. The options you have will depend on the size of your gardening area, of course, but keep in mind that north-facing slopes and low-lying or shaded areas are cooler and so more subject to frost or freeze damage, potentially increasing the risks presented by climate change. For some woody perennials, changing the timing and/or severity of winter pruning might minimize potential losses from a premature bloom followed by a spring frost event. For shrubs, small trees, or groundcovers, covering with freeze-protection mulches or reusable fabrics can be an emergency option. Poling (2008) outlines several strategies used by commercial fruit growers, and some gardeners might find one or more these (wind machines, heaters, overhead sprinklers) feasible options for them.

Improved water management. Increases in both short-term flooding and short-term droughts are projected to become more frequent in many regions. Site selection and modification are the first steps toward adapting to these challenges. Identify which parts of the garden are more prone to prolonged wet or dry periods. Chronic wet sites can be modified by reconfiguring the topography to keep water from pooling in low spots, or by using raised beds to minimize "wet feet" during flooded periods. Soil amendments can be used to improve drainage during wet periods or improve water holding capacity during dry periods. Climate change is an added incentive to maximize the rooting volume of urban trees. "Structural soil" (typically an 80:20 stone:soil mix) beneath sidewalks allows for the necessary compaction prior to pouring cement, while also allowing expanded root growth under the sidewalk. The use of permeable asphalt reduces runoff and overfill of urban storm drain systems, and provides water to plant roots beneath the asphalt. Irrigating is an obvious adaptation to increasing frequency of water deficits. Use of drip irrigation systems and tensiometers or other devices to monitor soil water status will improve water use efficiency. Finally, use of flood- or drought-tolerant plant varieties will become essential in some areas.

Growing a greener garden: becoming part of the solution

While gardening tends to attract individuals concerned about the environment, it is easy to become a bit obsessed with having the perfect garden and end up making a significant contribution to greenhouse gas emissions. There is much gardeners can do to reduce their "carbon footprint" and become part of the solution. Here are several win-win strategies, which not only will

tend to move your garden toward a more "carbon neutral" state but also often reduce costs or labor associated with gardening.

Improve nitrogen fertilizer use efficiency. Many farmers, gardeners, and homeowners are surprised to learn that often the "lowest hanging fruit" when it comes to greenhouse gas mitigation has little to do with use of tractors or mowers, but rather with nitrogen fertilizer. One reason for this is that synthetic nitrogen fertilizers (e.g., urea, ammonium nitrate) are very energy-intensive to manufacture (often involving temperatures exceeding 700°F and emitting as much as 4 to 6 tons of CO_2 equivalents for every ton of nitrogen manufactured). Thus, just purchasing a bag of synthetic fertilizer contributes to your carbon footprint.

Being very strategic in terms of the timing and amount of synthetic nitrogen fertilizers applied is one aspect of improving efficiency. Better yet, reduce dependence on synthetic sources. One option is to integrate legumes (beans, peas, clovers) into your garden or lawn instead of relying on fertilizers. Through their symbiotic relationship with nitrogen-fixing bacteria in their roots, legumes accomplish the same thing nitrogen factories do (converting atmospheric N_2 gas into ammonium) but at common soil temperatures and with fewer emissions (Wolfe 2001). For supplemental additions, preference should be given to organic sources, such as manures or compost when available.

In the nitrogen cycle diagram of Figure 3 you can see that whether we add organic nitrogen sources, or synthetic ammonium or nitrate fertilizers, some of the nitrogen is inevitably lost to the atmosphere as nitrous oxide (N_2O), a potent greenhouse gas with three hundred times more warming potential than CO_2, during natural soil biological processes that are part of the nitrogen cycle. The point here is that even

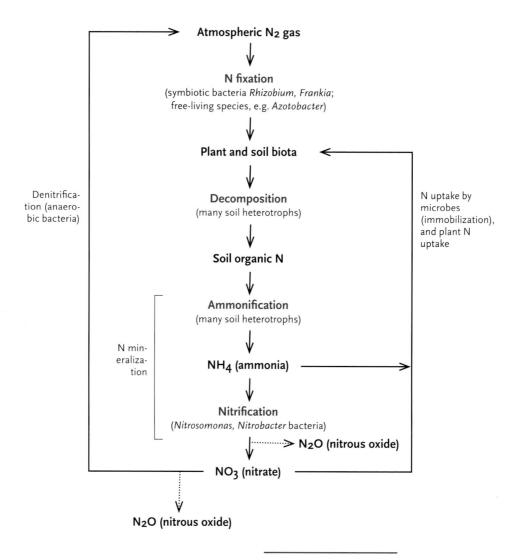

Figure 3. The nitrogen cycle.

in an organic garden relying exclusively on manure and composts, these inputs should be used strategically and sparingly to minimize emission of N_2O and contributions to global warming.

Increase soil carbon sequestration. When plants die and decompose, much of the carbon that they have taken up as CO_2 from the atmosphere during photosynthesis becomes part of the soil organic matter

NITROGEN MANAGEMENT FOR LAWNS (TURF)

There is considerable acreage of public and private lawns throughout the developed world, and most of these are poorly managed when it comes to nitrogen. Specific recommendations for improving nitrogen use efficiency for lawns include the following:

- Select grass species with relatively low nitrogen requirements. For example, Kentucky bluegrass has a relatively high nitrogen requirement, so preference should be given to mixes with lower percentages of this variety, replaced by fine fescues.
- Consider clover (legume)-grass mixtures. Clovers show the effect of foot traffic more than grasses so these mixtures are best suited to low-traffic areas. Also note that if you repeatedly apply nitrogen fertilizers to these mixes the clovers will be less competitive and not survive.
- Mow high (i.e., greater than 3 inches). This promotes good root growth and exploration of more soil for nitrogen.
- Recycle lawn clippings. These hold nitrogen and other nutrients that you should recycle to your soils.
- If using synthetic nitrogen fertilizers, urea is preferable to ammonium sulfate or ammonium nitrate. This is because greenhouse gas emissions during manufacture

are smaller for urea compared to the others. Also, urea is more slowly released in the soil, thus available to plants as they grow and need it.
- Organic nitrogen sources are preferable because they do not have the high carbon footprint associated with manufacture. However, these too should be used judiciously to minimize nitrous oxide (a potent greenhouse gas) release from soils as they degrade (see main text and Figure 3).
- Avoid very early spring nitrogen applications. Be patient and allow soils to warm sufficiently to stimulate soil microbial activity that will convert nitrogen in stored soil organic matter into ammonium and nitrate that plant roots take up (see Figure 3). If you must use an early spring pre-emergent crabgrass weed control, try to find one without nitrogen fertilizer unless it is really warranted.
- Healthy mature lawns and shaded areas may need only two applications of supplemental nitrogen per year (early summer and late fall), and lower total annual amounts of applied (1 or 2 pounds per 1,000 square feet) compared to new lawns.
- Consider replacing high-maintenance turf lawn with a no-mow lawn, meadow, or other sustainable planting.

pool. Building up and maintaining the organic matter in soils is something gardeners should be doing anyway for soil health and crop growth, but this also serves to sequester carbon in the soil that otherwise would be in the atmosphere as CO_2 gas.

One way to build up soil carbon is to till (turn) the soil less. This a great example of how by doing less, you do more for the environment! Tillage over-aerates the soil, literally fanning the flames of microbial breakdown of organic matter (and release of CO_2 into the atmosphere). Both farmers and gardeners often go overboard with tillage, perhaps stemming from a misguided notion that a well-prepared seed bed should look like a fine powder and be free of any small clods or debris. Other times an "addiction to tillage" begins with the legitimate need to till a compacted soil, but because this ends up burning off organic matter the soil structure becomes more vulnerable to future compaction. Low organic matter reduces soil flora and fauna overall, and these soil organisms are essential for good soil aggregate stability because they release sticky substances that help hold soil particles together. Poorer aggregate stability makes soils more prone to compaction, and the downward spiral continues.

Darwin was the first to document that earthworms "till" the soil, but in a gradual process that does not lead to rapid organic matter or carbon loss. Earthworms can move 20 to 30 tons of soil per acre per year (Wolfe 2001). Managing soils to promote beneficial soil organisms such as these is how we should approach gardening and farming. Use of rotation or cover crops with deep root systems to break up compacted layers and move organic matter deep into the profile is another biological approach to alleviating soil compaction while minimizing CO_2 losses to the atmosphere.

Plant a tree. Planting a tree has perhaps been overhyped by some politicians and city planners as a panacea for global warming, but certainly trees do take up CO_2 from the atmosphere and also can have a cooling effect in urban areas, thus reducing emissions associated with air conditioning and fans for cooling of residences and offices in summer. Pataki et al. (2006) estimated the combined direct CO_2 uptake plus "avoided" emissions benefits of urban trees in several U.S. cities and found a range of about 75 to 550 pounds of CO_2 equivalents per tree per year. Depending on where you live, the annual per person emissions for much of the developed world ranges from about 10,000 to over 40,000 pounds of CO_2 equivalents per person per year. You can do the math and see we will not solve the problem with tree planting, but it can be a part of the solution, and trees have many other benefits, such as contributing to human well-being (both mental and physical) and serving as habitat for birds and other species.

Recycle and reduce use of disposable products. Use of organic mulches and reusable products rather than disposable plastics is an example of a green approach in the garden. It usually takes more fossil fuel energy to build a product from scratch than to start with recycled materials. Every time we throw something away, whether it be a garden product or something in the home or office, it means more energy spent creating its replacement, and also energy spent in transporting waste.

Reduce fossil fuel use. This is the obvious one, in all our activities, including gardening. For those with large lawns who use power mowers, mowing less often and keeping engines well tuned is a specific thing we can do.

Use renewable energy sources. In the commercial horticulture sector there are some great examples of growers using farm-generated renewable energy—biodiesel from soybeans or corn pellets, wind energy—to heat greenhouses or provide energy for other operations.

To summarize, there are many adaptation and mitigation options for growing healthy and "greener" lawns, gardens, and urban landscapes in the face of climate change. Gardeners represent a large fraction of the population, and collectively we can be part of the solution and serve as important role models for creative citizen action to confront the challenges of climate change.

CHAPTER 7

Waterwise Gardens

by Thomas Christopher

WATER IS THE STUFF of life, in the most literal sense. Almost two-thirds (by weight) of every gardener's body is water. And the proportion is even greater in most of our plants. Herbaceous plants—a category that includes annual and perennial flowers, grasses, most herbs and vegetables—are typically 80 to 90 percent water by weight, and in some especially succulent ones, such as lettuce and cacti, the water content is as high as 95 percent. Even woody plants, our seemingly solid trees and shrubs, are about half water.

Plants are rich in water for a very good reason: it's fundamental to almost every aspect of their life and growth. It's water that carries minerals up from the soil and into their roots; and it's water that carries the nutrients from the photosynthesizing leaves to nourish the rest of the plant. Water inflates the cells to give the plant's tissues rigidity. It also provides

This designed meadow does very well without irrigation: a bioswale helps to conserve water on site. Photo by Saxon Holt.

the plant with a cooling system. By evaporating water off the surface of the leaves during hot weather, plants protect themselves from the botanical equivalent of heat stroke, much as you cool yourself by sweating. This last, the cooling process botanists call transpiration, accounts for most of a plant's water use: in warm, sunny weather, each leaf may transpire an amount of water equivalent to its own weight in just one hour. Most of the damage a plant experiences during periods of drought, at least initially, isn't caused by dehydration so much as by the switching off of its cooling system and the consequent overheating of the plant's tissues.

Understanding how a plant uses water might seem to be of interest only to botanists, but in fact it's also your secret for turning irrigation into a precise and potent gardening tool. Some mention was made in the introduction to this book about the huge wastage of water that is intrinsic to conventional gardening methods, and the role this plays in draining rivers, lakes, and aquifers. It's essential to understand, however, that this wastage of water is just as harmful, in the long run, to the garden. Overwatering of the sort practiced by most American gardeners washes the fertility out of the soil (and into nearby waterways, where it becomes a major source of water pollution). Giving a plant excessive amounts of water encourages soft, overly lush, plant growth that makes your garden a target for all kinds of pests, ranging from aphids to deer. It also encourages the spread of plant diseases.

In addition, overwatering promotes invasion by those opportunistic, aggressive plants we categorize as weeds. It's worth noting in connection with this that weeds are, overall, one of the best indications of whether you are gardening sustainably. They are a class of plants that has evolved in partnership with mankind, adapting to take advantage of the environmental disturbances we promote, and to seize on the resources we waste through such behavior. When a farmer strips a field of vegetation with his plow, weeds rush in to claim the unoccupied soil. When you over-fertilize your plantings, weeds spring up to make use of the nutrients that your shrubs or flowers cannot absorb. Likewise, if you apply more water to your garden than it needs, weeds will surely spring up to claim the excess. If, therefore, you find yourself devoting much time and effort to weed control, it is probably an indication that, among other things, you are too free with your irrigation.

Reducing water use in the garden

As shortages in the public water supply system have become chronic in many parts of the United States, especially in the Southwest, over the last generation, gardeners in the affected regions have developed strategies and new types of design that minimize the need for irrigation. So far, however, this has remained for the most part a regional movement. "Xeriscaping" and "desertscaping" may have attracted a good deal of attention in Arizona and New Mexico, just as "prairiescaping" has won popularity in the drier areas of the Plains states, but gardeners in the moister parts of the country have typically paid little attention, taking the attitude that landscape water conservation is something to be practiced in the desert or arid West, but not in New England, Georgia, or Minnesota.

What these holdouts are discovering, however, is that unsustainable landscape practices can stress water supply systems even where natural rainfall is abundant. After all, the decisive point when it comes to irrigation is not just the scope of the local water supply, but also the quantity that can be delivered (sustainably) through the local supply system. In many cases, these delivery systems have failed to keep pace with local development; suburbanization not only creates an increased demand for water in formerly rural communities, it also makes difficult or impossible the condemnation of land to create new reservoirs. Meanwhile, industrial development has often polluted streams, rivers, and aquifers that were once useful sources of fresh water, so that they are no longer potable. The net result has been that areas that wouldn't seem likely to suffer shortages, do. Dade County, Florida, for instance, the home to the Miami metropolitan area, enjoys an average of 53 inches of rainfall annually, distributed over 131 days of storms. Yet because of an undersized storage system and groundwater pollution, the local water utility finds it difficult to satisfy its customers' needs and regularly imposes landscape watering restrictions.

One reason that landscape and garden irrigation has become a bugaboo of water managers is that irrigation tends to create seasonal spikes in water consumption. Typically, watering increases dramatically in summertime—in many areas of the West, it temporarily doubles the demand on the public water supply system. In

Waterwise garden at a school in forward-thinking Portland, Oregon.

many regions of North America, the summer season of warm weather, when temperatures are suitable for plant growth, is also a dry season, when reservoirs are not being replenished by rain or melting snow. The problem this creates for a water utility is obvious: peak demand coincides with a period of reduced supply.

Even if you and your neighbors draw your water from private wells, your landscape irrigation may have an impact on the public water supply. The Ipswich River, for example, a source of drinking water for fourteen towns in coastal Massachusetts, runs dry every summer now in part because of water pumped from private wells—this pumping may keep plantings green, but it sucks the underground reservoir, the aquifer, dry, which in turn drains moisture from the adjacent river. Nor is this an isolated instance. Many streams and even rivers that once ran year-round now disappear in summertime because of unsustainable demands on the local aquifers.

To keep your garden from becoming this sort of environmental burden, you should free it, as much as possible, from its dependence on irrigation. It's unlikely that you will ever entirely eliminate the need for this sort of support. It would be difficult (if not impossible) to garden without injecting at least some extra water into the landscape. New plantings, even if they are of species adapted to the local climate, are going to need some judicious watering until their roots have grown out into the surrounding soil. You'll greatly enhance both the quantity and quality of vegetable and fruit crops by keeping the soil around their roots moist through periods of drought. Timely, just-enough irrigation also boosts the floral display of annual and perennial flowers. Besides, even the water-thriftiest gardener may want to enhance with some extra water the lushness of the plantings immediately surrounding a deck or terrace used for outdoor entertaining and dining, or relaxing on weekends. Still, even with all these uses for your hose, it is possible as a gardener to reduce your water use dramatically, by 75 percent or more.

Weaning your garden off the irrigation habit begins with a detailed analysis of your particular situation.

GETTING THE MOST OUT OF IRRIGATION

To create an impression of lushness, concentrate irrigated plantings around the area of your landscape where you spend the most time. A couple of lavishly flowering tubs placed on a deck, or a band of colorful flowers encircling a terrace make a disproportionate impression. Outer, less prominent areas of the landscape can be left to more self-sufficient but less decorative plants, such as ornamental grasses and deep-rooted shrubs.

Assessing local climate

It's revealing that the traditional guides created to help gardeners find plants appropriate to their local climate deal solely with temperature. For example, the USDA Plant Hardiness Zone Map (the map you find in the back of every nursery catalog) divides the United States into different numbered "climate zones" solely on the basis of the average low temperatures experienced in wintertime in each area. Of course, availability of water is at least as crucial to plant growth as tolerance to cold, but clearly, the presumption is that unlimited water for irrigation may be had just by opening your tap. In other words, the USDA map classifies Naples, Florida, as identical with Victorville, California, even though Naples receives 51.9 inches of precipitation annually, while Victorville gets less than 7.

Fortunately, it isn't hard to develop a better profile yourself. You can download the necessary information for free from the National Climatic Data Center website. Go to its homepage, at www.ncdc.noaa.gov/oa/ncdc.html, and click on "Free Data" (you'll find this under the "Data & Products" menu). Scroll down to "Free Data C" and then select your state, and after that the weather station nearest to your place of residence. What you'll get for this is a list of monthly averages over a thirty-year period (1971–2000). These include the average high and low temperature experienced at that station each month, but also the average precipitation in inches and—this is important—the average number of days each month on which rain, snow, or ice fell, and how many days on which the total accumulation was 0.01, 0.1, 0.5, or 1 inch. This may seem like more information than you want, but it will give you an idea of how evenly distributed the precipitation has been. That is crucially important, after all. Even if your average rainfall during the summer is 4 inches a month, if this falls in just a few big storms, your plants (unless you have chosen only deep-rooted, drought-resistant species) are going to suffer from thirst during the hot, dry intervals between the storms.

Perhaps the most important knowledge to be gained from this website, though, is the total annual precipitation received in your region. This number provides a very useful clue about what sort of vegetation will do best in your garden.

■ Less than 10 inches of annual precipitation qualifies your region as desert, although Americans tend to stretch this definition, labeling as "desert" locations such as Tucson, Arizona, that typically receive an inch or two more per year than the official maximum. When planting a garden in an area of this sort, you should use drought-adapted plants, and space your plantings in the manner of a desert, where the roots of individual plants occupy extensive spreads of soil so that they can tap more of the moisture that does fall from the sky. Groundcover plants and turf are out of place in such a setting, and trees should be planted very sparingly and should be of a desert-adapted species such as palo verde (*Parkinsonia* spp.) or mesquite (*Prosopis* spp.).

■ Annual precipitation of 10 to 20 inches, in most of the United States, indicates a steppe or grassland climate. Precipitation in the lower part of that range is typical of shortgrass prairie, while precipitation toward the upper part defines a tallgrass prairie. Both types of prairies are dominated by grasses and perennial flowers, which protect themselves from the extremes of the prairie climate by investing most of their growth in their roots (as much as 90 percent by weight of a prairie grass is found below the surface of the soil). Any nursery that specializes in prairie plants can help you distinguish which species of plants will thrive in your climate. The important thing to remember is that trees and most shrubs are, from the perspective of water consumption, a luxury in such a climate because most will require regular irrigation. As a designer, you should think hard about where you need shade and how to dispose the trees so that you get the maximum advantage from each. One of the great joys of a steppe garden is that it provides an ideal setting for many kinds of bulbs, most of which evolved in grassland habitats.

■ Annual precipitation in excess of 20 inches will generally support a woodland garden. Conifers such as pines tend to be more successful in harsher climates with less rainfall and where seasonal droughts are a regular occurrence. Hardwood forest is more typical of regions where annual precipitation ranges from 30 to 50 inches. Keep in mind that in an area where woodland is the natural flora, meadow or any other kind of grassed area will probably require regular cutting to keep trees and shrubs at bay.

When the rain or snow falls is also a crucial factor to consider when planning your garden. Coastal central and southern California, for example, has what is commonly classified as a Mediterranean climate. That is, most of the precipitation falls in the wintertime, while summers are hot and dry. Cultivating plants from the traditional palette American gardeners adopted from northern Europe is possible, but only with constant summertime irrigation. A far more sensible solution is to cultivate plants native to the area, which naturally go dormant in the summer, or else plants from areas with similar climates such as the Mediterranean basin, western and southern Australia, or southwestern South Africa.

Assessing topography
How quickly and completely your garden absorbs any precipitation that falls on it is

determined by the soil and topography of your site. These two factors also influence how long your garden stays moist.

Topography is the shape of your garden—the slopes, dips, and level spots. These features affect how much moisture tends to settle into the ground at each spot. Slopes shed water, so the soils on slopes tend to remain drier. The steeper the slope, as a rule, the drier it is. Depressions, areas lower than the surrounding terrain, collect water. Level areas don't shed water like a slope but don't collect it, either. The orientation of the slopes is also important: south- and west-facing slopes receive the most intense sunlight in the northern hemisphere, so plants growing on them are particularly prone to drought.

The best way to get a feeling for the topography of your garden is to make a tour of inspection right after a heavy rain. Bring a spade and use it to cut a slice of soil 12 to 18 inches deep in the different areas, on the slopes, dips, and levels, to see how deeply the water has penetrated at each spot. Repeat this inspection a couple of days later, to assess how quickly the moist areas dry.

Track the runoff to determine which areas of your garden tend to shed the precipitation that falls on them and identify the route the water follows off site. In the north, this is easiest to do during a late winter or early spring thaw. The ground is frozen and non-absorbent then, so any water produced by melting snow or ice is likely to end up as runoff. Pay special attention to downspouts from your roof, since these are particularly abundant sources of runoff during storms. The important point to remember is that runoff is a natural irrigation source for your plants, if you can redirect and trap it.

Assessing and improving the absorption rate of your soil

Soil, specifically its absorption rate, is the other major factor that determines what your garden will do with any moisture that falls on it. To identify the rate at which your soil absorbs moisture (what gardeners have traditionally called "drainage"), perform the following five steps.

1. Dig a hole 18 inches deep and 6 inches wide at the proposed location.
2. Fill with water and allow to drain completely.
3. Wait twenty-four hours, then refill the hole with water to the top.
4. Stick a yardstick upright in the middle of your hole, and with it measure how far (in inches) the water level drops at one-hour intervals until the hole is empty.
5. Divide the depth of the hole (18 inches) by the total amount of time required for all the water to be absorbed to identify the average rate of absorption.

The rate at which the water is absorbed into the soil reveals a couple of important things. First, it indicates how much your garden is likely to benefit from storms. If your soil absorbs water slowly, at a rate of only 0.5 inch per hour for example, then most of the water dumped on it by a heavy rain storm—one that deposits several inches of rain in a few hours—is likely to be lost as surface runoff or to pool in low-lying areas, creating boggy conditions that are fatal to most non-wetland plants.

Knowing the absorption rate of your soil also helps you calibrate your irrigation.

> It is possible as a gardener to reduce your water use dramatically, by 75 percent or more.

If you know that your soil absorbs water slowly, then it makes sense to water in a couple of brief sessions, leaving an interval between the waterings for the moisture to be absorbed, rather than in one intensive irrigation. Trying to make that soil absorb a lot of irrigation all at once is likely to result in surface runoff and waste.

Knowing its absorption rate also provides a clue about how long your soil will retain moisture. As a rule of thumb, porous soils that absorb water rapidly (more than 4 inches per hour) also dry out more quickly. One way to correct such fast-drain-

ing soils is to boost the amount of decomposed organic matter, or humus, they contain. Humus acts like a sponge, absorbing and retaining many times its own weight in water, so a humus-rich soil loses moisture more slowly. At the same time, humus also encourages the mineral particles in the soil—particles of clay, silt, and sand—to combine into large particles, or "crumbs," which aggregation makes the soil more porous. In this way, humus can also improve soils with slower rates of absorption.

To boost the water absorption and retention of your soil significantly, you must apply a considerable quantity of humus. The most practical way to accomplish this is to identify some locally abundant (and so inexpensive) raw organic material, such as wood chips, autumn leaves, or spoiled hay. Spread this as a mulch, a couple of inches thick, on any area of soil you intend to plant. Mulch insulates the soil beneath it, keeping it cooler, and by reducing the evaporation of moisture off the soil's surface, it also keeps the soil moister. These conditions enhance root growth; they also favor the proliferation of earthworms who feed on the mulch, eating particles of it as it decomposes, then carrying them down into their tunnels, to incorporate the organic material into the topsoil. Replenished as it decomposes, a mulch of this sort will, over time, substantially boost the organic content of the soil, which helps to aerate it, increasing its ability to absorb water while also increasing the soil's ability to retain moisture. In the short term, an organic mulch will reduce soil fertility, because it will absorb nitrates (a major plant nutrient) from the soil as it decomposes. For this reason, the application of such a mulch will probably increase your plants' need for fertilization in the short run. As the organic matter finishes its decomposition into humus, however, it releases back into the soil the nitrates it absorbed earlier. What's more, the maturing humus releases these nutrients at a slow, steady rate that is much more beneficial for plants than the quick flush of nutrients released by most commercial fertilizers.

Working with your topography and soil

The highest skill in gardening is the ability to recognize and take advantage of the opportunities that nature presents. Rather than selecting plants that appeal to you during trips to the garden center and then imposing them on your site, try to match plants to appropriate settings. A drought-prone, south-facing slope, for example, would be a good place to plant deep-rooted, drought-tolerant shrubs, or herbs, perhaps together with spring bulbs that flourish during the late winter or spring when temperatures are moderate (and the soil's still moist from snowmelt or spring rains) and then go dormant during the heat of the summer. A low-lying, damp spot is an obvious location for ferns and other moisture-loving plants, or floodplain shrubs and trees such as swamp azalea (*Rhododendron viscosum*), witch hazels (*Hamamelis* spp.), pin oak (*Quercus palustris*), and sweetgum (*Liquidambar styraciflua*).

One excellent source of information about plants adapted to your climate, soil, and topography is the Native Plant Database maintained by the Lady Bird Johnson Wildflower Center (www.wildflower.org/plants). Though based in Austin, Texas, the database offers detailed information on more than 7,000 native plants suited to every region of the United States, so that you can find the right species not only for your climate but also for the conditions found on your site. And because of their interest in reducing landscape irrigation, local water companies and utilities can often provide lists of regionally adapted, drought-tolerant plants. Inquire at your municipal water department for the availability of such information.

Often, identifying native plants that thrive with minimal irrigation in your garden will provide clues about exotic (nonnative) species that will thrive there as well. If American witch hazel (*Hamamelis virginiana*) performs well in your garden, chances are good that any of the spectacular Asian witch hazels and their hybrids will feel at home there, too. This can be crucial to broadening the appeal of your plantings: whereas the American witch hazel blooms in fall to early winter, the Asian witch hazels bloom from late winter through early spring.

Local botanic gardens and arboreta are also fertile sources of information about plants adapted to the regional climate and different degrees of soil moisture. For addresses about such public gardens in your region, contact the American Public Gardens Association (see under Chapter 7 in "References, Resources, and Recommended Reading"). The New England Wild Flower Society, one of the oldest and most active native plants organizations in the United States, also maintains a directory of regional plant societies operating within every region of the country. This list is available online, at www.newfs.org/publications-and-resources/native-plant-societies.html.

Water harvesting and rain gardens

Capturing and storing storm runoff is an ancient but still very effective technique for boosting garden moisture in areas with dry climates. Recently such water harvest-

CLUES TO WATER-CONSERVING PLANTS

- Gray or silvery foliage. These colors reflect sunlight rather than absorbing it, so that the plant doesn't use as much water for cooling itself.

- Downy or hairy foliage. The hairs shade the leaves, which reduces the amount of water the plant uses to cool itself.

- Small leaves or needled foliage. By reducing the surface area of its leaves, a plant reduces the amount of water lost through its foliage, tending to make the plant more drought resistant.

- Fleshy, thick stems and leaves. These are another clue to drought-tolerance, especially if the foliage and stems are covered with a glossy, waxy skin, such as is found in cacti and sedums.

- Ephemeral growth pattern. Many wildflowers and most flowering bulbs are genetically programmed to emerge from dormancy and flower during a season that typically experiences moist, cool weather in their native habitat. The plants then go dormant and retreat back underground during the drier, hotter season that follows. Such plants require little irrigation and are highly drought resistant. Spring ephemerals (crocuses, daffodils, trilliums) are more common in northern regions; in the South, there are also fall or winter ephemerals, such as schoolhouse lilies (*Rhodophiala bifida*) and the different species of *Lycoris* (lily-like relatives of amaryllis).

- Cool season annuals. Plants that flourish and bloom during the spring or fall in the North and in the winter in the South typically require far less irrigation than flowers that bloom during the summer heat.

ing has been attracting attention even in regions with wet climates as a way to protect and enhance the water supply. Not only does water harvesting reduce the need for other forms of irrigation, thus lightening the demand on the public supply system, it also minimizes a major source of water pollution. As storm runoff washes over the surface of the soil and down the gutter, it picks up all sorts of pollutants, from excess lawn fertilizers and pesticides to animal feces and oil leaked from automobiles.

Clearly, if the runoff pours without treatment into local waterways, this promotes pollution. It can cause even greater harm to local water supplies if, as is the case in most cities and towns, the runoff is channeled through storm drains into the municipal sewer system. Then the big surge of runoff that follows any major storm is likely to overwhelm the water treatment system and sweep raw sewage into streams, rivers, or coastal waters.

For this reason, the U.S. Environmen-

A roadside swale in Portland, Oregon.

tal Protection Agency has been encouraging cities and towns to trap runoff near the source in "rain gardens." These are shallow, unlined basins that collect and hold the excess water until it infiltrates the ground, where it is cleansed by plant roots and soil microbes. Progressive communities such as Portland, Oregon, have begun to include plantings of this sort into the green strips that flank their roads. But private gardeners have an even more important part to play in this effort, because the cumulative effect of their efforts can be immense. Besides, their rain gardens, each reflecting individual inspiration, will surely be more interesting.

Siting your rain garden

The first, and most important, principle of sustainable gardening is to work with nature rather than trying to dominate it. In the case of rain gardening, this means bringing the garden to the water, rather than vice versa. In most yards the most considerable source of stormwater runoff is the roof of your house. As a rule of thumb, a roof, whether flat or pitched, yields about 0.6 gallons of runoff for every square foot of ground space it covers for each inch of rainfall. In the case of a modest structure measuring 20 feet by 50 feet, that's 600 gallons (approximately 80 cubic feet) of water. Most yards include other sources of runoff as well: the water that washes off the surface of the driveway, for instance, or the water that washes down a slope. The object of a rain garden or gardens is to capture and absorb these flows before they exit your property.

The study you made of surface drainage in the course of your garden site analysis of topography (see page 147) will help you select the most effective site for this new landscape feature. Be sure to test the drainage in any spot you select:

1. Dig a hole 18 inches deep and 6 inches wide at the proposed location.
2. Fill with water and allow to drain completely.
3. Refill the hole with water to the top.
4. Measure how far the water level drops at one-hour intervals.

If the level drops an inch or more per hour, the soil is suitable for a rain garden. Here are some more dos and don'ts of siting a rain garden:

- A flat spot is ideal—excavating a basin that will retain water on the side of a slope requires digging deep on the uphill side and banking up the downhill margin.
- A slightly sloping site, one with as much as a 10 percent slope (i.e., the ground drops 1 foot for every 10 feet you move downhill) is also acceptable.
- Do not place a rain garden within 10 feet of your house—otherwise, the collected runoff may seep in through the foundation.
- Do not locate a rain garden over a septic field.
- To ensure vigorous growth of the

rain garden's plantings, don't locate it under the canopy of a tree. Instead, set it out in the open, where it receives direct sunlight at least half of each day.

It is possible to redirect runoff by excavating a broad, shallow channel, or swale, that intercepts the flow and leads it off in a direction different from the one it would naturally follow. However, unless you aspire to the role of canal-builder, it is best to locate the rain garden as close as possible to the natural flow of the runoff. Keep in mind that a swale must run downhill to move the water—a carpenter's level set on a long, straight board or a string with a line level (available at most hardware stores) stretched tight between two stakes will help you read the incline of your topography accurately. Keep the swale shallow to avoid creating a hazard for walkers; a channel 4 inches deep and 2 feet wide should be adequate, especially if you bank up the edges of the swale with the earth excavated from the middle. To keep the swale from turning into a source of soil erosion, line it with turf or with coarse gravel and rounded stones so that it resembles a creek bed.

When diverting water from a downspout to a rain garden, you may find a length of buried, corrugated polyethylene drain pipe more efficient than a swale. In any case, you must adapt your downspout to make sure that the runoff doesn't infiltrate your foundation. Tapping a downspout is easy:

■ Use a hacksaw to cut the downspout 9 inches above the ground.

■ Attach a 90° downspout elbow (obtainable at most hardware stores) by inserting the upper end of the elbow into the bottom of the downspout. Secure the joint with sheet metal screws.

■ Slip the end of a length of corrugated plastic drain pipe over the other end of the elbow; the drain pipe should be of a slightly larger diameter than the elbow (4-inch pipe should serve, but check the width of the elbow before purchasing). Secure this joint, too, with sheet metal screws.

This type of pipe is flexible, so you can use it to direct the water in any direction, as long as it runs downhill from the mouth of the downspout elbow. If you are feeding the water into a swale, the pipe should extend at least 5 feet from the house. Alternatively, bury the pipe in a shallow trench, extending it all the way to the uphill edge of the rain garden. Use a level to make sure that the drain pipe runs continuously downhill, with no upward interruptions that will impede the flow.

Designing, contouring, and digging

The size of the rain garden you create depends in part on the size of the space available but also on the amount of runoff you intend to harvest. A good rule of thumb is to make the area of the rain garden 10 percent of the area that drains into it. In other words, if you intend to capture and infiltrate all the runoff from your roof, and the footprint of your house is 1,000 square feet, then the area of your rain garden should be 100 square feet. If you feed the water from different downspouts into different rain gardens, the *total* area of those rain gardens should still be 100 square feet.

A garden hose is a useful tool for designing the perimeter of the rain garden—you can lay it out on the ground, trying different shapes and curves until you find a contour that pleases you. If you are installing a rain garden on a sloping site, you'll save yourself a lot of digging if you make the basin of the rain garden long and thin, following the contour line of the hill. Use a carpenter's level or a string with a line level to ensure that the length follows a level line across the face of the slope.

Moistening the soil (if it's dry) before you dig will make excavation easier. If the basin sits on a slope, all the excavated earth

PLAY IT SAFE

At least seventy-two hours before you start excavating, place a call to 811. This national clearinghouse will contact utility companies in your area who will, if necessary, send a locator out to mark the route any buried utility lines (gas, electric, water) take through your yard.

should be piled outside the downhill side to raise that edge so that the basin will hold water. Your line or carpenter's level will help you match the heights of the uphill and downhill edges, as well as helping you to keep the floor of the basin level.

How deep you make the basin of the rain garden depends partly on the character of your soil. The goal is not to create a pond. The water must drain out of the rain garden within a couple of days of the storm so that the garden doesn't become a breeding ground for mosquitoes (mosquito eggs take a minimum of seven days in standing water to hatch). In general, a basin 4 to 8 inches deep works well, but you should excavate a couple of inches deeper than the basin's intended final depth, to make room for a generous layer of coarse sand and compost (or some other organic material, such as decomposed bark). Dig this into the basin floor to enhance water absorption and create a good bed for the roots of the rain garden plants.

Give the basin a saucer-like profile with gently sloping walls, piling the excavated earth around the edge of the basin in a shallow berm. Pat the enclosing berm firm with the sole of your shoe or the blade of your shovel—the berm must resist the outward pressure of the water when the rain garden fills with runoff. To further protect it against washouts, plant the berm with grass seed or drought-tolerant prairie and ornamental grasses tucked in with straw or some other mulch.

Planting your rain garden

A rain garden actually provides two different types of habitat, and to make its planting a success, you must select species suited to each. The upper edge of the rain garden's side and the berm that encloses it are designed to be impervious to water; the soil there will tend to be dry and any plants you grow in it must be drought tolerant. The floor of its basin, on the other hand, with its cycle of flooding and draining, requires plants that can thrive in both wet and dry soils.

Unfortunately, because of regional variations in climate and soil, it isn't possible to prescribe a single list of rain garden plants for the whole of the United States. It is possible, however, to suggest the classes of plants that will perform well. In general, perennials and shrubs are better choices for a rain garden than annuals; their roots persist year-round, helping to stabilize the soil even

Ornamental grasses and other plantings protect this City of Portland vegetated swale from washouts.

SHOPPING FOR PLANTS

To stabilize the soil in the rain garden and protect it from erosion, it's essential that the plantings spread their roots quickly. For this reason, it's best to start with well-rooted, container-grown plants. Use only nursery propagated plants; never use plants collected from the wild.

during seasons when they are dormant. In arid climates, a rain garden provides an ideal planting opportunity for a deep-rooted, drought-tolerant tree; the water that collects in the basin will soak deep into the ground and provide a long-lasting reservoir for the tree, and surrounding the tree with a gravel mulch will reduce water lost from the soil through surface evaporation. Deep-rooted, drought-tolerant prairie or meadow grasses and flowers, where adapted to the local climate, are good choices for the berm and lip of a rain garden.

Rain garden in a residential development, Portland, Oregon.

For the floor of the rain garden, perennials native to seasonal wetlands (areas that flood for part of the year but dry up, typically, during the summer and autumn) are good choices; examples include swamp milkweed (*Asclepias incarnata*), blue flag iris (*Iris virginica*), and swamp sunflower (*Helianthus angustifolius*). Floodplain shrubs (shrubs native to areas along rivers and streams that flood during times of high water) also do well in the rain garden floor; examples include red osier dogwood (*Cornus sericea*), buttonbush (*Cephalanthus occidentalis*), and meadowsweet (*Spiraea alba*). Many sedges (*Carex* spp.) and rushes (members of the genera *Scirpus* and *Juncus*), with their attractive, grass-like appearance, make a good background to these wetland and floodplain flowers and shrubs. Check with local native plant nurseries for species adapted to your region.

Landscaping your rain garden with native plants will make it an oasis for butterflies, birds, and amphibians, and ensure that it doesn't serve as a nursery for invasive plant species.

Maintaining the rain garden

Until they extend their roots into the surrounding soil, your new plantings will be very vulnerable to drought. Immediately after planting, water the new plants thoroughly, moistening the soil to a depth of several inches. Repeat this treatment weekly during periods of rainless weather throughout the first growing season. By the second season of growth, such irrigation should be unnecessary.

The other care you must provide while the plants establish themselves is to keep the rain garden free of weeds. Periodic hand-pulling is the best way to accomplish this. Again, the need for this care should be temporary: as the rain garden plants infiltrate the soil with their roots and spread to fill the available space, they will gradually crowd out any invading weeds.

After the plants have root in and knit together, virtually the only care the rain garden should require is periodic pruning. Leave the stalks and seedheads of the perennials, grasses, rushes, and sedges in place through the winter. They'll provide food and valuable cover for wildlife through that season of scarcity. In early spring, though, just before growth resumes, cut the dead material back to a height of 6 inches or so with a string trimmer or hedge shears. This will stimulate vigorous new growth and eliminate overwintering pests.

CHAPTER 8

Green Roofs in the Sustainable Residential Landscape

by Edmund C. Snodgrass and Linda McIntyre

GREEN ROOFS, ALSO KNOWN AS ecoroofs, living roofs, planted roofs, and vegetated roofs, use plants to improve a building's performance, appearance, or both. They mitigate the urban heat island effect and provide stormwater management, energy efficiency, and habitat for urban wildlife, among other environmental benefits. The layers of plants, growing medium, and other materials that make up the green roof also protect the waterproofing membrane of a flat roof from the degrading effects of ultraviolet light and extreme temperature swings. Green roofs that are visible from inside the building, or from neighboring buildings, are a pleasing visual relief from the usual rooftop landscapes of asphalt, tar, and ballast.

A green roof system comprises plants,

most often sedums or other hardy succulents; growing medium, a lightweight, long-lasting, mineral-based alternative to soil; material or mechanical means of draining excess water; and a waterproofing membrane. The green roof components above the membrane, including the plants, are often referred to collectively as the green roof assembly. Green roofs can be installed directly on the building, one layer at a time, or laid on base materials as sod-like mats or pre-grown modules. Modules usually take the form of plastic trays filled with growing medium and plants.

Used for decades in parts of western Europe, green roofs are increasingly popular in North America, where they are most often installed on large commercial or multi-unit residential buildings. This makes sense because many of their benefits are most pronounced on large buildings or when they are implemented on a big scale. Stormwater running off the roof of a single-family house is not a big contributor to the combined sewer overflows

Green roofs aren't just for large buildings, or those with flat roofs. This green roof, at a Baltimore marina, makes a small utilitarian building a thing of beauty.

that plague many urban areas, and a lone residential green roof provides little in the way of heat island reduction or wildlife habitat.

But green roofs can also be installed on small buildings such as rowhouses or single-family houses, on dormers or overhangs, or even on small outbuildings such as garages, sheds, or carports. Projects like these don't provide substantial environmental benefits on their own—they're too small to have much impact. But they can provide enormous satisfaction for their owners and help promote greater acceptance of and enthusiasm for green roof technology.

One of the reasons green roofs and rain gardens are not yet commonplace is that for many people, they seem to go against much of what we have come to expect from the built environment. Soil and plants on a roof? A garden in which water is supposed to pool up? Curbs that stop and start, or no curbs at all? Small-scale residential projects, which in many cases can be installed more easily and inexpensively than their commercial counterparts, can show just how limited, and even wrong, the conventional wisdom can be.

Is a green roof right for you?

On a big commercial development project, deciding whether to include a green roof will often depend on the owner's estimated return on investment—since a green roof is usually more expensive to build and

maintain, the owner or developer will consider whether the green roof might offset other costs, such as the need to buy extra land to build alternative stormwater control measures or the frequent replacement of the waterproofing membrane that protects a flat roof deck. Stormwater code requirements and municipal incentives for green building might also come into play in the planning and design of such projects.

But for the homeowner, these issues will rarely be relevant. A residential green roof is essentially a labor of love—a way to extend the reach of a garden, improve the view from the house, or showcase green roof technology to friends and neighbors—not a bottomline-driven proposition, even if modest incentives are available. That doesn't make it less valuable, but it does affect the analysis and planning necessary for a successful project.

While the quantifiable environmental impact of a small green roof is usually negligible, its less tangible benefits can be significant. Looking out a window and seeing foliage and flowers instead of asphalt shingles can make a room much more pleasant. In a city center or on a small building lot, a green roof can help make up for planted area taken away by the house or by an addition. In a more rural setting, a green roof can help a building blend in with its surroundings.

And even on a small scale, a green roof can effectively complement other sustainable home landscape features, such as a rain garden or porous paving. Working together, such measures can keep some or even all stormwater runoff out of the sewer system. While the financial rewards of such good citizenship are not particularly high, at least not yet, helping friends and neighbors get their minds around this new paradigm of buildings and landscapes working together—and away from the traditional but not very sustainable template of manicured lawns—is immensely valuable.

Scrutinizing your site

If you decide that you'd like to go forward with a green roof on your property, the first step is to conduct a thorough analysis of your site to determine its suitability for a green roof and whether its characteristics or situation will present any challenges that might make the project too difficult to be truly enjoyable. Even on a small project, you'll want to make sure the end result is structurally sound and won't require a level of maintenance that will make the roof more chore than pleasure.

Structural considerations. Like any roof, a green roof cannot exceed a weight that can be supported by the building. The components of the green roof, including soil or growing medium and plants, and the water held by the assembly after a rainfall, will weigh a lot more than most conventional roofing materials, though the weight of different green roof assemblies also varies a lot. Check your local building code for loading requirements. You should also consult a structural engineer, especially if the project under consideration is on a house or another building that's usually occupied.

Drainage and slope. Good drainage is a requirement for any structurally sound roof, green or not. A green roof has to drain properly: you should never see standing water. While the assembly will hold some water for a time after a rainfall, and some of the water will be taken up and used by plants, the retention capacity of any green roof, especially a small one, is limited. Poor drainage, in addition to killing plants,

A building buried in a hillside isn't a green roof; it's a more complex and expensive undertaking. But either approach helps a building sit comfortably in the surrounding landscape, making it more visually appealing.

can cause the roof to leak or even collapse. The plumbing section of the local building code will provide design information about the minimum slope, number of drains, and other requirements.

Green roofs are most easily installed on buildings with so-called flat roofs. Even these will have a slight slope, usually at least 0.25 inch per linear foot. Since water doesn't run off this kind of roof as easily as it does off a more steeply pitched roof, flat roofs usually have a secondary drainage system. Such a system might not be necessary on a tiny shed or carport, especially if there is enough pitch to effectively move water off the roof or to a gutter and downspout.

Green roofs can be installed on a slope, but beyond a 2:12 pitch (a "rise" of 2 inches over a "run" of 12 inches), extra supports

A green roof in a shady spot can be planted with tolerant species such as *Sedum ternatum*.

will be necessary to hold the assembly in place. Considerable expertise is necessary to design and install such a project. A sloped surface also exacerbates the already harsh, hot, dry, and exposed rooftop environment, complicating plant selection. A steeply pitched roof is unlikely to be a good candidate for a greening project, but flatter areas of a multi-surface roof, such as a shed dormer or porch overhang, can be planted on their own.

Shade. Shade is not necessarily a deal-breaker for a green roof project. It offers plants some protection against the heat and light that are so pronounced on a rooftop. Because of the free-draining properties of growing medium, however, shaded areas usually remain quite dry. Keep this in mind while selecting plants if you're planning a green roof on a shady site—they should be tolerant of dry shade.

The shade cast by buildings is different from the dappled shade cast by trees. Glass, metal, or light-colored surfaces can be highly reflective, creating a hot and stressful environment for plants. Such spaces are challenging and might not be good bets for small-scale green roof projects.

Situation. Sometimes a roof that seems a good bet for planting—relatively flat, high loading capacity, an enthusiastic homeowner—might be situated so as to make the project more trouble than it's worth. For example, if nearby trees, such as maples, throw off a lot of easily germinated seed, the effort required to keep the green roof free of unsightly and potentially damaging tree seedlings might be overwhelming. If you spend a lot of your gardening time pulling out weeds from sources that are likely to colonize a roof, you should consider this when deciding whether to install a green roof.

You can design and plant a green roof to provide a less hospitable environment for weeds, but weeding is a fact of life for most green roof owners, as it is for most gardeners. Be honest with yourself about how much work you want to put into a green roof before you decide to install one.

Logistics. Installing a green roof requires a means to get the components, including growing medium or soil and plants, up onto the roof. Think about how complicated this will be on your site. Will cranes or other specialized equipment be necessary? Will carrying trays of plants and sacks of medium or soil through a residence cause problems for someone living there? Some green roof designs include layers of fabric or rigid boards; these will have to be secured on the roof for the safety of the installers and people on the ground. These factors will affect the cost of the project as well as the degree of difficulty.

Logistical considerations will also remain relevant after the project is built and planted. How easy is it to get up on the roof to pull weeds and make sure the assembly is in good shape? Is there a source of water from which to draw to irrigate newly installed plants and keep them alive during dry spells? Often such issues can be addressed in the design process, making potentially burdensome activities much easier.

Before you start

Green roofs are often described as falling into one of two broad categories: intensive and extensive. There are no strict or technical definitions of these terms, but "intensive" usually refers to accessible roof gardens, with patio areas, deep planting beds, and a wide variety of plants, often including trees and shrubs. "Extensive" green roofs are lighter, thinner, and simpler in design, and are usually planted primarily with sedums and other hardy succulents. The course of growing medium supporting the plants is usually 6 inches deep at most and sometimes shallower. Extensive green roofs are popular in Europe and are increasingly common in North America. A small residential project will almost always fall into the extensive category.

Whether you intend to build your extensive green roof yourself or engage a designer and installer, it pays to learn as much as you can before starting your project. Are there a lot of green roofs in your hometown? Try to see some, and talk to the people who take care of them. If there aren't many, or the ones nearby are not accessible to the public, go online and look for projects in similar climates.

The industry association Green Roofs for Healthy Cities (greenroofs.org) and the resource portal greenroofs.com are good places to start looking for both general information and details of built projects. Check with local chapters of trade associations such as the American Institute of Architects (AIA), the American Society of Landscape Architects (ASLA), and the U.S. Green Building Council (USGBC) for information about projects and designers in your area.

Garden centers and botanic gardens can also be good sources of green roof information. Many have seminars featuring experts in green roof design and horticulture, and some have their own green roofs. In areas with an established green roof market, appropriate materials and components, including growing medium, should be available in small quantities. It's worth seeking out reputable suppliers and

Roof gardens are sometimes called intensive green roofs; they are most often found on large buildings such as offices, hotels, or apartments.

products with a good track record even for a small backyard project—doing so will give you a better quality and longer lasting green roof.

Roofing materials

A green roof shouldn't simply be built on top of a conventional roof laid with asphalt or slate shingles. A green roof assembly can be built over a waterproofing membrane or insulation layer, but it's important to make sure the material is compatible with the green roof components. Sometimes extra protection, such as a root barrier, will be needed. The membrane also has to be protected during the installation process to avoid damage that can cause leaks.

A built-in-place green roof assembly usually includes a drainage layer made up of a coarse-grained aggregate, synthetic fabric sheets, or rigid boards. If the roof has enough slope, a separate drainage layer might not be needed, but the edges should be designed to let water move off freely. A non-vegetated course of gravel around the perimeter can help.

Growing medium

Growing medium is to plants on a green roof what soil is to plants in a garden, and some people even call it "soil." But most green roof growing medium bears little resemblance to garden or field soil. It's not fine-textured, soft, and earthy—it looks and feels a bit like gravel. When it's wet, the medium doesn't get muddy or sticky. Its larger particles promote good drainage,

and its mineral character stays physically and chemically stable. It's surprisingly low in organic matter, usually just 10 to 20 percent by volume—most tried-and-true green roof plants don't need much in the way of nutrients, and a low organic content leaches fewer nutrients into the broader environment. This austerity also makes it harder for weeds to colonize a green roof.

While growing medium might seem expensive for a small project, it's not a good idea to simply throw some dirt on a roof and hope it works out. Garden soil is heavy, and its particles are too fine to promote good drainage and stability over a long period of time (and you don't want to be constantly adding soil to your green roof). Even the lightweight mix found in nursery

Workshops like this one at the Smithsonian Folklife Festival in Washington, D.C., provide useful information on designing and installing green roofs.

pots isn't good for green roofs—it becomes compressed and loses volume relatively quickly. Cutting corners on medium can produce an environment that over time becomes increasingly inhospitable to plants; ultimately you'll need to tear off most or all of the assembly and start over.

Look for a well-established vendor who understands the importance of keeping a clean site: good medium contaminated with weed seeds can spell disaster for a well-designed green roof. There are few standards in the North American marketplace, but many reputable vendors sell medium based on FLL guidelines, developed in Germany by the Landscape Research, Development, and Construction Society, known by its German initials FLL (for Forschungsgesellschaft Landschaftsentwicklung Landschaftsbau).

Plants

Green roof plants should be chosen with care. A rooftop environment, even one

The green roofs at this Colorado garden center help to brand the business as sustainable and attract customers with their good looks.

that's not especially high, is much more exposed to heat, light, and wind than that found in most gardens. Successful green roof plants can withstand these conditions and live a long time.

Other characteristics of good green roof plants include ease of establishment; a shallow lateral root system; low nutrient and maintenance requirements; resistance to damage from insects and disease; lack of windborne seeds; and light weight at maturity. These qualities are most easily found in hardy succulents such as *Sedum*, *Sempervivum*, *Talinum*, *Jovibarba*, and *Delosperma*, which effectively conserve and store water in their leaves. Some cacti, such as *Opuntia*, also make good green roof plants. Of these genera, *Sedum* species are the most widely adaptable and useful on green roofs; "sedum" has even become a kind of shorthand for any extensive green roof plant.

During dry spells, hardy succulents such as *Sedum* species suspend daytime evapotranspiration, effectively conserving water in their tissue, while most herbaceous plants, attempting to minimize surface exposure, wilt and soon die. Even plants that go dormant rather than dying completely, such as some grasses, take longer to regrow, and they produce a lot of dry biomass, which in addition to being unattractive can be a fire hazard in some areas.

Appropriate annuals and herbaceous perennials can certainly be used on an extensive green roof, but the effort and resources (water, nutrients, maintenance-related labor) necessary to maintain those plants will almost always be higher. Many of these plants also require a deeper course of growing medium with a higher organic content, which in turn might require that the building supporting the roof have a higher loading capacity. This kind of plant palette might also require irrigation to survive on a roof. This deeper, richer, more garden-like environment will be more hospitable to weeds as well as desirable plants.

A good solution is to plant most of the roof with tough hardy succulents, and use other species as accent plants. Some colorful and drought-tolerant flowering plants, such as *Talinum calycinum* and *Allium* species are easily incorporated into a typical extensive plant palette, and some shallow-rooted herbaceous perennials, such as species of *Petrorhagia*, *Dianthus*, *Phlox*, *Campanula*, *Teucrium*, *Potentilla*, *Achillea*, *Prunella*, *Viola*, and *Origanum*, can also be used on an extensive roof, depending on the regional climate and the exposure on the site.

Annuals, usually planted as seeds, add quick color to a green roof and can help fill in bare spots, making it harder for weeds to get a foothold. Perennials and grasses can be planted in protected or mounded areas on roofs that are primarily planted with hardy succulents to add color and texture. Small bulbs such as *Muscari* and *Crocus* bring a welcome pop of color in early spring.

Choose plants carefully when seeking

Colorful accent plants and stones were included in the design of this green roof, on a porch overhang, to add visual interest. Green roof plants are usually installed as small plugs but will quickly establish and fill in open areas.

to expand your plant palette. What works in your garden will not necessarily work on your roof. The hardiness and heat zone maps used by gardeners can provide some broad initial guidance when selecting green roof plants, but conditions are so different on top of a building, and microclimates are so important, that their utility is limited. And while native plants are popular with many gardeners, it's important to remember that no plant is native to a rooftop environment. Those concerned about the impact of invasive exotic plant species should note that common green roof plants pose no threat—on the ground, they are easily outcompeted by other species.

Many people, especially those with little room at grade for a garden, dream of growing vegetables on a rooftop. But successful cultivation will almost always require a deeper course of medium, irrigation during dry periods, and relatively high organic content, meaning weed pressure and maintenance requirements (as well as loading) will be much higher than for a more typical green roof planted primarily with hardy succulents. Turfgrass, for those seeking lawn space, is similarly demanding.

Green roof plants, like garden plants, best adapt to their new environment and are most successful over the long term when they are planted at a juvenile stage. Sedums and other hardy succulents are usually sold as plugs (tiny plants, usually 36, 50, or 72 per tray) or cuttings (small bits of plant that root easily when scattered on the surface of the growing medium). Plugs do well and are economical when purchased at the 72 size; up to four plugs can be planted per square foot. Cuttings are usually broadcast at the rate of 25 to 50 pounds per 1,000 square feet. Cuttings are less expensive, while plugs can be planted to form articulated designs. These small plants will usually establish and fill in quickly, but more dense applications will provide more instant gratification for the homeowner.

While it might seem as if bigger plants in large containers would jumpstart a green roof project, reducing weed pressure and making it look lush right away, these containers do not work well on an extensive green roof. The exposed nursery soil can carry in weeds and dry out completely, becoming a zone of horticultural death. If you're using perennials on your green roof, remove as much of the nursery mix as possible before planting.

Pre-vegetated options. For those who want fast results or don't want to navigate the marketplace of plants, growing medium, and other components, other options are available. Pre-grown mats, like sod but featuring sedums rather than turfgrass, can be laid over a course of growing medium. Modular systems, usually plastic trays with built-in drainage, are like green roof container gardens: the growing medium and plants are already in place.

On big projects, mats and modules have downsides that can be significant: they are expensive in large quantities, and some experts believe the stormwater management performance of a series of plastic trays is inferior to that of a built-in-place green roof. Design options are limited with this approach. But on a small residential project, they can greatly simplify the installation process. Some modules have exposed plastic edges that might be considered unattractive, but some systems have no visible edges, providing a more monolithic appearance.

Installation

Some established green roof designers and design-build firms take on only bigger projects. If you're looking for a contractor for a small job, it's best to use someone with green roof experience. But this might be difficult in some areas. A contractor with enthusiasm and the willingness to seek out specialized information and quality components should be able to work with you to design and build a quality green roof. Local chapters of the AIA, ASLA, and USGBC can help find potential candidates.

Can I build a green roof myself? On a small project, installing a green roof should be a fairly quick and straightforward process. But attention to detail will give you the best result. If you have the skills to build a small structure such as a shed, you will probably be able to add a green roof. But it's crucial to accommodate the weight of the green roof assembly, to ensure that water in excess of the assembly's holding capacity drains properly, and to make sure the components are properly secured during and after installation. The National Roofing Contractors Association (2009), in their online bookstore at www. nrca.net, sells the useful *Vegetative Roof Systems Manual*, which includes detailed information about design and installation. Some vendors are also producing do-it-yourself kits, including plans, lists of readily available building materials, installation instructions, and suggested suppliers for specialty components.

Safety is an obvious concern on any elevated space, and homeowners unaccustomed to being on rooftops should take precautions to avoid falls and injuries. When in doubt, call in an experienced contractor to help.

Pages 171 and 172 show an example of a simple, do-it-yourself green roof project:

Caring for your green roof

An extensive green roof planted primarily with hardy succulents doesn't require a lot of maintenance, but regular attention is a good idea and will often stop small problems from escalating. Make sure the depth of the growing medium remains consistent. A roof on an occupied building should be checked regularly by a knowledgable contractor to make sure drains and other components are functioning as needed. Plant-related maintenance is usually easy for homeowners with enthusiasm and gardening experience. If you prefer to outsource maintenance, make sure the people doing it understand the requirements of a green roof—they are not the same as those of gardens at grade.

Protecting newly installed plants. Sometimes plugs will heave out of the medium, or be pulled out by birds looking for insects. Often hardy succulents will root in place anyway, or they can simply be stepped on to secure them. Biodegradable netting is available to help keep plants in place.

On this project, plug trays with different hardy succulent species are laid out before planting to make sure the right plants are in the right places—tougher varieties in more exposed spots, shade-tolerant varieties in shaded areas, and so on.

This carport was designed with extra loading to bear the weight of a green roof: note the large number of arching supports.

A layer of synthetic fabric protects the water-proofing membrane; bricks hold it in place during installation. Additional drainage components aren't needed because of the vaulted shape of the roof. A strip of coarse gravel, added next, will efficiently move excess water through spaces between the bricks and off the roof.

The roof was planted with assorted hardy succulents and drought-tolerant ground-cover perennials such as thyme, talinum, and silene to provide extra color.

The finished project is both beautiful and useful, and it shows you don't need a proper building to have a green roof!

Watering. Right after planting, or right after mats or modules are installed, some watering is usually necessary to help the plants grow strong root systems and adjust to their new environment. Irrigation systems are unusual on small green roofs, but it's helpful to have a source of water nearby for the establishment period and to help plants survive dry spells. This is a good use for harvested rainwater. On a tiered roof, downspouts can open onto planted areas, which can use some rainwater and slowly discharge any excess. Green roofs with a lot of perennials, grasses, or vegetables will need regular watering in most climates.

Weeding. If the roofing components are intact and functioning well, the primary task of green roof maintenance is usually weeding. Even when they don't look bad, weeds will often outcompete desired plants, and some, especially tree seedlings, can damage the waterproofing membrane and other components.

Weeding is most important just after installation, when there are areas of open growing medium. Hand-pulling weeds when they're small is the best way to eradicate them; this is usually easy since growing medium has a looser texture and is less subject to compaction than garden soil. Horticultural vinegar or a carefully wielded blowtorch can also be effective. Chemical controls such as glyphosate and pre-emergent weed killers should be avoided if possible and used only with extreme caution: they were designed for use in clay soils. No herbicides are currently labeled for green roof use.

A dense cover of plants is the best defense against weeds. A thriving, well-established extensive green roof usually requires little weeding. A deeper, more garden-like green roof, with richer growing medium and plants that might have longer dormant periods, provides a more favorable environment for weeds and will demand more attention.

Fertility. On a green roof, your objective is to maintain enough fertility for your chosen plants, but not so much that a lot of nutrients leach off the roof or create an attractive environment for weeds or disease. In a garden, extra fertility rarely causes much direct harm to plants, but on a green roof it's better to err on the side of caution. During its first growing season, good growing medium has enough organic matter for plants to get started. After that, a light annual application of slow-release fertilizer is usually sufficient to keep them healthy.

CHAPTER 9

Flipping the Paradigm: Landscapes That Welcome Wildlife

by Douglas W. Tallamy

NOT LONG AGO a prominent horticulturist was interviewed in the *Wall Street Journal* about her garden designs in various Manhattan landscapes. The article celebrated the way her traditional use of color and texture brightened drab city plots that others had deemed unsalvageable. When asked why she did not use plants native to the Northeast, she bristled, "I will not be pressured into the latest fad." The irony of that statement still gives me heart palpitations. Have we really traveled so far down the road of contrived landscaping that we consider plant communities that evolved in concert with their region, its weather, and the mind-boggling diversity of life they support a "fad"? Has the pursuit of artistic expression so completely twisted our perception of reality that we believe the plants that have thrived here for millennia no longer have a place in our landscapes?

For better or worse, I often use my wife as a sounding board. One day, when I was ranting about the relegation of native plants to fad status, she turned, met my eyes with her it's-time-to-listen look, and said slowly and clearly, "Horticulturists are artists, and their medium is the garden. Their goal is to paint the landscape with beautiful plants, and they have a larger palette to work with if they use plants from all over the globe." What a polite way of suggesting that I dismount my high horse long enough to consider another point of view! Quite so. Horticulturists are indeed artists, and there is no question that when the landscape is viewed as a canvas that exists solely for our creative expression, a large plant palette will produce a more effective result than a small palette. And let's face it: it's easier to paint a picture on a blank canvas than on one already filled with existing plant communities. No won-

Nearly all the plants in this yard belong to a native plant community. Very little space is devoted to lawn or heavily mulched beds. The result is a beautiful, highly functional landscape in which nature is happy.

der Step #1 in landscaping so often is to re-move the natives and start from scratch.

But surely this approach to landscaping is based on a myopic view of what land-scapes are, of what they do for us every sec-ond of every day, and of what they should be. Landscapes are not art constructs to be arranged solely for our pleasure, and the plants in our lives are not mere ornaments. Instead, plants are the foundations of our ecosystems. Neither we nor any other ani-mal can live without them. As unfortunate for our freedom of expression as it might be, it is a biological fact that plants are only able to run ecosystems well when they re-main within the ecosystems in which they evolved. When a plant is removed from its evolutionary history, its indispensable role in supporting food webs disintegrates. In the coming pages we will explore why this is so, and how our wholesale replacement of native plant communities with disparate collections of plants from other parts of the world is pushing our local animals to the brink of extinction—and the ecosystems that sustain human societies to the edge of collapse.

Plants matter

Many people feel that I am given to out-landish statements, like "We wouldn't be here today if it weren't for native plants, and we won't remain long without them." Maybe, but allow me to defend myself. What may appear apocalyptic at first glance has been supported without con-troversy by thousands of ecological stud-ies since the late 1950s. My claim simply recognizes plants as the foundation of all the food webs on earth (with the minor exception of sulfur-based food webs near volcanic vents at the bottom of the ocean). What does that mean? It means that, in addition to producing oxygen (something I still view with relief), in addition to re-moving carbon dioxide from our carbon-laden atmosphere, in addition to moderat-ing our weather systems, and in addition to cycling, cleaning, and holding water on the land—all vital ecosystem services, to be sure—it is plants, and only plants, that harness energy from the sun and lock it in

Plants are the foundations of our ecosystems. Neither we nor any other animal can live without them. Ruby-crowned kinglet on gray dogwood (*Cornus racemosa*).

the carbon bonds of simple sugars and carbohydrates. That is, it is plants that make the food that allows us and our fellow creatures to exist. Think about it. Plants enable us to eat sunshine! I am convinced that if we truly internalized this remarkable fact, we would never again cut down a tree because we have grown tired of raking its leaves. Bulldozing a forest to erect another strip mall, or logging thousands of square miles of the great boreal forests of North America to make toilet paper and newspaper inserts, would not be rational options. We would never again risk importing a devastating plant disease like chestnut blight, or an alien insect like the hemlock woolly adelgid, so that we can garden with beautiful plants from elsewhere. If we acknowledged the essential role of plants in our lives, we would know that every time we add another member to our human population we need to add enough plants to our ecosystems to support that person. Instead, we do the opposite: we invariably respond to each additional soul by removing more plants from the earth in order to produce more stuff for that person—the quintessential example of unsustainable behavior. And when we reduce the amount of plant life in an area, we lower that area's carrying capacity.

Carrying capacity

You may be thinking that I am referring only to agricultural plants—the plants we humans eat directly—when I talk about the value of plants as food sources. I am not. Surely our corn, wheat, rice, and soybeans are the base of the simplified food web that feeds humans, but they do not support the millions of other animal species on earth. Rather, it is native plant communities all over the globe that harness the energy that permits the existence of other animals. In fact, humans have been competing with other animals for the energy fixed by plants ever since we learned how to farm. We have been competing, and we have been winning. Every new acre of land that is put to the plow creates more food for humans but reduces the amount of food available for local animals. And lately—that is, in the last hundred years or so—we have even worked hard to transform nonagricultural land from what it wants to be to what we want it to be. Picture your neighborhood, for instance. Chances are, the diverse native plant communities that once thrived there have been replaced with expansive lawns dotted with sparse plantings of ornamentals from Asia or Europe. If that is true, your neighborhood is no better than an Iowan cornfield at supporting local animals.

So what, exactly, do I mean when I talk about an area's carrying capacity? Carrying capacity is an ecological term that describes the amount of life that can be supported sustainably in a given place—that is, without degrading the life support systems of that place. Because plants make all the food and much of the shelter that animals need, we can use the amount of plant life in an area as a rough measure of that area's carrying capacity. For example, an eastern deciduous forest has a very high carrying capacity compared to a suburban lawn because it has a much greater amount and diversity of plant life.

It may help to think of carrying capacity as the principal in an ecological bank account. Do you remember when we used to have bank accounts? They used to generate interest that we could live off of as long as we didn't touch the principal. If we withdrew some of the principal in our account, the account generated less interest and we could not live as well as we did before. The same is true for the carrying capacity of your yard. If you have many plants (your

ecological principal) making much food and shelter (your ecological interest), your yard will have a high carrying capacity and be able to support lots of birds, butterflies, and other creatures. But if your yard is largely lawn, it has almost no principal and consequently generates very little interest; a yard that is largely lawn supports very little life.

Understanding the carrying capacity of human-dominated landscapes is critical if we are interested in the future of other species. This is because we have converted nearly all the natural areas in the United States for our own use without making an effort to share those spaces with other creatures. We have made no effort to share because for most of our history there was so much undisturbed nature out there that no one thought to worry about it. Those days, however, are long gone. As of 2007, 40.8 percent of the land area in the lower forty-eight U.S. states had been converted to some form of production agriculture (www.ers.usda.gov/StateFacts/US.htm). All but 5 percent of the rest of the land is now a giant matrix of urban, suburban, and exurban landscapes (Rosenzweig 2003). Only 3.6 percent of the United States is protected within the National Park Service (www.nps.gov/aboutus/quickfacts. htm). We have turned five times the area of New Jersey into 4 million miles of paved road surfaces (Hayden 2004) and another eight New Jerseys into manicured lawns (Milesi et al. 2005).

And we have great plans for the future.

Plants are the foundation of nearly all the food webs on earth. Here a hairy woodpecker (left) and red-bellied woodpecker search for insects on a young sycamore tree.

In the next fifty years we are projected to develop 75 million acres of forestland in the United States, an area equal to sixteen times the size of New Jersey (Little 2009). I am not talking about building houses on farmland from which forests were removed two hundred years ago, but on land that is currently home to healthy, mature forests. Why? Because we are still adding 5,647 people to the United States every day, with no recognition of ecological limits (www.census.gov/popest/national/NA-EST2008-01.html). In short, we have converted almost all the natural areas that once defined the United States into the cities, suburbs, and farmland that we need in order to live as we do.

What has happened to the species that depend on those natural areas? Exactly what you would predict would happen. Plants whose habitat is paved or plowed have disappeared, and so have the animals that depend on those plants for food. These species may not be globally extinct—not yet, anyway—but local extinction is rampant. To appreciate just how widespread local extinction is these days, look out your front window and count how many species you see. Now imagine how many species of plants and animals lived in the area you are looking at before your property was cleared and your house was built. If you counted even 1 percent of the original flora and fauna, I will be surprised. "Oh, they live in the park down the street," you say. I hope you are right, but experts at our State Natural Heritage centers across the coun-

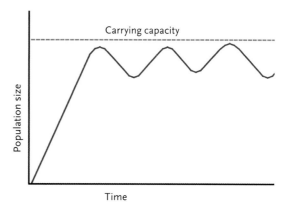

Because plants provide all the food and much of the shelter for animal life, we can estimate the carrying capacity of an area by measuring how many plants it contains (orange line). Here animal populations (green line) can cycle forever on the resources (food and shelter) produced by those plants, as long as they don't reduce the amount of plants in the area.

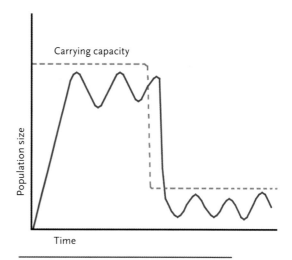

If the amount of plants in an area (the basis of the carrying capacity) is reduced (orange line), the amount of food and shelter in that area will also be reduced, and so there will be fewer animals that can survive there (green line).

try have been busy measuring the conservation status of all the species in that park down the street, and they are not as optimistic as you are. They estimate that as many as 33,000 species of plants and animals have not only disappeared from our yards, but also from so many parks and preserves across the country that these species are "imperiled"—no longer common enough to perform their roles in their ecosystems (Stein and Davis 2000; Wilcove and Master 2005). Yes: 33,000 species are now considered to be functionally extinct in the United States.

Lest you think it's only ugly insects and weeds that are in trouble, consider the 2009 results of a comprehensive survey of bird health in the United States. Data were collected by competent people in the U.S. Fish and Wildlife Service, the U.S. Geological Survey, the American Bird Conservancy, the Cornell Lab of Ornithology, and participants in the National Audubon Society's Christmas bird count, among others. The report's unhappy conclusion was that nearly a third of our eight hundred bird species are endangered, threatened, or in significant decline (www.stateofthebirds.org). If this is not a wake-up call, I don't know what is.

Who cares?

"Well, too bad for plants and animals! Too bad for our natural heritage! We humans have to eat, and we need places to live and work. Who cares about animals, or the plants that feed them, anyway?" That, of course, is strictly a human perspective, and a commonly held one at that. So, for argument's sake, let's stick with what is best for humans. Do humans need other species? Do humans need nature? Will our quality of life improve if we increase our own population to the point that no resources are left for anything else?

Although you wouldn't know it from listening to the evening news, we do, in fact, need nature and *all* its components to continue our journey on Spaceship Earth far into the future. Why? Because it is nature that runs our ecosystems. Perhaps everything you need can be found at the mall, but everything in the mall comes from a functioning ecosystem. A great deal of research has shown that ecosystems are more stable (they will not collapse as easily), more productive (they make more oxygen, clean more water, sequester more carbon, filter more pollution, pollinate more plants, and buffer extreme weather systems better—that is, they deliver more ecosystem services for humans) and are less susceptible to invasion by foreign organisms when they are built from more species of plants and animals than when they are species-poor (Duffy 2009). And so, for our own well-being, it behooves us to be good stewards of the species that run our ecosystems.

Do ecosystems ever really collapse? Indeed they do, whenever the resources generated by an ecosystem are used up faster than they can be produced—that is, whenever the carrying capacity of an ecosystem is exceeded. If you are interested in a highly detailed accounting of when and why carrying capacity of various ecosystems has been exceeded in the past, I refer you to Jared Diamond's book, *Collapse* (Diamond 2005). Ecosystem collapse is not just an unhappy event that occasionally overtook pre-industrial societies. What we call "political unrest" or a "failed state" today is often just a symptom of ecosystem collapse. This is particularly true in sub-Saharan regions of Africa, like Darfur and Somalia, where low rainfall makes plant communities and everything that depends on them too fragile to support large human populations. But ecosystems also collapse at home. The fifty-five ecological communities that once made Manhattan Island a sustainable home for six hundred people have all been replaced by pavement, steel, and concrete. Manhattan's carrying capacity is now nearly zero (Sanderson 2009). People can live in Manhattan only by importing resources created by ecosystems that have not collapsed elsewhere. What will happen to the inhabitants of Manhattan, or Philadelphia, or Atlanta, or Denver, or all our great cities if we do allow their support ecosystems to collapse?

Restoring suburban food webs

If human societies need healthy ecosystems to remain healthy themselves, and if species-rich ecosystems are better at sustaining humans than species-poor ecosystems, it is clear that, from a selfish perspective alone, we need to do a better job of

sharing the spaces in which we live, work, and farm with as many other organisms as we can. The best way to do this at home is to raise the ability of our yards to support life by increasing the amount and diversity of our landscape plants. Is that it? Is it really that easy to bring nature back into our lives? Well, yes, but there is a catch. We have to put the *right* plants back into our yards, or our best intentions won't work. Remember our goal: we are trying restore the carrying capacity of the spaces we have taken for our own needs by rebuilding the food webs required to support the natural world. Yes, it is plants that support food webs, but unfortunately, all plants are not equal in their ability to provide food for the life that needs it. If all plants were

Populations of neotropical migrants like this black-throated green warbler have declined precipitously in the past two decades.

equally good at supporting food webs, we could move them around the world with impunity, and global food webs would remain intact. One plant species would work as well as any other in providing food and shelter for our fellow creatures. But this is not the case.

Although plants harness energy from sunlight and pass it on to animals in the form of food, they do so reluctantly, if I may anthropomorphize just a bit. Plants want to save the energy they have captured for their own growth and reproduction. In fact, they go to great lengths to protect their photosynthetic products from ani-

Not all plants are equally good at supporting food webs. Native plants, like these featured at the University of Delaware's Lepidoptera Trail, support larger, more diverse, and more complex food webs than do plants that evolved elsewhere.

mals that eat plants by loading their tissues with bitter chemicals like cucurbitacins, or toxic chemicals like cyanide and nicotine, or digestibility-reducing compounds like tannins. Larger herbivores are further discouraged by thorns, spines, trichomes, or dense hairs on leaves. In short, nearly all plant leaves are protected by elaborate chemical and physical defenses that effectively discourage most creatures that would otherwise eat them.

Despite these defenses, all herbivores have found a way to eat at least some species of plants. Ungulates like deer and goats, for example, have enlisted the help of symbiotic bacteria that ferment plant tissues in a complex series of stomach chambers until the chemical defenses have been destroyed. Insects have taken a different route. Rather than evolve ways to circumvent all phytochemical defenses, insects have made the job easier by specializing on just one, or a few, types of chemical defenses (Berenbaum 1990). The monarch butterfly is a perfect example. Over eons, monarch larvae have developed enzymes capable of detoxifying cardiac glycosides, the defensive compounds in milkweeds. They also have evolutionarily "discovered" how to eat milkweed leaves without triggering the flow of the milky latex sap that gives milkweeds their name. These physiological and behavioral adaptations enable monarchs to reduce competition for food by specializing on a plant that is toxic to most other animals. The down side of specialization, however, is that the monarch is now restricted to eating only milkweeds. If you mow down your milkweed patch, the monarch larvae cannot crawl over to the nearest violet, or aster, or oak tree, and resume eating. They will starve. The same is true for 90 percent of the insect herbivores in the world (Bernays and Graham 1988): without the host plant lineage with which they co-evolved, they will disappear.

Insects are key

Most of us have been taught from childhood that the only good insect is a dead insect. In fact, one of the traits we have favored when selecting our landscape plants is that they be "pest-free." We should hardly be surprised that we now live in landscapes with very few insects. Since the late 1800s, we have been busy replacing the native plants on which insects develop with plants that evolved outside of our local food webs—plants that our local insects cannot eat. We have been wildly successful at creating the gardener's dream: a land without insects. Unfortunately, like the tragic costs associated with W. W. Jacob's monkey's paw, our wish for insect-free landscapes has come with an enormous unanticipated price: it has created a landscape without nature.

Why can't nature be happy without those pesky insects? Like it or not, insects are an essential part of every terrestrial ecosystem because they are the primary way most animals get their energy from plants. Plant tissues typically contain very little protein, and so most creatures do not depend directly on plants for their nutrition. Instead, they eat the insects that converted plant tissues to protein for them. In contrast to plants, insects are a superior source of protein and fat (DeFoliart 1992). Birds provide an excellent example of animals that are heavily dependent on insects for protein. Ninety-six percent of the terrestrial birds in North America rear their young on insects (Dickinson 1999). No insects, no baby birds. People think of birds as seed- and berry-eaters, and many birds do eat seeds and berries during the fall and winter. But when they are reproducing, birds need the high-quality protein and

Insects that specialize on one plant often are no longer able to eat other plants. This monarch butterfly larva has become adapted to detoxifying the cardiac glycosides in milkweed plants, but those adaptations prevent it from eating anything but milkweeds.

energy-rich fat bodies produced by insects to succeed. Bottom line: if you want birds, or toads, or salamanders, or countless other species in your yard; if you want your kids to develop an emotional connection with the wonders of nature (Louv 2008); if you want your landscape to do something, rather than just look like something, you must put the plants that support your local insects back in your yard.

Build a balanced community

There are many misconceptions about using native species as landscape plants, but one of the most pervasive is the fear that natives will be defoliated by the very insects we are trying to attract with them. After all, that's one of the reasons "pest-

Our wish for insect-free landscapes has come with an enormous unanticipated price: it has created a landscape without nature.

free" plants from Asia and Europe appeared to be the logical choice. No gardener wants favorite plantings to be riddled with insect damage. It may seem paradoxical, but planting natives that are part of local food webs is the best way to prevent insect outbreaks. It is true that native plants attract more species of insect herbivores than non-native ornamentals—fifteen times more species by some measures (Tallamy and Shropshire 2009). What we must remember, however, is that all those insects attract a diversity of predators, parasites, and diseases that keep their populations in check. To have a diverse community of natural enemies present in your yard at all times, you must have a diversity of prey available at all times. When one prey species becomes too uncommon to support a predator, other species will be present for it to eat and will therefore prevent the predator from leaving the area. The key to controlling insect outbreaks is to nip them in the bud. This can only happen if natural enemies are ready to pounce whenever an insect becomes too numerous.

We run into trouble when we landscape with plants that support very few herbivores, because then there usually is not enough food to keep insect predators and parasitoids, as well as hungry birds, nearby. When there is an outbreak of one of the many insects we have imported along with our Asian ornamentals—insects like the Japanese beetle or euonymus scale—there are not enough natural enemies to control them. This helps explain why as much as four times more pesticide by weight is applied to suburban landscapes than to the agricultural landscape in the United States (Pimentel et al. 1991).

Hearing that a diversity of native plants will create an ecological community in your yard that will keep the abundance of herbivores and their enemies in balance is one thing, but I know for a fact that many of you are from Missouri and won't believe it until you see it. That is one reason I convinced Erin Reed, one of my graduate students at the University of Delaware, to study insect damage in native and non-native plantings. Erin compared the amount of damage sucking and chewing insects made on the ornamental plants at six suburban properties landscaped primarily with species native to the area and six properties landscaped traditionally. After two years of measurements Erin found that only a tiny percentage of leaves were damaged on either set of properties at the end of the season (1.5 percent of the leaves had sucking damage while 4.5 percent had chewing damage). Earlier studies have shown that homeowners do not notice and react to insect damage until about 10 percent of the leaves are damaged (Sadof and Raupp 1996), so the damage levels in Erin's study were well below the aesthetic injury level in both native plantings and traditional plantings. Erin's most important result, however, was that there was no statistical difference in the amount of damage on either landscape type. If Erin's study proves to be the rule and not an exception, you need not worry that your native plants will be eaten to a nub. Your bluebirds and chickadees, parasitic wasps and toads, assassin bugs and ladybird beetles, fireflies and hover flies, lacewings and ground beetles—all will keep your plant-eating insects in check before they cause perceptible damage to your beautiful landscape.

Flipping the paradigm

If you are convinced that the benefits of landscaping with native plants far outweigh the costs, then you are ready to start restoring the functional aspects of your property. There are two things that you can do that will enable you to raise the carrying capacity of your property successfully: in-

Ninety-six percent of our terrestrial birds rear their young on insects and the spiders that eat insects. No insects means no baby birds!

crease the percentage of plants in your yard that contribute to local food webs; and, increase the amount of plant life on your property. Increasing the percentage of native plants is easy. You can replace non-natives with more functional natives that are similar in habit, flower type, and fall color by digging up the old and putting in the new, or you can simply replace your plants from Asia and Europe as they die.

Increasing the amount of plant life on your property without losing control of your landscape is a bigger challenge. Perhaps the best way to accomplish this is to flip on its head the landscaping paradigm that has dominated our culture for the past century. The traditional approach to landscape design has been to clear the land of most or all existing vegetation (properties built on farmland have already been

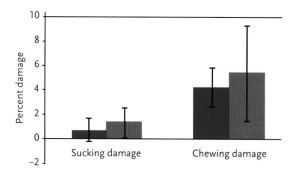

The percentage of leaves damaged by insects on ornamental plants is no greater in yards landscaped primarily with native species (green bars) than it is in yards landscaped traditionally (red bars). Both landscapes maintain damage well below the aesthetic injury level of 10 percent.

cleared), plant the entire property in lawn, and then carve out small spaces for flowerbeds. This approach renders most of the property an ecological wasteland. But if we do the opposite, we can use lawn as it should be used, while turning most of our property into a vibrant landscape. Instead of designing where our plantings will go in a sea of lawn, our new approach will be to carve out necessary lawn spaces from a property that is otherwise entirely planted.

Where do we need lawn? The cool season European grasses that make up our lawns are ideal for walking spaces because they can bear our weight without being crushed to death. So start by deciding where you will need grass paths to allow movement from one place to another: a path to the backyard vegetable garden, paths on either side of the house to allow passage from the front yard to the back, and so on. Next, decide where you would like spaces for small social gatherings. These are often positioned in a private, cozy space near the house in the backyard, but can just as easily be placed in the front or side yard, depending on your property size and shape and on your personal preference.

The biggest change in our new approach to landscaping will occur in the front yard. Today it is almost universally accepted that the front must be entirely lawn. Real estate agents will tell you that you need to see the entire house from the street to preserve curb appeal. Knowledgeable landscapers say hogwash to that notion. Your property can have curb appeal whether you can see all, part, or none of your house from the street, if you use your plantings to direct the eye to the most aesthetically pleasing parts of your yard. That may be your front door, your front flowerbed, or a magnificent oak off to the side of your house. Less appealing areas of your property can be screened with dense plantings of natives. Where these plantings are placed will be defined by where you build a view (a landscape "window," if you will) with lawn. Your lawn will no longer be your landscaping default—what you do with your yard when you don't know what else to do—it will become a useful landscaping tool that helps you define the use of various parts of your property.

What should we do with all those spaces that are no longer lawn? If you are lucky enough to build on property that already has native plant communities, take care to protect those communities from the start. You may want to reshape them when you have designed your lawn spaces, but that's okay. At least you don't have to start from scratch. Most yards already exist, however, and most are already lawns, so you will need to replace those with the plant communities that once thrived there. Planting large areas can be daunting tasks, so I recommend making your restoration a long-term project. Move from one manageable area to the next, as time and resources permit. You will start to reap the benefits of your new plantings almost immediately as you look forward to your future designs.

My research has shown that, in areas of the country where there is enough water to support them, woody plants like trees and shrubs serve as hosts for many more species of Lepidoptera (moths and butterflies) than herbaceous plants and in doing so provide more types of food for birds and other insect-eaters. Supplying birds with the caterpillars they need while they are nesting will bring just as many birds to your yard during the spring and summer as a bird feeder does during the winter. You can find a complete list of all plant genera in the Mid-Atlantic states, ranked by their potential to support nature, at http://copland.udel.edu/~dtallamy/host/index.html.

It's not just the *type* of plants we use in suburbia that is killing nature, it is the *amount* of plants in our landscapes as well.

The traditional approach to landscape design is an ecological wasteland.

In this schematic of the new approach, lawns are used for social spaces and paths for movement; the rest of the property is planted with productive native plant communities.

Plant densely

We are so used to landscapes nearly devoid of the plants that support life that dense plantings such as those typically found at forest edges may seem too "wild" for many homeowners. But remember: the more plants you put in your yard, the more food and shelter you are creating for other living things. A garden that requires yards of mulch and constant weeding is one that wants more plants. When you are restoring nature in your yard, keep your focus on the animals that will come to your plants, not on the individual plants themselves. This means that all trees don't have to be treated as specimen trees, isolated from other trees by seas of grass. Trees planted close enough to create a closed canopy are exactly what most of our charismatic animals prefer. Garden beds edging your property should be so packed with high-value plants that you cannot see the ground. This reduces maintenance effort by leaving little room for weeds in your beds, protects the ground from the extremes of summer heat and winter cold, prevents the soil from drying out, and allows a complex community of soil organisms to flourish.

Leaf litter is the best mulch

As with many parts of nature, we have demonized the leaves that fall from deciduous trees every year. We rake them up, stuff them in bags as if they were garbage, and put them out for the trash man. Then we go to Home Depot and buy fertilizer to replace the nutrients we have just thrown away, mulch to protect the plant roots we have just exposed, and hoses to water our plants after the bare soil dries out. We engage in this curious practice because leaf litter is not compatible with grass, and because of the fear that some of our leaves might blow onto the neighbor's lawn. But if you convert much of your lawn into trees, shrubs, and flowering plants, you now have a home for those leaves each fall. Mulch all your expanded beds with leaves from your tress. Healthy forest floor is built from layers of dead leaves, and the arthropods that live in it are the primary food for our thrushes and several warblers. Did you know that our terrestrial birds get most of the calcium they need to build eggshells from the shells of land snails they find in leaf litter (Graveland and van Gijzen 1994)? You can make your yard a haven for breeding birds by mulching your beds with leaves. (If your beds are too small for the amount of leaves that fall in your yard, you need bigger beds!)

Plant a butterfly garden

Butterfly gardens are one of the easiest and most effective ways to incorporate more natives into your landscape. When you are planning your garden, remember that butterflies need two kinds of plants: plants that produce nectar for the adult butterflies, and plants that serve as food for the larvae. Many people plant only nectar plants in their butterfly gardens, but without larval host plants, they are not making any new butterflies. One of the most interesting things a butterfly garden offers to young and old alike is the opportunity to observe all stages of metamorphosis. Kids are fascinated by the process of a single individual transforming from egg to larva to chrysalis to adult, something they will miss if you do not include larval hosts in your garden. Many people assume that butterfly larvae eat the same plants that provide nectar for the adults. This is true in some cases, such as the pearl crescent on black-eyed Susan or the monarch on milkweed. More often than not, however, butterfly larvae develop on woody plants that don't supply any nectar. Black

Butterfly gardens are a wonderful way to bring beauty into your yard and your life. Here a buckeye nectars on *Clematis virginiana*.

cherry, for example, is the host plant for tiger swallowtails, coral hairstreaks, and red-spotted purple butterflies. Native willows are hosts for the viceroy and morning cloak. Avoid planting butterfly bush (*Buddleia*). It is a good nectar plant, but it is not recorded as the larval host for any butterfly species in the United States, and it has joined the long list of ornamental plants that have escaped our gardens and invaded our natural areas. Also, remember to mass your larval host plants. If you have only one milkweed plant in your garden, a single monarch larva may eat all its leaves before reaching its full size. This leaves you with a bare stalk and the larva with nothing to eat. But if you have thirty milkweed plants, you won't even notice that you have a larva on your plants unless you look carefully—and your milkweed patch will thrive.

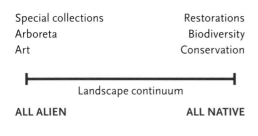

Special collections   Restorations
Arboreta   Biodiversity
Art   Conservation

Landscape continuum

ALL ALIEN   **ALL NATIVE**

The percentage of native plants in your landscape depends on what you would like your gardens to accomplish. If you are not constrained by the needs of a special collection, consider using more natives to restore the food web that once thrived in your yard.

Are natives for everyone?

The indelible connection between native plants and the health of nature herself is often troubling to horticulturists at all skill levels because it creates a conflict between the two things many of us like most about gardening: the challenge of growing new and beautiful plants from all over the world (and the status associated with succeeding) versus the ability to share our landscapes with the life that was once common around us. Many people want the best of both worlds, but they wonder how many native plants they need to have to make a positive difference and how many non-natives they can enjoy without degrading the landscape. The answer depends on your goals. If your primary goal is to make a special collection of Japanese conifers, you had better use non-native conifers from Japan. If your goal is to restore your local food web to conserve biodiversity, you will need to use the indigenous plants that contribute the most energy to that food web. If you want to have collections of exotic plants *and* to landscape sustainably at the same time, you will need to compromise your expectations for both goals.

Our problems are not coming from horticulturists who want to express themselves with non-native ornamentals. There aren't that many serious gardeners, and they do not impact enough land to make a big difference. Rather, our problems come from the millions of typical homeowners and corporate land managers who have no particular aspirations for their landscapes other than to fit in with the neighbors. These are the people who determine the biotic richness of thousands of square miles of suburbia, yet they don't even know that there is an alternative to exotic ornamentals. And they are encouraged in their ignorance by nurseries that limit their selections and by gardening publications that discuss no alternatives.

In the past we have embraced a landscaping paradigm that was based only on aesthetics because we did not see our yards as parts of natural systems. In fact, we found satisfaction in creating unnatural landscapes and were reluctant to share our spaces with nature. After all, who needed to share? Nature was healthy elsewhere—or so we thought. Today nature is very unhealthy. But we can nurture her back to health within our managed ecosystems—within our yards—if we use the plants that are her lifeblood. It won't be easy, because it will require a shift in attitude: a new consciousness about the consequences of landscaping with non-native plants. Still, I am optimistic that we can and will do this. Humans are adept at using new information to modify previous perceptions and have made many impressive reversals in the past as the consequences of our choices became clear (Reed 2010). The SUVs that looked so good to us when gas was cheap have lost their appeal. We banned DDT when we learned that it was no longer killing our pests but *was* killing our birds (Carson 1962). In the same way, we can learn to value our native plant heritage by recognizing how poorly non-native ornamentals compare with native species in one of the most important ecological functions performed by plants, that of supporting food webs. Today we value a plant only for what it looks like in peak bloom, fall color, or mature habit. I am hopeful that tomorrow we will also see it, and hold it in reverence, for the complex web of life it supports: the luna moth, the blue-tailed skink, the painted bunting . . . the diversity of life that enriches us daily.

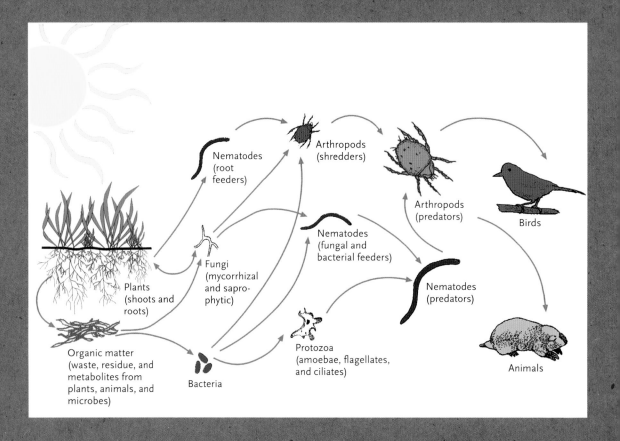

CHAPTER 10

Nematodes (root feeders)

Arthropods (shredders)

Arthropods (predators)

Birds

Plants (shoots and roots)

Fungi (mycorrhizal and saprophytic)

Nematodes (fungal and bacterial feeders)

Nematodes (predators)

Organic matter (waste, residue, and metabolites from plants, animals, and microbes)

Bacteria

Protozoa (amoebae, flagellates, and ciliates)

Animals

Managing Soil Health

by Elaine R. Ingham

SOIL HEALTH—WHAT COULD BE more basic to the sustainability of your garden? Healthy soil supports healthy plants, just like eating healthy plants supports healthy people. Yet many—or even most—home gardeners employ practices that tend to degrade rather than improve the health of their soil. A visit to the nearest gardening center or nursery too often gives the impression that the key to plant health is to apply the right chemical fertilizers and pesticides in the proper sequence. Nothing could be further from the truth, but if you don't understand soil biology you risk being taken in by the claims of the chemical companies.

The purpose of this chapter, then, is to educate you about what's known as the soil food web. The soil food web is the living component of soil, the community of organisms that live all or part of their lives underground. As these organisms interact, eat, grow, and move through the soil, they directly affect the growth, diversity, and health of plants in the soil.

The soil food web can be compromised by many different types of disturbances, some of which are imposed by humans. Unfortunately, industrial agriculture today has created so many disturbances that it has done an outstanding job of killing most of the beneficial organisms in agricultural soil. With an understanding of soil biology, you can avoid the mistakes of the toxic chemical approach to raising food or flowers. Let's look, then, at the organisms and processes that determine soil health. We'll next explore the range of possible disturbances and their effects on the soil food web. Finally, we'll lay out some practical steps you can take to improve the health of your soil and thus the sustainability of your garden.

The soil food web is the community of organisms living in the soil. This diagram shows the series of conversions (represented by arrows) of energy and nutrients that occur as one organism eats another. Courtesy USDA-NRCS.

Organisms that make up the soil food web

An incredible diversity of organisms make up the soil food web. They range in size from the tiniest one-celled bacteria, algae, fungi, and protozoa to the more complex nematodes and microarthropods to the visible earthworms, insects, small vertebrates, and plants.

One way to think about these organisms is to classify them according to the level of the food chain they belong to. As shown in the soil food web diagram, all food webs are fueled by the primary producers, the photosynthesizers, at the first level: the plants, lichens, moss, photosynthetic bacteria, and algae that use the sun's energy to fix carbon dioxide from the atmosphere. Bacteria and fungi and possibly a few microarthropods obtain energy by consuming organic compounds released by plants (exudates) or consuming dead plant material. A few notable species of bacteria and fungi attack plants while they are living, and these we call pathogens, or disease-causing organisms.

The various organisms that inhabit the soil have developed close and, in many cases, mutually beneficial relationships with plants over the last billion years. For this reason, a gardener aiming for sustainability needs at least a basic familiarity with the different types of subterranean flora and fauna. What follows is a brief introduction to the main categories of these biological actors and the parts each plays.

Soil bacteria. Bacteria are tiny one-celled organisms, visible only by microscope, that range in diameter from 1 micrometer (roughly 1/25,000 of an inch) to 5 micrometers, depending on the spe-

cies. Most bacteria are round (cocci) or rod-shaped (bacillus); some have one or two flagella and thus can move under their own power. What bacteria lack in size, they make up for in numbers. A teaspoon of productive soil generally contains between 100 million and 1 billion bacteria.

Bacteria were the earliest organisms on this planet, and they perform a broad array of functions. Most bacteria (and fungi) are *decomposers*: they consume simple carbon compounds, such as plant root exudates and fresh plant litter. By this process, bacteria convert easy-to-use energy in organic matter into forms useful to the rest of the organisms in the soil food web. A number of decomposers can break down pesticides and pollutants in soil. Decomposers are especially important in retaining nutrients, such as nitrogen, in their cells so the nutrients are not lost from the rooting zone. Another group of bacteria and fungi, the *mutualists*, form partnerships with plants; the most well known of these are the nitrogen-fixing bacteria or mycorrhizal fungi. A third group, *pathogens*, attack living plant material and cause diseases. A fourth group, *lithotrophs* or *chemoautotrophs*, obtain their energy from compounds of nitrogen, sulfur, iron, or hydrogen instead of from carbon compounds; some of these species are important to nitrogen cycling and degradation of pollutants.

A fifth category of bacteria are *photosynthesizers*, such as cyanobacteria. They tap the energy in sunlight, just like plants or algae do. These bacteria dissolve min-

SOIL ORGANISMS AND OXYGEN

Healthy soil is perforated with passageways built by soil life that allow water and oxygen to move freely through it. These are the conditions required by the majority of beneficial organisms in soil. When soil is compacted—for example, following agricultural tillage—then neither water nor oxygen can easily move into the soil. As the organisms in the soil use up the oxygen that is already there, an anaerobic (without air) condition develops, with dire consequences for plant roots. The organisms that can grow in reduced oxygen conditions (certain anaerobic bacteria and fungi) make some very nasty waste products that harm plants. The tip-off to this condition is the bad smells that develop only when anaerobic organisms grow.

From an oxygen point of view, then, there are three types of soil organisms:

- *Aerobic organisms* require oxygen to survive and grow. For aerobic organisms to flourish, the oxygen concentration within the soil should be above 6 milligrams of oxygen per liter or kilogram of soil. In general, aerobic organisms decompose organic materials, breaking them down ultimately into carbon dioxide and water, although a wide range of organic compounds are produced as stepping stones along the way.

- *Facultative anaerobes* can function and survive either in the presence of oxygen or without it. In the sorts of concentrations of oxygen that are ideal for aerobic organisms, the facultative anaerobes cannot compete successfully. But if the level of oxygen in the soil drops, aerobes become dormant or die, and facultative anaerobes will take over. In this category are actinobacteria, which decompose organic materials in reduced oxygen conditions and thus tie up nutrients so they are not lost from the soil, but which also release compounds that may harm plants. They help in the formation of humus and, incidentally, produce a majority of the antibiotics used by humans. Actinobacteria make the typical "before the rain" soil smell, indicating that the soil is likely perfect to grow cabbage, mustard, and kale crops, but not all that beneficial for other vegetables or grain crops.

- *Anaerobic organisms* do not need oxygen to thrive and in many cases grow only in the absence of oxygen. When the oxygen concentration in the soil falls below 4 milligrams of oxygen per liter or kilogram, the anaerobes win the competition with facultative anaerobes for food and space. Anaerobes generally produce extremely acidic waste products, which is why soils that are deprived of oxygen for prolonged periods (as in bogs and swamps) tend to become strongly acidic. This combination of lack of air and extreme acidity makes anaerobic soils highly inhospitable to most terrestrial plants and animals.

So you can see that having enough oxygen in the soil is a key condition for plants to thrive. We will come back to this later when we talk about soil disturbances.

eral materials from rock, sand, silt, and clay, producing oxygen as a byproduct of their photosynthesis. In fact, it was anaerobic cyanobacteria that more than 2 billion years ago began to change the earth's atmosphere from one without oxygen to one in which there was a sufficient level to support the sort of plant and animal life familiar today. In addition, most cyanobacteria fix nitrogen, and can be used instead of legumes to replenish nitrogen levels in soil.

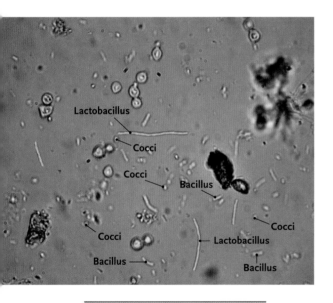

Bacteria come in many different shapes and sizes but typically are 1 to 2 micrometers in diameter. Shown in this sample of compost are bacillus (rod-shaped), lactobacillus (same shape as bacillus but longer and skinnier), and coccus (round) species. Most bacteria of the genus *Bacillus* are beneficial for plants; lactobacillus are often found in milk products and are helpful to human digestion but not beneficial for most plants. Magnified 400 times.

There are possibly more than 5 million species of bacteria on this planet, each species adapted to a very narrow set of conditions where it wins the race for food, space, and nutrients. Each species wakes up and grows rapidly while conditions are right, but years or decades may elapse between times when conditions are right and it performs its function. Most bacteria go dormant in conditions where they can't win the competitive game. Some species make spores, some make cysts, and some others just wrap themselves in layers of slime and slow their metabolism for a while. Only two things kill bacteria in natural conditions: being eaten by predators and rapid change (where the organism cannot respond fast enough to protect itself, as in a sudden freeze, a fire, or a sudden loss of oxygen or water).

Most bacteria in soil are fed by plants through release of foods directly from plant surfaces. Foods for bacteria are typically "fast foods" or exudates, which are simple sugars, proteins, and carbohydrates. The exudates released by plants vary from one species of plant to another, which means that different plants, and even different parts of plants, support different types of bacteria.

Soil fungi. Fungi grow as long threads or strands called hyphae, or as single cells called yeasts. Yeasts mostly occur in reduced-oxygen conditions, while hyphae are indicative of aerobic conditions. The majority of fungi are decomposers. Hyphae, which can have cross-walls called septa, are usually only several thousandths of an inch (a few micrometers) in diameter; a single hypha can span in length from a few cells to hundreds of yards. Fungal hyphae physically bind soil aggregates built by bacteria into larger crumbs, creating pore structure in soil, which allows water and air to move into, and be held in, the soil.

Soil fungi can be grouped into the same three general functional groups we talked about with bacteria, based on how they get their energy: decomposers, mutualists, and pathogens.

- *Decomposer* (or saprophytic) fungi convert dead organic material into fungal biomass, carbon dioxide (CO_2), and small molecules, such as organic acids. These fungi often compete with bacteria for the simple food resources in soil. While bacterial enzymes are much more efficient at scavenging

USING BACILLUS AS A PESTICIDE

Bacillus are bacteria that are beneficial for plants most of the time. Certain species of bacillus produce materials repugnant to many insect pests or inhibit the growth of specific fungi. Be careful, however, when buying single-species bacillus products (such as Serenade). No single species of bacteria functions outside a relatively narrow range of conditions, so any single-species product will work for only a limited time, in limited conditions. A greater diversity of species is really needed to provide plant protection throughout all the conditions that occur in a growing season. Thus, when a disease outbreak occurs, the real message being sent is that your soil lacks the full range of species needed to keep your plants healthy.

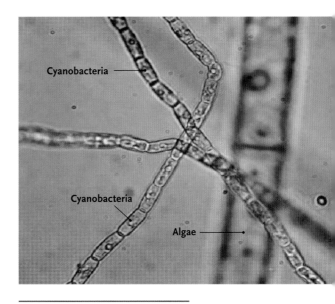

Cyanobacteria contain chlorophyll or other types of photosynthetic pigments, so they may be golden, tan, or reddish. The three strands of cyanobacteria shown here are typical of the cells-within-a-filament manner in which these bacteria grow. For a long time, they were considered fungi because of how closely their form resembles that of fungi, but each of the cells in the filament is actually a bacterium. Magnified 400 times.

simple sugars, proteins, and carbo-hydrates, fungi usually win when it comes to decomposing more complex organic molecules, like lignin, cellulose, and humus. Bacteria also need more nitrogen than fungi, and thus materials containing more nitrogen than carbon, such as green grass clippings, fruits, vegetables, and animal manures are generally bacterial foods.

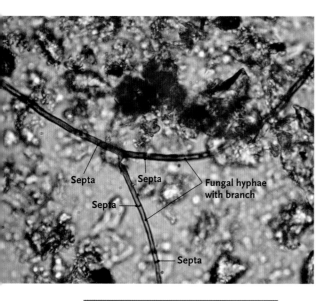

Fungal hyphae look like threads, and their color and diameter can indicate whether they are beneficial or detrimental to plants. Clear, narrow-diameter (1.5 to 2 micrometers) strands typically belong to disease fungi, while colored (tan, golden, red, brown), wider-diameter (2.5 to 10 micrometers) fungi are typically the beneficial species. The brown, wide-diameter (3.5 micrometers) strand of fungus in the photo is most likely highly beneficial for the growth of plants. Magnified 400 times.

Fungi make the enzymes and have a lifestyle that allows them to do well on materials with little nitrogen relative to carbon, such as wood, sawdust, paper, and brown, dormant, or dead plant material.

- *Mutualist* (or mycorrhizal) fungi form a mutually beneficial partnership with plants. These fungi colonize root systems, with visually distinctive structures in the root. The plant then provides energy (sugars mostly) to the fungus so it can digest rocks, pebbles, and soil particles as well as plant material and exchange the nutrients from those materials with the plant. The health and vigor of most crop plants, shrubs, and trees are greatly enhanced by the presence of appropriate mycorrhizal fungi in the soil. One exception: the brassica (kale, cabbage, and mustard, for example) are harmed if they are colonized by mycorrhizal fungi.

- *Pathogens* cause reduced production or death when they colonize their host. Root-pathogenic fungi (such as *Verticillium*, *Pythium*, and *Rhizoctonia*) and foliar fungal pathogens (such as *Fusarium*, *Phytophthora*, and *Taphrina*) cause major economic losses in agriculture each year. In soil, such harmful fungi tend be more competitive in habitats with low oxygen concentrations and high nitrate levels. Many disease fungi are clearly opportunists, in that they attack only an already weakened, unhealthy plant, one whose ability to protect itself and fight off infection has been compromised.

Soil protozoa. Protozoa are single-celled microorganisms that feed primarily on bacteria but also eat other protozoa, soluble organic matter, and sometimes fungi. They are several times larger than bacteria, ranging from 1/5000 to 1/50 of an inch (5 to 500 micrometers) in diameter. As they eat bacteria or fungi, protozoa release many different nutrients that their prey extracted from organic materials and retained in their cells. The nutrients released by protozoa can then be used by plants and other members of the food web. Protozoa are classified into three groups based on their shape:

- *Ciliates* are the largest and move by means of hair-like cilia. They eat the other two types of protozoa, as well as bacteria.
- *Amoebae* can also be quite large. They move by means of a temporary foot, or pseudopod, that oozes out and then pulls the rest of the body along. Testate amoebae make shell-like coverings for themselves; naked amoebae do not. Amoebae with stiff, straight, very slender pseudopods are described as stellate.
- *Flagellates* are the smallest of the protozoa and use one to two whip-like flagella to move.

Soil flagellates and amoebae are, for the most part, strict aerobes. Ciliates, on the other hand, bloom in conditions of reduced oxygen, often aided by rapid bacterial growth that uses up available oxygen. Ciliates are thus useful indicators of anaerobic conditions hostile to most plant growth.

Nematodes. Nematodes are nonsegmented worms typically 1/500 of an inch (50 micrometers) in diameter and 1/20 of an inch (1 mm) in length. Nematodes have gotten a bad reputation with most gardeners as plant pests, though in fact only one of the four major groups of nematodes is harmful to plants. Most nematodes in soil play beneficial roles in plant production.

ENCOURAGING MYCORRHIZAL FUNGI IN YOUR SOIL

Making certain that mycorrhizal fungi are present in your soil benefits most garden and crop plants (notable exception: the brassica). The habitats where mycorrhizal fungi do best are those with lots of air, which means good soil structure. These habitats contain plenty of aerobic bacteria and decomposer fungi to build aggregates and open up passageways to allow oxygen and water to move easily into the soil. To create conditions where mycorrhizal fungi win, and disease fungi lose, supply lots of humus and organic matter, and don't compact the soil.

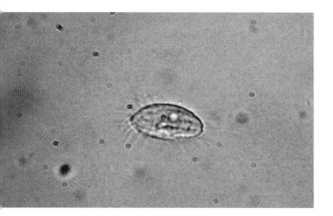

Ciliates move rapidly through the soil, using the many short hairs—or cilia—to zoom around. Their rather distinctive motion and usually larger size (compared to amoebae and flagellates) make them relatively easy to identify. Ciliates prefer reduced-oxygen conditions, especially since their more competitive oxygen-requiring brothers, the amoebae and the flagellates, can't challenge them for their bacterial foods when oxygen is limited. Magnified 400 times.

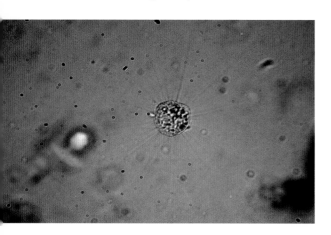

The many bacteria consumed by this stellate amoebae can be seen inside its round central body. Magnified 400 times.

While some nematodes feed on plants and algae (first level), most nematodes are grazers that feed on bacteria and fungi (second level), and some feed on other nematodes (higher levels).

Agronomists have focused on the harmful group, the root-feeding nematodes, because of the damage they do to crops. These pests cost growers millions of dollars every year. The truth is, though, that these plant parasitic nematodes would never reach high levels in the soil if the food web were in proper balance. A balanced, healthy web includes other organisms that compete with and inhibit the proliferation of root-feeding nematodes, so that they do not become a problem. Unfortunately, the sorts of soil disturbances that are intrinsic to conventional agriculture upset the web and release the root-feeding nematodes from natural constraints.

Nematodes that are free-living in the soil (not plant parasites) can be divided into three broad groups based on their diet:

- *Bacterial feeders* consume bacteria. These nematodes have a simple mouth structure adapted to consuming bacteria. If a protozoan or two happens to also be pulled in, they don't object at all. These predators release plant-available nutrients of all kinds.
- *Fungal feeders* feed by puncturing the cell wall of fungi and sucking out the internal contents. There is some evidence for certain nematodes being able to home in on specific fungal spe-

cies, such as fungi that cause mildew or blight. These are attracting interest for use as biocontrol agents.

- *Predatory nematodes* eat all types of nematodes and protozoa. Again, some observational information suggests that some species are attracted to root-feeding nematodes, so once again, there is potential for use in biocontrol.

Microarthropods and annelids. Microarthropods (bugs with jointed legs) and annelids (earthworms) are also part of the soil food web, and like nematodes, they consume prey based on what their mouth-parts allow. They grind up any organism they can and consume the juices released from the crushed organisms. Both groups therefore also release nutrients in plant-available forms.

Processes that take place in the soil food web

Now that you've met the full cast of characters living belowground in your garden, we turn to considering what they're doing down there. Growing and reproducing are the primary activities of all living organisms. As individual plants and soil organisms work to survive, they depend on interactions with each other. Foods released from growing roots and plant residues feed soil organisms. In turn, these soil organisms support plant health as they cycle nutrients, build soil structure, hold water and nutrients, and control the populations of soil organisms, including crop pests.

Nutrient cycling. Soil organisms perform nutrient cycling, the process by which nutrients in the soil are made available to plants. Nutrients are present in rocks, sand, silt, clay, and organic matter, but in these forms, the nutrients are not available to plants. Nature figured out a way to convert from not-plant-available to plant-available through the work performed by the soil food web.

Another important fact to understand is that different kinds of plants require nutrients in different forms; one size does not fit all when it comes to healthy plants. For example, although all plants require nitro-

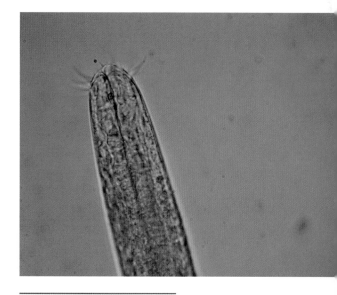

Bacterial-feeding nematodes have simple mouths, making it easy for them to scoop up loads of bacteria. The other types of nematodes have different mouth structures adapted to their diets. Magnified 400 times.

gen, you need to know how much of each of the two plant-available forms—nitrate or ammonium—is needed by the particular type of plant you want to grow. Annual plants require more nitrate than ammonium; perennials, by contrast, require mostly ammonium and very little nitrate. Understanding which forms of which nutrients favor the growth of different plants, and which sets of soil life produce those balances, is therefore critical.

Each of the nutrients that plants require—such as nitrogen (N), phosphorus (P), and potassium (K)—go through cycles in the soil. We won't go into detail about each of the nutrient cycles here but will leave it to you to search out more literature if you're interested. You should, however, understand the nitrogen cycle (see sidebar), since nitrogen is the nutrient most likely to be limiting to plant growth. When you understand how nitrogen cycles, you won't feel a need to apply bagged inorganic fertilizer from the garden center (chemical salts containing nitrogen are commonly the single largest active ingredient in these fertilizers).

Soil structure building. Soil organisms are responsible for creating the large- and small-scale soil aggregates and pore spaces that determine soil structure. Microaggregates (collections of sand, silt, clay, and organic matter) are built by aerobic bacteria as they produce copious amounts of "glue" to bind themselves and the food they eat to the protective surfaces of the sand, silt, and clay. Macroaggregates (larger crumbs of soil) are built by filamentous fungi binding microaggregates together with the threads and strands of their hyphae. The larger critters in soil—protozoa, nematodes, microarthropods, and earthworms—rearrange these aggregates to make bigger pore spaces in the soil, the "swimming pools" where water is held through the driest of summers. The ability of roots to grow deep into the soil, searching for nutrients or water, is very dependent on having these organisms performing their soil-building function.

Water and nutrient holding. Water, oxygen, and nutrient movement through soil are directly related to the structure built by bacteria and fungi, and the pore spaces maintained by predators. Bacteria and fungi also hold nutrients in their biomass, preventing the loss of otherwise leachable forms of nutrients. Food web organisms control the rate at which nutrients are turned into soluble forms that are absorbable by plant roots—but also vulnerable to loss if washed out of the soil by a heavy storm or irrigation.

An ideal balance of organisms results in the release of sufficient nutrients at seasons of peak plant growth but leaves nutrients banked in an insoluble form during dormant seasons. When plants are not growing, nutrients need to be held in non-leachable forms by bacteria and fungi, plus the organic matter produced by their activity. When plants are growing, then protozoa, nematodes, microarthropods, and earthworms must perform their job of

THE NITROGEN CYCLE

Nitrogen makes up roughly 75 percent of the earth's atmosphere but is not usable by plants in the gaseous form. Soil life changes the nitrogen in air (N_2) into ammonium and nitrate, the two forms that can be used by plants. It is a multistep process that requires the participation of all the soil food web organisms introduced earlier.

First, a variety of nitrogen-fixing bacteria—such as legume-colonizing *Rhizobium*, free-living azotobacters, photosynthetic cyanobacteria, algae, or lichens—use very specific enzymes to break N_2 bonds and create amino acids, the building blocks of protein. Because it takes a lot of energy to make the enzymes, nitrogen-fixing bacteria such as *Rhizobium* and the azotobacters have to rely on plants to provide them with energy (sugars). Plants feed sugars to these bacteria by excreting root exudates into soil (in the case of the free-living bacteria) or into root nodules (in the case of *Rhizobium*). In return, the bacteria feed amino acids and proteins to the plant.

When the higher-in-protein plant materials die and are decomposed by bacteria and fungi, those bacteria and fungi now contain more protein, and there are more bacteria and fungi than there would have been without that highly nutritious plant material. So far, no inorganic, soluble (plant-available) forms of nitrogen have been produced. Next, these bacteria and fungi are consumed by protozoa, nematodes, microarthropods, and earthworms. Because the nitrogen concentration in the bacteria and fungi is so much higher than in their predators, the predators release that excess nitrogen as ammonium (NH_4)—a soluble, inorganic form of nitrogen that perennial plants require.

What happens to this ammonium in the soil depends on the balance of fungi and bacteria present. If the soil is dominated by aerobic fungi, ammonium remains as ammonium. If the soil is dominated by aerobic bacteria and the bacteria have the right food (from root exudates mostly), nitrifying bacteria will use their enzymes to convert ammonium to nitrate (NO_3), the other soluble, inorganic form of nitrogen that plants, especially annual plants, require. Plants then take up the nitrate and ammonium, and convert them into protein inside the root. When that plant material dies, bacteria and fungi decompose it, and the cycle goes 'round again, thousands of times per day per gram of soil.

The only way to complete the cycle back to nitrogen gas is if conditions become anaerobic. In reduced-oxygen conditions, the soluble, inorganic forms of nitrogen (ammonium, nitrite, and nitrate) are converted by denitrifying bacteria, or ammonia-producing bacteria, into ammonia and nitrous oxide, which are both gases. In the atmosphere, these gases are converted to nitrogen gas by ozone and sunlight. If ozone is depleted, these gases can be washed out of the air when it rains and end up back in the soil as nitric acid, a highly toxic material that is very destructive to life. It would be much wiser to prevent nitrogen loss to the atmosphere by not allowing soil to become anaerobic through compaction.

eating bacteria and fungi and thus releasing plant-available nutrients.

Control of disease and pest organisms. If the full diversity of soil life is present, a plant can protect itself from diseases and pests through mechanisms that have been in place for billions of years. The root exudates that plants put out feed certain, very specific species of bacteria and fungi. These bacteria and fungi help the plant by preventing diseases and pests from finding the root, or aboveground leaf, blossom, or fruit/seed surfaces.

Given all these processes that require different species to be present so some organism is growing, protecting the plant, building soil structure, holding each nutrient in place in the soil, doing nutrient cycling, then it is no wonder that hundreds of thousands of species of bacteria, fungi, protozoa, and nematodes are needed in each and every gram of soil. If people slowly but surely destroy these species and do not replace them, as has occurred in agriculture today, plant health will be perpetually at risk.

Before looking at some of the ways these species can be destroyed, we'll discuss succession, the evolutionary movement forward that happens as soil organisms enact their processes day by day.

Succession: driven by the soil food web

Each field, forest, pasture, or garden has a unique soil food web with a particular proportion of bacteria, fungi, and predators and a particular level of complexity within each group of organisms. These differences are the result of soil, vegetation, and climate factors, as well as land management practices. We will look at the results of climate factors and land management practices a little later when we focus on soil disturbances. For now, let's discuss how the proportion of soil organisms and thus the vegetation supported by the soil changes in a natural process known as succession.

Any undisturbed land will naturally evolve toward more complexity, from bare soil to grass to shrubs to trees to climax forest. What drives this process of succession from one group of plant species to the next is a change in the balances of bacteria and fungi and their predators in the soil. In essence, the soil food web shifts over time from being dominated by bacteria to being dominated by fungi. What controls this shift is the plants themselves as they release exudates and dead plant materials that favor first bacteria and then fungi.

Let's look at succession in more detail. Before plants can grow on sterile soil, the bacterial community must establish first, starting with photosynthetic bacteria. These fix atmospheric nitrogen and carbon, produce organic matter, and immobilize nitrogen and pull other nutrients out of the rocks. As the bacterial community builds microaggregates, more species of bacteria have a place to live and survive. At some point, there will be enough bacteria, and protozoa will therefore initiate nitrogen cycling in the young soil. Once nitrate is in high enough concentration, early successional plant species can start to grow. These early successional, disturbance-requiring plants are plants that we would call weeds. But these early colonizers add bacterial and fungal foods and therefore, a different microbial community develops. As fungi begin to perform their functions, soil structure is improved, the amounts and types of nutrients change, and more predators survive and grow. Nutrient cycling is then enhanced, which will eventually lead to the next stage of succession,

with different plant species that better utilize the new soil conditions and outcompete the earliest weed species.

As the food web becomes more complex, and as the fungal component increases slowly but surely, weeds no longer rule. Instead, vegetables, then row crops, and productive pasture species are the winners, as the balance shifts from completely bacterial-dominated, to ever more fungi, ever closer to balance, and to high levels of both bacterial and fungal biomass. As this bootstrap process of building soil life continues, new forms of nutrients become avail-

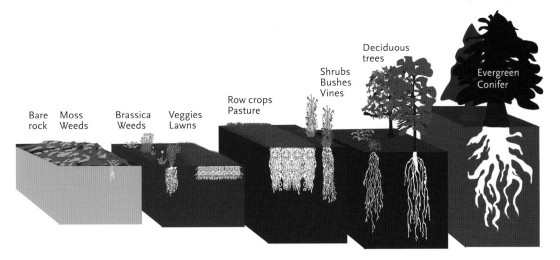

Bacteria	. . . .	A few fungi	. . . .	Balanced	. . . .	More fungi	. . . .	Fungi
Bacteria: 10 µg		100 µg	500 µg	600 µg		500 µg		700 µg
Fungi: 0 µg		10 µg	250 µg	600 µg		800 µg		7000 µg

Soil biological succession causes plant succession. The increasing levels of fungal foods in dead plant material brings about the shift to greater fungal biomass, which in turn changes the habitat so that later successional plant species are selected.

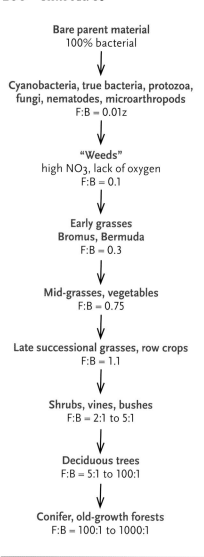

Bare parent material
100% bacterial

↓

Cyanobacteria, true bacteria, protozoa, fungi, nematodes, microarthropods
F:B = 0.01z

↓

"Weeds"
high NO3, lack of oxygen
F:B = 0.1

↓

Early grasses
Bromus, Bermuda
F:B = 0.3

↓

Mid-grasses, vegetables
F:B = 0.75

↓

Late successional grasses, row crops
F:B = 1.1

↓

Shrubs, vines, bushes
F:B = 2:1 to 5:1

↓

Deciduous trees
F:B = 5:1 to 100:1

↓

Conifer, old-growth forests
F:B = 100:1 to 1000:1

Soil foodweb structure through succession, increasing productivity. The proportion of bacteria to fungi in the soil determines the types of plants that will grow there. Bare soil where plants cannot grow is typically 100 percent bacterial. Weeds like ratios of 10 units of bacterial biomass to 1 unit of fungi (0.1), while vegetables like ratios of 1 to 2 units of fungi for 3 to 4 units of bacteria (0.5 to 0.8). Old-growth forests are healthy when soils have ratios of fungi to bacteria in the range of 1,000:1. What does your plant need?

able and soil structure improves, letting air and water move deeper and deeper into the soil. And thus, plant species will shift again. As the soil supports more fungi than bacteria, more fungal predators than bacterial predators, shrubs, bushes, perennial herbs, deciduous trees, and then conifers are favored to be the winners.

Besides the ratio of fungi to bacteria, two other factors are important in understanding food web structure. First, levels of fungi and bacteria must be high enough for healthy soil. For adequate processing of nutrients and building of soil structure to occur to support healthy plants, at least 300 micrograms of both bacteria and fungi must be present per gram of soil. Second, protozoa and nematodes must be present in adequate numbers and activity.

Succession can take eons the first time through, but from then on, the speed of successional shift can be rapid, depending on what exactly happens to favor the growth of soil organisms. Note also that while the broad continuum of succession is clear, detecting the subtle shifts from one stage of succession to the next is a bit more difficult. And systems can go backward in succession if disturbances occur.

The important point to take away from the discussion thus far is that the complexity and diversity of the soil food web in any particular plot of land has far-reaching consequences for what can grow there. Complex food webs with a diversity of organism groups favor healthy plants that have well-balanced and maximum levels of nutrients. Food webs low in complexity and diversity favor early successional, weedy species of plants. If the soil organisms that cycle nutrients from plant-not-available to plant-available are not present, nutrients will not be available when they are needed to germinate seed, grow leaf tissue or strong stems, produce flowers, or set seed.

Disturbances that compromise soil health

Now that you understand how and why plant health depends on the soil food web, we'll explore what happens to soil life when disturbance occurs. First, let's define *disturbance*: typically, a disturbance is any unusual event that can cause groups of organisms to stop functioning. A disturbance can remove plants, or groups of organisms on plant surfaces, either above- or belowground. Disturbances can be natural, as in weather and climate events or wildfires, or they can be the result of human management practices.

Disturbances due to weather and climate include extremely low or high levels of water (as in a drought or flood) and

SUCCESSION AND SOIL PH

Most gardeners are familiar with pH, which is a measure of the concentration of hydrogen ions in the soil. Soil pH plays an important part in determining whether nutrients present in the soil will be in the specific form for particular plants to take up.

Before life starts to work building soil structure, pH is dependent on the bedrock, or parent material. The first colonizers, the aerobic bacteria, produce waste and "glues" that are alkaline. Thus, early in succession, aerobic, bacterial-dominated soils are alkaline. As long as nutrients are cycling through bacteria and being consumed by protozoa and bacterial-feeding nematodes, nitrifying bacteria do their job of converting ammonium to nitrate, and the predominant form of inorganic, soluble nitrogen is nitrate for these early successional stages.

As succession proceeds and fungi eventually overtake bacterial biomass levels, the organic acids produced by aerobic fungi will result in a soil pH between 5.5 and 7.0 (acid soil). In acid soil, nitrifying bacteria do not convert ammonium to nitrate: they don't need the hydrogen ions from the ammonium since hydrogen is free in the soil solution. The soluble form of nitrogen remains as ammonium. This is perfect for perennial plants.

Thus, through the exudates plants produce, the plants themselves drive succession by altering soil balances of aerobic bacteria and fungi, and thus nitrate versus ammonium as the predominant forms of inorganic, soluble nitrogen for plants to take up. As the plant species shift because these balances shift toward more fungal, then more fungal foods are made.

extremely low or high temperatures (as in unusual heat or freezing conditions). Typical weather patterns favor species that win in competition for food, space, and ability to reproduce in those specific combinations of conditions. As the climate changes and higher temperatures become the norm, for example, different species of soil organisms will be favored if they are present. Those soil organisms that grow better in the new conditions will now rule. If those new ruling species behave in very different ways, or if balances of major functions change, the plant community has no choice but to shift.

Disturbances caused by agricultural management include compaction of the soil by tillage, and applications of toxic chemicals, herbicides, pesticides, copper, sulfur, or high concentrations of salts or sugars. Tillage and toxic chemical application result in the death of beneficial organisms in agricultural soil. The organisms left are those adapted to these specific disturbances. Basically, nonbeneficial and pathogenic soil organisms are favored by chemical agricultural methods. In a moment we will take a closer look at how this happens.

For now, note that the speed of change imposed by a disturbance determines whether the active soil organisms will be able to respond in time to stay alive. If temperature shifts from warm to freezing in a few hours, many organisms will die because they can't go dormant fast enough.

If diversity was low to start with, complete functional groups of organisms can be lost. When all species in a functional group are lost, plants will be susceptible to disease, pests, poor nutrient availability, or loss of soil structure. Without organisms to perform the work, the health of the plants will be harmed. As more and more groups of soil species are lost, plant health can be completely compromised.

The type and amount of organic matter added or lost with a disturbance is also important to consider, since this affects which soil organisms can function and do their jobs. The more types of food and the greater amounts of each food present, the greater the number of species and individuals of each species that are active to support soil health.

The effects of soil compaction. As noted earlier, aerobic habitats, those with lots of oxygen present, tend to favor beneficial, disease-suppressive sets of organisms. Unfortunately, over the last hundred years, human management has driven oxygen from soils through compaction in nearly all agricultural systems and in most urban or suburban environments. As water moves through a soil and encounters a zone where soil has been compacted by the plow blade, discs, or bars, it accumulates at that compacted layer. As aerobic organisms continue to grow, they consume oxygen faster than it can diffuse into that waterlogged, compacted area. When they run out of air, the beneficial organisms either die or go dormant, and anaerobic organisms, present in their dormant stages up until now, begin to grow.

Anaerobic soil organisms turn plant-available forms of nitrogen, phosphorus, and sulfur into gaseous forms, such as ammonia, phosphine gas, and hydrogen sulfide; these gases escape from the soil and thus the fertility of that soil is lost. In addition, anaerobic microorganisms produce highly acidic organic acids that cause soil pH to inexorably drop to lower and lower levels if anaerobic conditions persist long enough. Addition of materials like lime or gypsum is ultimately ineffective at dealing with the reduction in pH that occurs when anaerobic organisms grow, since the lime or gypsum is merely neutralized and the soil soon drops back to a low pH.

Moreover, anaerobic organisms produce alcohol, formaldehyde, and phenolic compounds, all extremely toxic to plants. While wetland and riparian plants have specific mechanisms to deal with these anaerobic products, terrestrial plants do not. The roots of terrestrial plants die when they come into contact with areas where anaerobic organisms are active.

The soil organisms that can rebuild soil structure are the very ones that are killed, slowly and inevitably, by tillage and by overuse of toxic chemicals. Without beneficial soil biology present, plow pans, anaerobic black layers, and bad smells develop, and roots become restricted to the top few feet or inches of the soil. Thus, compaction imposed by inappropriate human management is the real reason behind the common misconception demonstrated in many scientific papers that plants do not send roots below the first few feet of topsoil.

The effects of applying chemicals. Applying chemical fertilizers has a harmful effect on plants. To see why, you need to understand how plants take up nutrients. It is impossible to know exactly which mix of nutrients a plant requires on a day-to-day basis. Applying the "full season's" supply of inorganic nutrients means too much is present early and too little will be present later in the season. The plant does not receive exactly what it needs; it gets an excess of some nutrients and a lack of others, leading to imbalance and stress.

Loss of the excess soluble nutrients by leaching is impossible to avoid as well. As soil organism numbers and diversity are lost, in part from the application of high concentrations of inorganic fertilizers, the ability to keep nutrients in the soil is lost as well. The dead zones in the Gulf of Mexico, the Great Barrier Reef, and numerous oceans of the world are clear evidence of the runoff of soluble nutrients, as well as toxic chemical pesticides, from chemical agriculture.

Besides, inorganic fertilizers are all salts with the potential to take water away from any organism, including plants. At low concentrations (a pound per acre, for example), salts do not have significant impacts, but at more than 100 pounds per acre, the impact is extremely detrimental to any living organism in the soil. Use of inorganic fertilizers at modern levels results in the death of millions of individuals and potentially hundreds of species each time the salt is used. By the same token, pesticides are used because they kill things, and this includes soil organisms.

Because not all species of soil organisms are active at any one time, the dormant individuals are generally not harmed when a toxic chemical is applied to soil any one time. But when the use of toxics becomes routine, more and more life is destroyed, to the point that nearly all the beneficial organisms are lost. Chemical companies can claim that their products don't harm soil life only because the methods they use to measure soil life are not capable of revealing the majority of organisms in soil.

Regenerating disturbed soil

In essence, soil disturbances cause succession to go backward. Complexity and diversity are lost and must be rebuilt if plants are to thrive once again in the soil. Lost species do not just magically reappear but must be reintroduced. Given how widespread the practice of applying toxic chemicals has become today, the likelihood that the needed organisms are close by, and can rapidly and easily move back in, is extremely low.

Disease-causing organisms tend to return more quickly than beneficials following toxic chemical applications because these organisms become dormant rapidly and escape the death-dealing effects of toxic chemicals. The strategy of diseases is to grow rapidly, produce a huge number of offspring, and spread rapidly by wind and water, so if even one pathogen survives application, the organisms will soon be back in force. Since beneficial organisms are in balance with living plants, beneficial organisms grow at rates dictated by the plant, quite often produce few offspring, and do not spread rapidly by wind or water.

To correct a situation where life has been severely reduced by toxic chemical use, all the food web organisms, in the proper balances for the desired plants, need to be returned to the soil. The easiest way to do this is to add compost containing the full diversity of life, in either solid or liquid form, depending on what is most efficient and least expensive. If compaction is an issue, forking in the compost, or injecting a liquid form of compost, at the depth of compaction will likely be necessary until good soil structure is built. If compaction is not present, applying compost to the soil surface should be adequate.

Regardless of how life is added, check to make sure all the life that is lacking in the soil, or on your plant surfaces, is present in the compost. Find a neighbor who can use a microscope, or take a course that teaches you how to look at soil life. It takes most people a single day to get the basics down, and then all you need to do is practice watching these willing workers. Alternatively, you can send a soil sample to a Soil

Foodweb Inc. (SFI) lab, where the organisms will be looked at and their biomass and activity reported back to you.

It should go without saying that the use of toxic chemicals and constant tillage needs to be sharply curtailed. When beneficial organisms are added back to the soil, we cannot afford to kill them again.

What plant problems say about your soil

You should understand by now that when a pest or disease attacks a plant in your garden, the information being conveyed is that the plant is stressed and unhealthy. Your response should be to find out what is wrong in the soil and bring the soil back into a condition where nutrient cycling is controlled by the plant's influence on life in the soil; then pests will not attack. Following is a list of typical plant problems, along with their underlying cause and how to use soil know-how to fix the problem.

Symptom: Weeds (thistles, dandelions, and composites; chickweed, nutgrass, nutsedge, and crabgrass)
Underlying cause: These disturbance-selected plants are clear indicators of compaction; many produce strong taproots, which allow them to punch through compacted layers. All require strongly bacterial-dominated soil.

Thistles, dandelions, and composites typically require high levels of nitrate in order to germinate. For particular species, other nutrients may need to be very low,

which suppresses other competitor plants; for example, most thistles win if calcium is completely tied up in unavailable forms.

Chickweed, nutgrass, nutsedge, and crabgrass typically require out-of-sync nutrient cycling, which results in short pulses of excessive levels of nitrate followed by longer periods of nearly no soluble nitrogen. Low levels of ammonium but loss of nitrogen as ammonia gas can also be indicators of these early successional soils.
How to fix: Build soil structure by applying compost with the full diversity of soil life and high levels of protozoa, nematodes, and microarthropods. Maintain a permanent cover of a mixture of plant species to suppress weeds.

Symptom: Aphids, whiteflies, caterpillars, leaf miners, scale, mites, sucking insects, leaf feeders
Underlying cause: The plant is stressed, usually because the roots are being attacked by root-feeding pests as a result of poor soil structure and compaction zones, both of which prevent oxygen and water from moving properly into the soil. As a result of these conditions, some nutrient is not available to the plant. A secondary problem is often that the leaf material does not decompose through the dormant season (dry season in tropical areas).
How to fix: Reestablish the full food web in the soil by applying compost, making sure the balance of bacteria, fungi, proto-

zoa, and nematodes is what the plant requires. If the plant needs the support of mycorrhizal fungi, provide conditions for those fungi to flourish (see the sidebar on page 199). Send roots into a lab that can assess whether mycorrhizal colonization of the roots has occurred.

Symptom: Boring insects (such as elm and pine bark beetles)
Underlying cause: The plant is stressed and unable to protect the stem and bark from adult insects attempting to find a place to lay their eggs.
How to fix: To prevent the current crop of pests from killing the plant, spray the outside of the plant until dripping with compost tea and let naturally occurring microarthropods carry the full set of soil organisms inside the galleries excavated in your tree by the beetles. The eggs will be consumed by the soil organisms carried in by the beetles, and the larvae, if the eggs survive, will have no food to eat that they like and will typically die. Reestablish the full food web in the soil by applying compost, making sure the balance of bacteria, fungi, protozoa, and nematodes is what the plant requires. If the plant needs the support of mycorrhizal fungi, provide conditions for those fungi to flourish (see the sidebar on page 199). You may need to add the microarthropod community as well by finding compost with good arthropods, if insecticides have destroyed good-guy insect life.

Symptom: Foliar fungal diseases such as botrytis, mildew, leaf spots of various kinds, and leaf curling (*Taphrina*)
Underlying cause: The plant is stressed. Typically some nutrient is out of balance as a result of poor life in the soil. A secondary problem is often that dead plant material does not decompose through the dormant season (the dry season in tropical areas) and provides the perfect place for disease fungi, bacteria, and insect pests to overwinter, protected from weather.
How to fix: Establish the full food web on any dead plant material or residues. Observe the rate of disappearance of any bit of plant material once it is dropped on the ground; if decomposition is not rapid, apply compost, compost extract or compost tea, whichever is least expensive or easiest to apply. Do not burn dead plant material; instead, compost it in aerobic piles.

Symptom: Root rots (such as *Phytophthora, Pythium, Armillaria*), crown rot (such as *Fusarium*)
Underlying cause: There is an inadequate supply of bacteria and/or fungi around the roots, along with too few protozoa, beneficial nematodes, and beneficial microarthropods. Compaction may have led to a condition where roots are being harmed by toxic anaerobic materials.
How to fix: Establish the full food web in the soil by applying compost, making

sure the balance of bacteria, fungi, proto-zoa, and nematodes is what the plant re-quires. Make sure any compaction zones in the soil are inoculated with a good set of organisms, typically by injecting a well-made compost tea. If the plant needs the support of mycorrhizal fungi, provide conditions for those fungi to flourish (see the sidebar on page 199).

Symptom: Root-feeding nematodes, root-feeding grubs, insects
Underlying cause: The plant is stressed. Compaction and lack of needed nutrients in plant-available form have made the plant susceptible to pest and disease attack.

How to fix: Reestablish the full food web in the soil by applying compost, making sure the balance of bacteria, fungi, pro-tozoa, and nematodes is what the plant requires. The protective layer around the root should be actively growing, and the organisms around the root should be so dense that it is physically impossi-ble for root feeders to find the root. If the plant needs the support of mycorrhizal fungi, provide conditions for those fungi to flourish (see the sidebar on page 199). Remove any undecomposed plant mate-rial that may harbor eggs or larval stages of pests.

CHAPTER 11

Landscapes in the Image of Nature: Whole System Garden Design

by Toby Hemenway

THE AUTHORS OF THE PREVIOUS chapters of this book have told, in compelling words, why we need a new way of gardening. The subjects have ranged over wide and fertile ground, and reveal how rich and ecologically vibrant is the new American sustainable garden compared to a traditional vegetable bed or flower border. Each writer has offered a glimpse of his or her own view of this new garden, letting us see its magic and importance. In this final chapter, I will try to link these pieces together.

In this new way of gardening, we're creating landscapes that live, that behave like natural ecosystems but have room for people in them too. The secret to doing this, as much of this book has hinted at, is to connect the pieces of our landscapes together, and also to the larger world of nature, in patterns that help each part work harmoniously with the others. Microbes break down leaf litter to create soil that stores water and feeds our plants; plants offer leaves, pollen, and fruits that nourish insects but also sequester greenhouse gases; insects pollinate plants and provide food for birds; and on and on. Each thread ties to the others and makes the whole web stronger.

If a garden's pieces aren't linked together, they cannot connect us and our landscapes to nature. An immaculate lawn, pretty as it may be, is a sink for resources, lacks wildlife habitat, and grows no food. A brace of raised vegetable beds is inhospitable habitat for songbirds and most native insects. In turn, a natives-only garden offers little sustenance for its principal tender: the gardener. Delicious as it may be, I rarely eat native camas-bulb cakes slathered in huckleberry compote.

This Flagstaff, Arizona, backyard blends annuals and perennials to offer an enormous food harvest and backyard habitat with only a few hours work per month. The yard and house also harvest rain, so this desert garden relies very little on municipal water.
Design and photo by Josh Robinson of Eden on Earth Landscaping, Sedona, Arizona.

My breakfast, though reliably from an organic farm, is often shipped to me from some faraway monoculture. Thus native habitat in my yard is offset by sterile farmland planted somewhere else to meet my needs, so what I gain in one spot is diminished by losses in another. A one-function garden won't bring people together with nature in a whole, living webwork.

Sadly, many existing gardens don't tie into the larger world. Why? One reason

---

"Put your salad garden between your front door and your car door."

---

is that most of our gardens are designed to do one thing. Since we have concocted some potent design methods, they do that one thing awfully well: our vegetable gardens are fabulously productive, our flowered borders look gorgeous, our native plant gardens nurture a blizzard of buzzing, soaring, scurrying wildlife.

To garden sustainably, our gardens need to behave the way nature does. A hallmark of a natural ecosystem is that nothing there does just one thing. Contrast that with our own designs, in which, when a conventional landscape designer chooses a tree for a yard, he would select it for one

quality: for shade, say, or for its foliage, or fruit, or spring blossoms. But in nature, no tree exists only for shade, or fruit, or any other single quality. Each tree is doing dozens of things at once. Yes, a tree in a woodland casts shade, and probably bears edible fruit or seeds. But it's also building humus via leaf litter, breaking heavy soil with its roots, and catching rain with its leaves and funneling that water toward its trunk. It's breaking the force of the wind with its mass, softening the impact of raindrops as they splash on its foliage, holding soil in place with a mass of fibrous roots, cooling the forest by its shade, seeding clouds via evapotranspiration and pollen, feeding an infinitude of soil organisms with root exudates and mulch, sheltering birds, nurturing insects, sprouting seedlings, sequestering carbon, exhaling oxygen, and on and on. Each one of these roles ties the tree to other life and to the larger environment, supporting hundreds of other species directly and indirectly. So when we plant a tree solely for foliage, we're quite literally missing the forest for the trees, and ignoring a wealth of opportunities to connect ourselves and our landscapes to the environment that we are dependent on for everything.

This is one reason why nature's designs show such resilience and abundance, and ours often don't. Have you ever wondered why a forest or meadow can survive months of drought or bad weather, while if we leave our garden for a brief two-week vacation we return to withered husks or a weed-tangled jungle, or, astonishingly, some of each? It's because our landscapes are disconnected pieces that lack the mutually beneficial relationships which nourish and preserve the rest of the living world. Even worse, now we're the ones stuck with the bill for fixing it. A lawn, for example, has been robbed of its natural connections to partners such as grazers and soil life, so we have to make up the deficit ourselves. We must clip, mow, fertilize, and irrigate relentlessly to replace the freely given work that those missing partners could happily provide.

The way to save ourselves a ton of work and—speaking of doing more than one thing—to save our environment, is to help our gardens to act more like nature does. Our gardens need to behave like ecosystems, and ones where our needs and nature's can both be taken care of. Fortunately, in the last few decades, tools have been developed for the gardener to design landscapes that do just that. These tools are called by various names: ecological design, whole-systems land management, regenerative design, and permaculture, to list a few of the better known methods. All have one critical thing in common: they offer ways to create relationships and connections among the pieces that make up our designs. By using these approaches, we can design landscapes that act like nature but also offer us the things we need from our gardens.

Instead of being a wasteland that taxes storm drains and uses resources for little yield, this Houston, Texas, parking strip harvests rainwater and grows beautiful carbon-sequestering plants that offer habitat for birds and insects. Design and photo by Kevin Topek of Permaculture Design, LLC, Houston.

To begin exploring these new design tools, let's look at the different kinds of connections that need to be made, and how these methods help us create them. To behave like an ecosystem, we need to create three kinds of connections.

First, it's obvious that the pieces of the landscape need to be connected to each other—in nature, as the environmentalists have been intoning for years, everything really is connected to everything else. Second, the parts of our garden also need to be properly connected to the larger environment, to forces like sun, shade, rain, and wind. And third, to involve us in our landscape, the pieces need to be connected to us, in ways that make it easy for us to take care of them and to get the rewards that will keep us returning to and renewing these vibrant landscapes.

My favorite approach to these new (and yet very old, as we will see) design methods is called permaculture, which is a contraction of the words "permanent" and "agriculture" and was specifically created to let us compose landscapes that act like ecosystems. It has grown to encompass tools for designing buildings, communities, and even businesses and schools, but I'll confine myself here to describing its ways of creating living landscapes. Permaculture offers handy tools that let us make all three of the types of connections just mentioned.

Connecting with zones

For tying the pieces of our landscape to each other, we can use what permacul-turists call the zone system. A zone is a roughly circular region around the house that contains the things in our yard that have similar frequencies of use. Here's how that works. The house is zone 0, and the other zones extend outward, from zone 1 to zone 5. Zone 1 is close to the house and also runs along the paths we traverse most often. It holds the plants and other elements in our landscape that we use every day, or that need our attention each day. What belongs in zone 1 varies with each gardener, but the basic rule is this: does it need a visit roughly every day? A typical zone 1 for a gardener with cosmopolitan interests might hold salad greens, culinary herbs, a cherry tomato plant, patio or deck, bird bath, and some colorful flowers, scented plants, or other species that are rewarding to be near. Don't forget the things that need us, too: for example, a place for tender seedlings that can easily dry out after just one day of hot sun.

This sounds only like common sense, but it's surprising how often gardeners ignore this basic wisdom, and it's why, languishing in the back corner of too many yards in August, lurk zucchini the size of watermelons. That's a shouting signal that the zukes are in the wrong place. If the parts of our yard that most need our attention are far away and not on the way to places we often visit, they will sap our energy and won't thrive.

Zone 2 contains the things we visit less than every day but more than once a week. Here could go a compost pile, production vegetables such as beans and sauce tomatoes, berries and small fruits, native species that draw insects and birds we'll enjoy watching, and perhaps a greenhouse, tool shed, and firewood storage. Zones 3 and 4 are visited—and maintained—less frequently, and zone 5 isn't managed at all; it's wilderness, where we go to observe, be inspired, and learn from nature. See the accompanying table for more details and for the contents and uses of the other zones.

How big are the zones? It depends on your own habits and the size of your yard. On a rainy fall evening, how far are you willing to walk in the dark to get some salad greens for dinner? For most people, that's no more than 20 to 40 feet—a handy

Grapes offer close-in food as well as seasonal shade for the residents of this California home. Zone 1 contains other food plants and herbs, plus flowers for scent and beauty. Farther from the house are fruit trees mixed with native plants.

The landscape gradually becomes wilder and less maintained as it touches the surrounding oak woodland, in keeping with the permaculture zone system. Design and photo by Larry Santoyo of EarthFlow Design Works, Los Angeles.

THE ZONE SYSTEM: FUNCTIONS, STRATEGIES, AND CONTENTS

	ZONE 1 (self-reliance)	ZONE 2 (domestic production)	ZONE 3 (farm and wildlife)	ZONE 4 (forage and natural)	ZONE 5 (natural)
Increasing intensity of management and use ←					→ Increasing amount of wildlife habitat
MAIN FUNCTION	Used for daily food and flowers, modifying house microclimate, social space, plant propagation, limited wildlife habitat	Main crops, market/income crops, plant propagation, bird and insect habitat	Grain and extensive crops, grazing, firewood, some timber, contiguous wildlife habitat	Timber, grazing, hunting, wildcrafting, extensive wildlife habitat	Extensive wildlife habitat
SITE PREPARATION	Intensive composted beds, full sheet mulch, near-total modification of hardscape	Some raised beds, full and spot sheet mulch, cover crops	Cover crops, manure and compost addition, spot mulch	Minimal	None
SPECIES TYPES	High-value, frequent-care and/or -harvest foods (herbs, medicines, flowers), seedlings, delicate natives	Storage and bulk crops, grafted dwarf and semi-dwarf trees, multi-functional plants, core natives	Large nut, fruit, and native trees, pasture crops, groundcovers, shelterbelts, extensive natives	Timber and native trees, forage crops, ecosystem support and habitat species	Native
PRUNING AND CARE	Polycultures, trellis, intensive pruning, espalier, cordon, multi-grafted dwarf trees	Trellis, seasonal pruning, coppice	Pruning at establishment only, select hardy seedlings	Occasional thinning, natural regeneration	None
STRUCTURES	Greenhouse, trellis, arbor, deck, patio, outdoor kitchen, bird bath, potting shed, worm bin	Greenhouse, tool shed, shop, barn, compost pile, wood storage	Feed storages, animal shelters	Tree belts as shelter	None
WATER SOURCES	Rain barrel, tank, pond, well, intensive irrigation, greywater	Tank, pond, well, directed catchment, irrigation	Tank, large pond, spring, extensive or flood irrigation, runoff, swales	Large ponds, natural sources, flood irrigation	Natural water features
ANIMALS	Small poultry, rabbits, fish, guinea pigs, worms, native insects and birds	Poultry, rabbits, fish, pygmy goats, native wildlife	Large grazing livestock, large poultry flocks, native wildlife	Grazing mammals, native wildlife	Wild

range, therefore, for zone 1. But remember that zones are not concentric circles. They are warped and shaped by topography and access. A flat backyard entered straight from the kitchen door might be mostly zone 1. But a steeply sloped side yard having no door near it might not get more than a few visits per year. That's zone 3 or 4.

Zones are also defined by our own activities. Los Angeles permaculture designer Larry Santoyo says, "Put your salad garden between your front door and your car door." If you follow Larry's advice, when you arrive home from work you can easily snag a dinner's worth of fresh greens as you stroll to the door, instead of getting settled into a comfy chair with glass in hand, and guiltily remembering that out there, in the dark, is the healthy salad you ought to be eating for dinner. This strategy of putting needed objects where we are already going is nothing new. In the days before indoor plumbing, families put the woodpile on the way to the outhouse, making it easy to answer nature's call and stock the cookstove on the same trip.

By using zones, we begin to think like an ecosystem. Most of us have been taught to think in static classes: this is a tree, this is a bug, this is a bluejay. In a dynamic system like nature, it's the interactions and relationships that count. The tree captures sunlight, the insect chomps the leaves, the bird eats the bug, and all this makes nutrients and energy cycle around vigorously, creating niches, diversity, habitat, and opportunities. When we start to think

in terms of relations and flows, instead of disconnected things and classes, we're learning to design landscapes that behave like nature's. The zone system doesn't just answer the designer's biggest quandary, "Where do I put stuff?" It also guides our answers toward creating relationships that breathe life into our landscapes.

Outside influences

Now that the zone system has helped us put the pieces of our design into smart, functional relationships with ourselves, let's look at another method, one that connects the plants and other objects in the landscape in useful, energy-saving ways with forces and influences coming onto our site. It's called designing with sectors.

Probably the largest outside influence on any landscape is the sun. Put a sun-loving plant in the shade, or a light-shunning understory plant such as pulmonaria in all-day sunshine, and you've got an unhappy specimen on your hands. That's basic garden design, but tracking the path of the sun isn't easy. Sun and shade shift with the seasons. A place that's in cool shadow during March or April planting season, such as the northwest corner of a house, can easily turn out to be blasted by fierce late-afternoon rays in July. The result is a fried plant. We need to know where the summer and winter sun sectors are so we can place our plants in the proper relation to sun and shade.

What are other sectors that gardeners need to consider? There's wind, another tricky one since it can often vary in force and direction over the seasons. Violent winter storms may roar in from one direction, so we want to block their ferocity in some way, perhaps by a planted windbreak or a building. But cool summer breezes that make our yards bearable on hot days might come from a very different direction. These we want to welcome and enhance. So we need to understand the seasonal wind sectors.

Other natural energies that originate from off our site might include wildfire, which often comes from downslope or from the same direction as hot summer wind, although it could also arrive from the direction of those kids next door who play with matches. Floods, noise, a beautiful view we'd like to "borrow," a nasty sight that we want to screen out, and wildlife corridors all count as sectors, and usually are attached to a specific direction originating offsite. With sectors, we can't directly affect the incoming energy itself. We can't turn off the sun or make our neighbor fix his ugly garage. But we can move the parts of our design around so they are in the best relationships with these sectors.

In designing with sectors, there are three principal choices. One is to place elements of our design so that they block the incoming influence. A shade tree to the south of our house, a windbreak, a berm to deflect floodwaters are all examples of ways to block sector energies. Or sector energies can be harvested: solar panels and sun-loving plants, wind generators,

and swales and water tanks all do this. And last, we can let the energy pass undisturbed, which we would do for wildlife or those cool breezes.

Don't forget the human-made sectors, too. Traffic, pollution, noise, utility lines and pipes, and even crime-prone areas count as sectors, since we can't directly affect them. Critical sectors also include codes, zoning, and covenants. You may want to grow a wildflower meadow in your front yard, but if zoning laws or the tastes of your neighbors conflict with that, you're setting yourself up for trouble. Sectors are among the most important influences upon any landscape, and a garden designer who learns to observe and work with them will labor less and enjoy more than one who doesn't.

Matching characters

The third major tool for creating gardens that work like ecosystems is called needs-and-yields design. It helps link the elements of the landscape to each other. It starts with asking, what does this plant (or animal, or other element, including the hardscape) need to thrive? What does it use up? What does it produce? What does it do? What harms it and thus should be kept away? Then, make a list of these characterisitics for the important elements of the landscape—for example, an apple tree. A sample listing of an apple tree's needs and yields appears in the sidebar.

Once these lists have been made, we can look for ways to satisfy the needs of one element by connecting it to the yields and products of others. If a plant demands copious doses of nitrogen, we can place nitrogen-fixing legumes near it. If it needs pollinators, we would put habitat and food plants for its favorite pollinators nearby. Is it a thirsty species? Perhaps it should be planted in a wet part of the yard, or it can reside near a faucet, or the soil under it could be kept moist by a mulch-producing plant close by. Or all three, for maximum drought-proofing.

This applies to more than just plants. Chickens will eat some of our kitchen scraps, right? So the compost pile can go near or on the way to the chicken coop, making choice chicken edibles easy to sort and toss to the birds when you empty the compost bucket. In this way needs-and-yields design means much less work for the gardener, since many of the needs of the landscape are already being taken care of. It takes less fertilizer, water, cleanup, pest prevention, and so on, to make the garden hum along happily. Every time we miss a link, the gardener has to step in to do the work. Each product not used by being connected to some other organism or feature means cleanup, waste, or pollution. Needs-and-yields helps us build opportunity and efficiency into the garden, and it's exactly how nature works.

Now we have three powerful tools for answering the most vexing question of any designer: where is the best place to put

THE NEEDS AND YIELDS OF AN APPLE TREE

Products and activities
fruit
leaves
wood
seeds
oxygen
carbon dioxide
water
shade
soil stabilization
dust collection
soil loosening via roots
nutrient transport
pollen
bark

sap
wildlife habitat
wind reduction
water purification
mulch and soil building
water transport

Needs
water
nutrients
oxygen
carbon dioxide
sunlight
soil
pollen

pollinators
protection from predators
and disease
pruning
harvest

Intrinsic qualities
color
shape
size
soil requirements
climate requirements
flavor
scent

everything? Zones tells us how to put the parts of our design in the best relationship to the user or center or activity. Sectors tell us where to place the pieces in the optimal relationship to influences we can't directly affect. And needs-and-yields helps us best connect the pieces to each other. Once we've applied all three of these methods to the landscape and its parts, most of the placements fall right out and are obvious. We won't have many pieces left that are still in question. For those few orphans, we can make a special effort to find the right place, knowing that they are the problem children of our landscape. And, if they are still giving us fits, we might want to ask if they should be in our yard at all.

First things first

This book has offered a broad array of approaches and ideas for gardening ecologically. For those just starting out on this new path, the scope of topics might seem a bit overwhelming. It's almost like you're being asked to design a whole ecosystem instead of a yard, what with the suggestions to think about water, native habitat, soil ecology, food, the effect on climate, and all the rest. That's a lot to bite off in one big chunk. My advice is, don't take it all on at once. Start small, and, even more importantly, start with the aspects of the garden that you're most excited and passionate about. Does a rain garden sound like fun? Or edible perennials? A native butterfly garden? Get successful with that, have a good time, and build on those suc-

cesses. But for those still wondering what to do first, and what pieces are most important to have in place to create a sustainable garden, here are some guidelines.

In keeping with the zone system laid out by permaculture design, start with the area you use the most often, or, in the vernacular, start at your doorstep. Okay, you say, but start doing what? Let's work backward to find the answer. Doug Tallamy has shown us compellingly that to have the birds, insects, and other wildlife that are the hallmarks of a happy ecosystem, we need a backbone of native and other supportive plants. Eric Toensmeier teaches us that to attract that other major species, *Homo sapiens*, to the garden, we want a tasty palette of edibles and further human-habitat plants present as well. And ample water is a staple feature of any healthy landscape, as Tom Christopher eloquently tells. To make all that happen, we need to go back to the foundation of any land-based ecosystem. That takes us to Elaine Ingham's realm: the soil. Fertile, living soil creates the conditions for everything else in a garden—or ecosystem—to occur.

A soil rich in organic matter stores far more water than a depleted one. Also, with a healthy soil food web, those microherds of bacteria, fungi, worms, insects, and other inhabitants release and cycle the nutrients needed for vigorous, lush plants to thrive. Plus, the soil food web is the basis for much of the aboveground food web. Countless birds, bugs, and mammals depend on both the life in the soil, which in many cases provides them with their meals, and on the fertility that is pumped from the soil into the plants, which they need for food, cover, and a home. Additionally, soil is one of the largest carbon sinks on the planet, so earth rich in organic matter and life helps sequester excess carbon dioxide and other greenhouse gases. Talk about multi-functional! The soil is the foundation of a whole pyramid of life, from microbes to plants to bugs, birds, and four-leggeds. The broader that pyramid's base—meaning, the more fertility and bio-diversity in the soil—the more life the rest of the pyramid can hold.

Thus a superb first step is to create a bed of rich soil, ideally close to the back door or other easily accessible part of the yard. This oasis of fertility and life is both the heart of the yard's zone 1, and the nucleus of abundance that can be expanded until it fills the entire yard (and, ideally, will ripple outward by inspiring your neighbors to do something similar). This first, close-in space will likely be the most densely planted, and for food gardeners, the most

This front yard in southwest Houston, Texas, has plantings between the sidewalk and street to create habitat and privacy. It includes native and drought-adapted species that need little maintenance or municipal water. In the foreground are rudbeckia, ruby grass, cassia, Mexican Turk's cap, almond verbena, bulbine, and thryallis. Design and photo by Kevin Topek of Permaculture Design, LLC, Houston.

frequently harvested, hence it will benefit from deep fertility.

There are many ways to jumpstart this zone of nutrient abundance. If the yard is being completely remodeled, then compost and other organic matter can be mixed in before planting. If plants are already installed, we can add topdressings of compost and manure, which the now-happy soil life will gladly draw down into the earth. We can also pour on organic mulches such as leaves, chipped tree trimmings, straw, stable bedding, or other materials that will break down into ideal soil while suppressing weeds. The humus created as this carbonaceous wealth breaks down will become superb storage for water, minerals such as calcium and potassium, and the other essentials for plant and other life.

Look at the great synergies that we're beginning to create, simply by building soil. Rich soil and a deep mulch that renews fertility allow plants to be placed densely without depleting nutrients. This dense plant cover increases yields if we are growing food, offers excellent cover for wildlife, and provides abundant pollen and other riches for insects. Now we have a zone of tightly interconnected soil, plant, and animal life that abounds with nutrients, water, habitat, organic matter, and all the other requirements of life.

The gardener, once he or she has learned the basics and has seen how successful this zone-1 strategy is, can easily and gradually expand this intensely planted area,

moving farther from the house. Now the area of thick interconnections enlarges, flows of nutrients and energy link up and fatten, new niches appear, and more species will thrive in this vibrant place. The living interconnectivity of the garden is so enhanced that it becomes a thick knot of life, virtually impossible to wound, invade, or otherwise destabilize.

This strength occurs for several reasons. When we have many species present from all life's kingdoms, they provide a broad array of food types, habitat, and other resources. This means each occupant of the garden has several places to feed or nest instead of a solitary "all-eggs-in-one-basket" source that could fail. Also, when so many habitats are present, each inhabitant has the best chance of finding the right microclimate, soil type, vegetation height, or other character it needs to survive. This tremendous biodiversity—many species—means that if one individual or species dies out, others that play similar roles are nearby, ready to plug the gap and keep the community functioning. Nature knows the value of redundancy and backup systems, and we can learn from that. Healthy, rich soil creates the foundation for the needed abundance and biodiversity.

A rich, multi-layered garden designed like this is hard to damage. A new species might enter from the wild or the nursery, but it's unlikely to become invasive. With so many other species present—potential competitors—it's not likely to find enough unused food or space to become a pest. If it breeds rampantly, it merely becomes a tasty, ample food for some of the myriad species of insects, birds, or other predators. For example, I used to have a serious slug problem in my garden. I kept my beds cleanly cultivated, with bare soil, because I'd been told that mulch was good habitat for slugs. Then I learned that mulch is also the habitat that predaceous beetles, carnivorous snails, lizards, garter snakes and other slug-eaters like. And birds are always coming by to check out what potential lunch lurks in the mulch. So I mulch, deeply and religiously. All the happy predators keep my slugs in check far better than bare soil ever did. This is what will occur in any balanced ecosystem when you create the conditions for diversity to occur.

Another reason that a diverse garden stays healthy is because almost any potential resource that shows up will be used by some waiting organism. This translates into fast growth and dense interconnections. In a conventional garden, with wastelands of bare soil and few species, fertilizer leaches out of uninhabited ground,

The warm microclimate created by the sunny southwest exposure of this 600-gallon rainwater tank protects the adjacent apple tree from late frosts. The tank, which gravity-irrigates a perennial front-yard garden in Prescott, Arizona, is made from galvanized metal culvert and features trellising for vines. Design and photo by Andrew Millison of Beaver State Permaculture, Corvallis, Oregon.

water evaporates, sunlight cooks empty earth. Many links are missing in both the soil food web and the one above ground. Thus many resources—from dead twigs to fallen leaves to eggshells in the compost—lie wasted because the organisms able to recycle and eat them are missing.

Compare this to a diverse garden, where almost nothing goes to waste. Some critter is always there to break it down. Every possible food or habitat is grabbed eagerly by at least one of the many species living there, and pulled into the expanding ecosystem of the garden. Once this framework for storing wealth is built—in this case, wealth being the "cash flow" of food, organic matter, water, sun, new species, or any other resource coming in, and the framework being fertile soil and a multi-storied assemblage of plants and animals—the garden just gets richer and more diverse. At every turn, the expanding wheel of life becomes better and better at harvesting and using nutrients and the constant stream of free energy from the sun, which powers still another round of expansion and connection.

The design itself ensures that not much goes to waste. Designing with zones ensures that the parts needing the most care are nearest to us, so we'll notice the bare spot that needs mulch, the scorched species crying for water, or the bindweed sneaking in. Using sectors effectively harvests free energy such as sunlight and reduces damage from wind or fire, releasing us for more productive work. A palette of insectary and wildlife plants carries the garden's reach beyond the plant kingdom into those of bacteria, fungi, birds, and other creatures. By inviting these allies into our garden, we're filling it with busy workers while we enjoy a barbecue with our friends instead of enlisting them in a weeding party.

Filling niches with plants

Now that we know that healthy soil is the foundation of a resilient garden, we can look at some of the kinds of plants to put in it. With virtually a whole planet from which to choose, an ecological gardener has a daunting assortment of plant selections. I narrow that down by setting priorities that tilt my landscapes toward acting like ecosystems. My first choice for a garden will almost always be a locally native plant that will do the job required and will fit the environmental conditions. That raises the chances that my plant choice will connect to, support, and be supported by the native insects, birds, and other wildlife nearby, as Doug Tallamy has told us. If a native won't fill the role I envision—say, if the focus of that bit of the garden is primarily to provide perennial salad greens—then I choose a tested exotic that's known not to be invasive (I prefer to call them opportunist) in my area. There are usually thousands of choices available, so there isn't much justification for introducing an unknown species, ever.

Earlier I suggested that we think in terms of the jobs or functions of the elements in our gardens, rather than focusing on names or other static classes. That will help us design landscapes that are dynamic and vibrant, like nature's. The roles that I've identified as helping a landscape act like an ecosystem are as follows.

Nutrient gatherers. These plants fall into two further categories: nitrogen fixers and dynamic accumulators. Nitrogen is often the limiting nutrient in a garden, thus nitrogen-fixing plants can cut fertilizer use, and at the same time add organic matter to the soil. Nitrogen fixers are perhaps the most important type of plant to have in a young garden. In poor soils, having 25 percent nitrogen-fixing plants to begin with is not too many. They can be culled as the garden matures. Remember to use nitrogen-fixing trees such as alders and black locusts, and shrubs such as pea shrub and bladder senna, too, not just perennial and annual herbs.

Dynamic accumulators are deep-rooted plants that shuttle minerals from the subsoil and concentrate them in leaves, which become leaf litter, and finally topsoil. These minerals balance the nitrogen and carbon added by other soil builders. Examples are yarrow, nettles, comfrey, and many other pioneer species.

Mulchers. All deciduous plants put mulch on the soil at leaf fall, but some do it faster. Plants with big leaves and thick canopies that can tolerate heavy pruning work best. Choices include artichoke, comfrey, canna lilies, and oak trees.

Soil busters. Compaction and heavy clay are common features of many human landscapes. Plants offer a natural way to solve these problems. Spike-rooted species such as wild carrot and daikon (Chinese white radish), and soil-loosening tubers such as potatoes and irises can help here. Also useful in creating good soil tilth are plants with large, fibrous root systems such as mustards and rapeseed.

This apple tree is partnered with comfrey plants, which aid the apple by attracting pollinators and pest predators; each comfrey plant builds soil (by accumulating minerals in its leaves and by creating a rich mulch) and breaks up heavy soil with its extensive root system. Comfrey is also an excellent medicinal herb.

Insectaries. These plants offer nectar or pollen, attract prey species (such as aphids and caterpillars), or provide homes for insects. The category should include native plants, to lure indigenous beneficial bugs, but exotic plants too, since a large fraction of the insects around us are imports that have been naturalized and need non-native hosts. A wide spectrum of insectaries should be included so they'll bloom over a long period. This way pollinators and pest predators will always be hovering near when needed.

Wildlife attractors. Herbs, shrubs, and trees that give food and shelter to birds, reptiles, amphibians, and mammals will create diversity in the garden and shrink pest problems. Select plants of differing heights, offering food at all seasons; include both woody and herbaceous plants, having diverse fruit, flowers, and leaves, with both thick and open foliage, to nourish many feeding styles. Natives are superb here.

If we select species from each of these categories, we're making sure that the most important jobs for a healthy ecosystems are being done. That stacks the deck in favor of our yard becoming a place that functions the way nature does, and benefits the earth rather than depletes it.

Payback time

One of the great benefits of gardening in the image of nature is that we are piggybacking onto over 3 billion years of design experience. Just by looking at a forest or prairie, we can see that nature has solved the problem of creating sustainable landscapes. If we follow her rules, we not only sidestep a huge amount of work, unsustainable resource use in the form of pesticides and chemical fertilizers, and poor yields, but we also boost our chance of success and drastically shrink the waiting period between initial planting and kicking back to admire and enjoy the fruits of our design work.

Ecological, sustainable gardens seem to just "click" in ways that old-style gardens don't. After an initial period of the usual slow growth and barely visible boosts in fertility and biodiversity common to any new garden, nearly all the landscapes I've seen that use these sustainable strategies suddenly "pop." All at once, they magically cease to be struggling and spotty yards demanding intensive care, and explode with life and surge with leafy lushness, the songs of birds, the glory of multicolored butterflies, and the buzz of pollinators. The soil is soft and dark, full of happy worms and supporting vigorous plant growth. The gardener suddenly finds that the hose, fertilizer, and weeding tools lie dormant in the tool shed, and are supplanted by pruners and harvest baskets to haul in the abundant yields. This usually happens between three and five years after beginning the process of soil-building and functional planting. The garden becomes a real ecosystem, nature takes over, and our main role seems to be eating the tasty produce and admiring the vibrant bloom of life from a comfy hammock strung between two now-vigorous trees. When we become students of nature, we're learning from the planet's most experienced teacher.

The authors of the preceding chapters of this book, with whom I'm privileged to share these pages, are some of the finest students of our master teacher, nature. By following the wisdom they have spent many years accumulating, our landscapes will be lush and nourishing, our labors fewer and more enjoyable, and our planet a richer and less burdened home for both ourselves and the more-than-human world.

At the Bullock brothers' homestead on Orcas Island, Washington State, an apple tree benefits from insect-attracting and soil-building plants that surround it. Other species offer additional food and herbs to the gardeners.

ABOUT THE AUTHORS

WILLIAM BURKHART

Thomas Christopher has been reporting on gardening and environmental issues for more than twenty-five years, writing for a wide range of publications including the *New York Times*, *Martha Stewart Living*, and Britain's *Daily Telegraph*. He is the author of *Water-Wise Gardening*, a guide to new styles of gardening emerging from the need to conserve this resource. A graduate of the New York Botanical Garden School of Professional Horticulture, he contributes a blog about sustainable gardening, "Green Perspectives," to the garden's website: www.nybg.org/wordpress2.

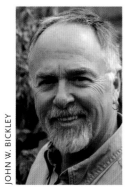

JOHN W. BICKLEY

JOHN W. BICKLEY

Plant pathologist and botanist **David Deardorff** was one of the earliest U.S. advocates of dry-land and native plant gardening, cofounding Plants of the Southwest in Santa Fe in 1977. Naturalist **Kathryn Wadsworth** shares her love for gardening and the outdoors through writing and photography. They are the authors of *What's Wrong With My Plant? (And How Do I Fix It?)*. Together, David and Kathryn present classes and workshops across the United States, with a focus on creating and maintaining gardens that sustain healthy natural systems. Visit them at www.ddandkw.com.

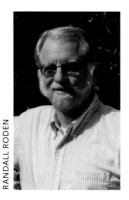

John Greenlee has been growing grasses and creating meadow gardens wherever there are meadows to be made since 1984. His California nursery changed the face of western gardens, and his books, *The Encyclopedia of Ornamental Grasses* and *The American Meadow Garden*, are best sellers. He can be reached at greenleenursery.com. **Neil Diboll**, since he began his involvement with Prairie Nursery in 1982, has championed the use of prairie plants and other natives in contemporary landscapes, designing private and public spaces throughout the Midwest and northeast United States.

Rick Darke is a Pennsylvania-based consultant, photographer, and lecturer whose work blends art, ecology, and cultural geography in the design and conservation of livable landscapes. He has authored and illustrated multiple award-winning books, including *The American Woodland Garden* and *The Encyclopedia of Grasses for Livable Landscapes*. His latest book, *The Wild Garden: Expanded Edition*, places William Robinson's classic concept of wild gardening in modern ecological context and illustrates its relevance for today's gardeners and landscape stewards. For more information, visit www.rickdarke.com.

Eric Toensmeier, an expert on the useful perennial crops of the world, has taught about permaculture and perennial food production systems in multiple languages and countries. He is the author of *Perennial Vegetables*, named the American Horticultural Society's Garden Book of the Year in 2008. Eric is also co-author, with Dave Jacke, of *Edible Forest Gardens*, which received a Garden Writers Association Silver Medal and *Choice* magazine Outstanding Academic Title in 2005. Eric's writing, teaching, and consulting practice is based at www.perennialsolutions.org.

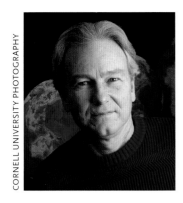

CORNELL UNIVERSITY PHOTOGRAPHY

David W. Wolfe is a professor of horticulture at Cornell University, a Faculty Fellow with Cornell's Center for a Sustainable Future, and an Honorary Research Associate with the New York Botanical Garden. He is a leading authority on the effects of climate change on plants, soils, and ecosystems, authoring or co-authoring many research papers and regional and national impact assessment documents on the topic. He is also author of the award-winning popular science book on soil ecology, *Tales From the Underground: A Natural History of Subterranean Life.*

GRAHAM SNODGRASS

EDMUND C. SNODGRASS

Fifth-generation farmer and nurseryman **Edmund C. Snodgrass** started the first green roof nursery in the United States and is owner and president of Emory Knoll Farms and Green Roof Plants. He is co-author of *Green Roof Plants: A Resource and Planting Guide* and *The Green Roof Man-* *ual.* Visit him at www.greenroofplants. com. Writer and editor **Linda McIntyre** specializes in ecology, urbanism, and design. She has served as a staff writer and contributing editor for *Landscape Architecture* magazine and is the co-author of *The Green Roof Manual.*

JON BALDIVIESO

Douglas W. Tallamy is a professor of entomology and wildlife ecology and director of the Center for Managed Ecosystems at the University of Delaware in Newark, where he has authored more than seventy research articles and has taught insect taxonomy, behavioral ecology, and other courses for twenty-nine years. Chief among his research goals is to better understand the many ways insects interact with plants and how such interactions determine the diversity of animal communities. He is the author of the award-winning book *Bringing Nature Home.*

SOIL FOODWEB INC.

Internationally respected soil microbiologist **Elaine R. Ingham** is president of Soil Foodweb Inc. in Corvallis, Oregon. This business, now with five labs around the globe, developed out of her very successful soil sample analysis service offered at Oregon State University. She is known the world over as an expert and enthusiastic speaker on the benefits of sustainable soil science; and her publication, *The Compost Tea Brewing Manual*, now in its fifth edition, is updated periodically to include the latest results in compost tea work. Visit her at www.elaineingham.com.

ART VARGAS

Toby Hemenway is an adjunct professor at Portland State University, Scholar-in-Residence at Pacific University, and a biologist consultant for the Biomimicry Guild. He teaches and lectures worldwide on permaculture and ecological design, and is the author of *Gaia's Garden: A Guide to Home-Scale Permaculture*, for seven years the world's best-selling book on permaculture. His writing has also appeared in *Natural Home, Whole Earth Review,* and *American Gardener*. He lives in Portland, Oregon, where he is developing sites and resources for urban sustainability. Visit him at www.patternliteracy.com.

References, Resources, and Recommended Reading

Chapter 1

Bradley, Fern Marshall, Barbara Ellis, and Ellen Phillips. 2009. *Rodale's Ultimate Encyclopedia of Organic Gardening*. Rodale Books.

Carson, Rachel Linda Lear, and Edward O. Wilson. 2002. *Silent Spring*, anniv. ed. Mariner Books.

Colborn, Theo, Dianne Dumanoski, and John Peter Meyers. 1997. *Our Stolen Future*. Plume.

Deardorff, David, and Kathryn Wadsworth. 2009. *What's Wrong With My Plant? (And How Do I Fix It?)*. Timber Press.

Fagin, Dan, and Marianne Lavelle. 2002. *Toxic Deception*, 2d ed. Common Courage Press.

Fillipi, Olivier. 2008. *The Dry Gardening Handbook*, illus. ed. Thames & Hudson.

Hemenway, Toby. 2009. *Gaia's Garden*, 2d ed. Chelsea Green.

Mizejewski, David. 2004. *Attracting Birds, Butterflies, and Backyard Wildlife*. National Wildlife Federation / Creative Homeowner.

Mollison, Bill, and Reny Mia Slay. 1997. *Permaculture: A Designer's Manual*. Tagari Publications.

Primrack, Richard B. 2008. *A Primer of Conservation Biology*, 4th ed. Sinauer Associates.

Shapiro, Howard-Yana, and John Harrisson. 2000. *Gardening for the Future of the Earth*. Bantam.

Tallamy, Douglas W. 2009. *Bringing Nature Home*, updated and expanded ed. Timber Press.

Wilson, Edward O. 1984. *Biophilia*. Harvard University Press.

Chapter 2

Sustainable Sites Initiative. 2009. *The Case for Sustainable Landscapes*. Available at www.sustainablesites.org/report.

———. 2009. *The Sustainable Sites Initiative: Guidelines and Performance Benchmarks 2009*. Available at www.sustainablesites.org/report.

Anyone can obtain both reports free of charge online or by mail for the cost of printing and handling from the

Initiative by calling the Lady Bird Johnson Wildflower Center store toll-free at 1.877.945.3357. We urge you to do so!

Chapter 3

Cullina, William. 2008. *Native Ferns, Mosses, and Grasses.* New York: Houghton Mifflin Harcourt.

Greenlee, John, and Saxon Holt. 2009. *The American Meadow Garden.* Portland, Ore.: Timber Press.

Lloyd, Christopher. 2004. *Meadows.* Portland, Ore.: Timber Press.

Ogden, Scott, and Lauren Springer Ogden. 2008. *Plant-Driven Design.* Portland, Ore.: Timber Press.

Pollan, Michael. 1992. *Second Nature.* New York: Delta Trade.

Chapter 4

Cronon, William, ed. 1995. *Uncommon Ground: Toward Reinventing Nature.* New York: W. W. Norton & Company.

Del Tredici, Peter. 2010. *Wild Urban Plants of the Northeast.* Ithaca, N.Y.: Cornell University Press.

Fernald, Merritt Lyndon. 1950. *Gray's Manual of Botany: A Handbook of the Flowering Plants and Ferns of the Central and Northeastern United States and Adjacent Canada,* 8th (Centenniel) ed. New York: Springer.

Goldsworthy, Andy. 1990. *A Collaboration with Nature.* New York: Harry N. Abrams.

Jackson, Kenneth T. 1985. *Crabgrass Frontier: The Suburbanization of the United States.* New York: Oxford University Press.

Kowarick, Ingo, and Stefan Körner, eds. 2005. *Wild Urban Woodlands: New Perspectives in Urban Forestry.* Berlin: Springer.

Kunstler, James Howard. 1993. *The Geography of Nowhere: The Rise and Decline of America's Man-Made Lanscapes.* New York: Touchstone.

Pyle, Robert Michael. 1993. *The Thunder Tree: Lessons from an Urban Wildland.* New York: The Lyons Press.

Ray, Janisse. 1999. *The Ecology of a Cracker Childhood.* Minneapolis: Milkweed Editions.

Stilgoe, John R. 1998. *Outside Lies Magic: Regaining History and Awareness in Everyday Places.* New York: Walker & Company.

Wolschke-Bulmahn, Joachim, ed. 1997. *Nature and Ideology: Natural Garden Design in the Twentieth Century.* Washington, D.C.: Dumbarton Oaks Research Library and Collection.

Chapter 5

Anderson, M. Kat. *Tending the Wild: Native American Knowledge and the Management of California's Natural Resources.* A history of Indian land management and implications for ecological restoration.

Apios Institute for Regenerative Perennial Agriculture. www.apiosinstitute. org. Promotes ecosystem mimicry, edible forest gardens, and perennial crops.

California Rare Fruit Growers. www. crfg.org. Fruit production enthusiasts and professionals.

Creasy, Rosalind. *Edible Landscaping*. A revised edition of this classic guide will be available in 2010.

Davis, Mark. *Invasion Biology*. Details the new findings in invasion biology and calls for a new perspective.

Desert Harvesters. www.desertharvesters.org. Helps communities plant native edible species in water-harvesting earthworks.

Ecology Action. www.growbiointensive.org. International headquarters of biointensive production.

Educational Concerns for Hunger Organization. www.echonet.org. Specialists in tropical agriculture, featuring many excellent resources on their website.

Jacke, Dave, with Eric Toensmeier. *Edible Forest Gardens*. Two-volume set on ecosystem mimicry and edible forest gardens.

Jeavons, John. *How to Grow More Vegetables than You Ever Thought Possible on Less Land than You Can Imagine*. The bible of biointensive production.

Kourick, Robert. *Designing and Maintaining Your Edible Landscape Naturally*. Detailed handbook on edible landscaping.

Lancaster, Brad. *Rainwater Harvesting for Drylands and Beyond*. Three-volume set, available from www.harvestingrainwater.com.

Mollison, Bill, and Reny Mia Slay. *Introduction to Permaculture*. Introduction to design principles and permaculture practices.

North American Fruit Explorers. www.nafex.org. Association of temperate climate fruit gardeners.

Northern Nut Growers Association. www.nutgrowing.org. Dedicated to all classes of nuts, as well as pawpaw and persimmon.

Rare Fruit Council International. www.tropicalfruitnews.org. Chapters of tropical fruit enthusiasts across Florida.

Reich, Lee. *Landscaping with Fruit*. Profiles low-maintenance, ornamental edible fruits.

Stamets, Paul. *Mycelium Running: How Mushrooms Can Help Save the World*. Revolutionary guide to mushroom production and "mycoremediation."

Toensmeier, Eric. *Perennial Vegetables*. Design ideas and profiles of over 100 perennial vegetable crops for many climates.

Chapter 6

Anisko, T., O. M. Lindstrom, and G. Hoogenboom. 1994. Development of a cold hardiness model for deciduous woody plants. *Physiologia Plantarum* 91:375–382.

Bradley, N. L., et al. 1999. Phenological changes reflect climate change in Wisconsin. *Proceedings of the National Academy of Sciences USA*. 96:9701–9704.

Cathey, H. M., and L. Bellamy. 1998. *Heat-Zone Gardening*. Alexandria, Va.: Time-Life Books.

Cayan, D. R., et al. 2001. Changes in the onset of spring in the western United States. *Bulletin American Meteorological Society* 82(3):399–415.

Fitter, A. H., and R. S. R. Fitter. 2002. Rapid changes in flowering time in British plants. *Science* 296:1689–1691.

Goho, A. 2004. Gardeners anticipate climate change. *American Gardener* 83(4):36–41.

Gu, L., et al. 2008. The 2007 eastern U.S. spring freeze: increased cold damage in a warming world? *BioScience* 58(3): 253–262.

Hayhoe, K., et al. 2007. Past and future changes in climate and hydrological indicators in the U.S. Northeast. *Climate Dynamics* 28:381–407.

Kimball, B. A. 1983. Carbon dioxide and agricultural yield. An assemblage of 430 prior observations. *Agronomy Journal* 75:779–788.

Levin, M. D. 2005. Finger Lakes freezes devastate vineyards. *Wines and Vines*, July.

Logan, J. A., J. Regniere, and J. A. Powell. 2003. Assessing the impacts of global warming on forest pest dynamics. *Frontiers in Ecology and Environment* 1(3):130–137.

Long, S. P, et al. 2006. Food for thought: lower-than-expected crop yield stimulation with rising CO_2 concentrations. *Science* 213:1918–1921.

Marris, E. 2007. A garden for all climates. *Nature* 450:937–939.

Montaigne, F. 2004. The heat is on: eco-signs. *National Geographic* 206(3):34–55.

Nakicenovic, N., and R. Swart, eds. 2000. *Intergovernmental Panel on Climate Change: Special Report on Emissions Scenarios*. Cambridge University Press.

Paradis, A., et al. 2008. Role of winter temperature and climate change on the survival and future range expansion of the hemlock woolly adelgid (*Adelges tsugae*) in eastern North America. *Mitigation and Adaptation Strategies for Global Change* 13:541–554.

Parmesan, C., and G. Yohe. 2003. A globally coherent fingerprint of climate change impacts across natural systems. *Nature* 421:37–41.

Pataki, D. E., et al. 2006. Urban ecosystems and the North American carbon cycle. *Global Change Biology* 12:1–11.

Poling, E. B. 2008. Spring cold injury to winegrapes and protection strategies and methods. *HortScience* 43(6):1652–1662.

Primack, D., et al. 2004. Herbarium species demonstrate earlier flowering times in response to warming in Boston. *American Journal of Botany* 91(8):1260–1264.

Primack, R. B., and A. J. Miller-Rushing. 2009. The role of botanical gardens in climate change research. *New Phytologist* 182:303–313.

Trenberth, K. E., et al. 2007. Observations: surface and atmospheric climate change. Ch. 3 in S. Solomon, et al., eds., *Intergovernmental Panel on Climate Change Working Group 1 Report: The Physical Basis*. Cambridge University Press.

Walther, G., et al. 2002. Ecological responses to recent climate change. *Nature* 416:389–395.

Westwood, M. N. 1988. *Temperate Zone Pomology*. Portland, Ore.: Timber Press.

Wolfe, D. W. 1995. Physiological and growth responses to atmospheric carbon dioxide concentration. Ch. 10 in M. Pessarakli, ed., *Handbook of Plant and Crop Physiology*. New York: Marcel Dekker.

———. 2001. *Tales from the Underground: A Natural History of Subterranean Life*. Cambridge, Mass.: Perseus Books.

Wolfe, D. W., et al. 2005. Climate change and shifts in spring phenology of three horticultural woody perennials in northeastern U.S.A. *International Journal of Biometeorology* 49:303–309.

———, et al. 2008. Projected change in climate thresholds in the northeastern U.S.: implications for crops, pests, livestock, and farmers. *Mitigation and Adaptation Strategies for Global Change* 13:555–575.

Ziska, L. H. 2003. Evaluation of the growth response of six invasive species to past, present, and future carbon dioxide concentrations. *Journal of Experimental Botany* 54:395–404.

Ziska, L. H, J. R. Teasdale, and J. A. Bunce. 1999. Future atmospheric carbon dioxide may increase tolerance to glyphosate. *Weed Science* 47:608–615.

Chapter 7

American Public Gardens Association
351 Longwood Road
Kennett Square, PA 19348
tel 610.708.3010
fax 610.444.3594
www.publicgardens.org

Lady Bird Johnson Wildflower Center
4801 La Crosse Avenue
Austin, TX 78739
www.wildflower.org

New England Wild Flower Society
Garden in the Woods
180 Hemenway Road
Framingham, MA 01701
tel 508.877.7630.
www.newfs.org

Chapter 8

Dunnett, Nigel, and Noël Kingsbury. 2008. *Planting Green Roofs and Living Walls*, revised and expanded ed. Portland, Ore.: Timber Press.

National Roofing Contractors Association. 2009. *Vegetative Roof Systems Manual*, 2d ed. Rosemont, Ill.: National Roofing Contractors Association.

Osmondson, Theodore. 1999. *Roof Gardens: History, Design, Construction.* New York: W. W. Norton.

Roy, Rob. *Stoneview: How to Build an Eco-Friendly Little Guest House.* 2008. Gabriola Island, B.C.: New Society Publishers.

Snodgrass, Edmund C., and Lucie Snodgrass. 2006. *Green Roof Plants.* Portland, Ore.: Timber Press.

Snodgrass, Edmund C., and Linda McIntyre. 2010. *The Green Roof Manual for Professionals: Define, Design, Install, and Maintain.* Portland, Ore.: Timber Press.

Stephenson, Ray. 1994. *Sedum: Cultivated Stonecrops.* Portland, Ore.: Timber Press.

Chapter 9

Berenbaum, M. R. 1990. Coevolution between herbivorous insects and plants: tempo and orchestration. In F. Gilbert, ed., *Insect Life Cycles.* Springer.

Bernays, E. M., and M. Graham. 1988. On the evolution of host specificity in phytophagous arthropods. *Ecology* 69:886–892.

Carson, R. 1962. *Silent Spring.* Houghton Mifflin.

Darke, R. 2002. *The American Woodland Garden* . Timber Press.

Dean, C. 2009. One-third of U.S. bird species endangered, survey finds. *New York Times,* 19 March.

DeFoliart, G. 1992. Insects as human food. *Crop Protection* 11:395–399.

Diamond, J. 2005. *Collapse: How Societies Choose to Fail or Succeed.* Viking Press.

Dickinson, M. B. 1999. *Field Guide to the Birds of North America,* 3d ed. National Geographic Society.

Duffy, J. E. 2009. Why biodiversity is important to the functioning of real-world ecosystems. *Frontiers in Ecology and the Environment* 7:437–444.

Graveland, J., and T. van Gijzen. 1994. Arthropods and seeds are not sufficient as calcium sources for shell formation and skeletal growth in passerines. *Ardea* 82:299–314.

Hayden, D. 2004. *A Field Guide to Sprawl.* W. W. Norton.

Little, J. B. 2009. Forests and climate change. *American Forests* (autumn): 9–11.

Louv, R. 2005. *Last Child in the Woods: Saving Our Children from Nature-Deficit Disorder.* Algonquin Books.

Milesi, C., et al. 2005. Mapping and modeling the biogeochemical cycling of turf grasses in the United States. *Environmental Management* 36:426–438.

National Park Service. 2009. "Quick facts." Department of the Interior. www.nps.gov/aboutus/quickfacts.htm.

Pimentel, D., et al. 1991. Environmental and economic impacts of reducing U.S. agricultural pesticide use. *Handbook of Pest Management in Agriculture,* 2d ed. CRC Press.

Reed, S. 2010. *Energy-Wise Landscape Design.* New Society Publishers.

Rosenzweig, M. L. 2003. *Win-Win Ecology: How the Earth's Species Can Survive in the Midst of Human Enterprise.* Oxford University Press.

Sadof, C. S., and M. J. Raupp. 1996. Aesthetic thresholds and their development. In L. G. Higley and L. P. Pedigo, eds., *Economic Thresholds for Integrated Pest Management.* University of Nebraska Press.

Sanderson, E. W. 2009. *Mannahatta: A Natural History of New York City.* Harry N. Abrams.

Sauer, L. 1998. *The Once and Future Forest: A Guide to Forest Restoration Strategies.* Andropogon Associates.

Silvertown, J. W. 2005. *Demons in Eden: The Paradox of Plant Diversity.* University of Chicago Press.

State of the Birds. 2009. www.stateofthebirds.org.

Stein, B. A., and F. W. Davis. 2000. Discovering life in America: tools and techniques of biodiversity inventory. In Stein, B. A., et al., eds., *Precious Heritage: The Status of Biodiversity in the United States.* Oxford University Press.

Tallamy, D. W. 2009. *Bringing Nature Home: How You Can Sustain Wildlife with Native Plants.* Timber Press.

Tallamy, D. W., and K. J. Shropshire. 2009. Ranking lepidopteran use of native versus introduced plants. *Conservation Biology* 23:941–947.

Wilcove, D. 2008. *No Way Home.* Island Press.

Wilcove, D. S., and L. L. Master. 2005. How many endangered species are there in the United States? *Frontiers in Ecology and the Environment* 3:414–420.

Chapter 10

Allmaras, R., J. Kraft, and D. Miller. 1988. Effects of soil compaction and incorporated crop residue on root health. *Annual Review of Phytopathology* 26:219–243.

Bolton, H., Jr., et al. 1985. Soil microbial biomass and selected soil enzyme activities: effect of fertilization and cropping practices. *Soil Biology and Biochemistry* 17(3):297–302.

Carpenter, S., et al. 1998. Nonpoint pollution of surface waters with phosphorus and nitrogen. *Ecological Applications* 8(3):559–568.

Clarholm, M. 1985. Interactions of bacteria, protozoa and plants leading to mineralization of soil nitrogen. *Soil Biology and Biochemistry* 17(2):181–187.

Jacke, D., with E. Toensmeier. 2005. *Edible Forest Gardens.* White River Junction, Vt.: Chelsea Green.

Kronzucker, H., M. Siddiqi, and A. Glass. 1997. Conifer root discrimination against soil nitrate and the ecology of forest succession. *Nature* 385(6611): 59–61.

For more information about Soil Foodweb Inc. and the closest SFI lab to you, see www.soilfoodweb.com. Contact your local lab to discuss how to sample, when to sample, and how to assess compost extract or tea to make sure you will apply what is needed to benefit your plants.

For books, CDs, papers about compost tea and extract, or to invite speakers to talk about the soil food web, contact Sustainable Studies Inc., a nonprofit educational organization, at info@sustainablestudies.com.

Chapter 11

Flores, Heather C. 2006. *Food Not Lawns*. Chelsea Green. Permaculture gardening and community organizing with an urban focus.

Fukuoka, Masanobu. 1978. *The One Straw Revolution*. Rodale. Nature as a model for agriculture.

Hemenway, Toby. 2009. *Gaia's Garden: A Guide to Home-Scale Permaculture*, 2d ed. Chelsea Green. Permaculture gardening for cities, suburbs, and small acreages.

Holmgren, David. 2002. *Permaculture: Pathways and Principles Beyond Sustainability*. Holmgren Design Services. Permaculture's principles applied to sustainability and energy descent, by the field's co-founder.

Jacke, David, with Eric Toensmeier. 2005. *Edible Forest Gardens*. Chelsea Green. The new bible on forest gardening, highly recommended.

Jeavons, John. 1991. *How to Grow More Vegetables (Than You Ever Thought Possible on Less Land Than You Can Imagine)*. Ten Speed. Biointensive (and labor-intensive) techniques that boost production; excellent for small spaces.

Kourik, Robert. 1986. *Designing and Maintaining Your Edible Landscape— Naturally*. Metamorphic. A comprehensive, well-researched book with great reference lists and tables.

Mollison, Bill. 1988. *Permaculture: A Designers' Manual*. Tagari. The fat bible on permaculture, worth many re-readings and perusings.

Mollison, Bill, and Reny Slay. 1991. *An Introduction to Permaculture*. Tagari. Concise coverage of permaculture's basic principles.

Toensmeier, Eric. 2007. *Perennial Vegetables*. Chelsea Green. The best book on growing perennial vegetables, covering most known species for temperate climates.

INDEX